Rebirthin

A Biography

How an Illinois Lawyer Kept Secret His Illegitimate Birth and Won the 1860 Presidential Nomination of the Northern States Republican Party.

By

Howard

Ray

White

Howard Ray White is an accomplished Southern Historian, author of thirteen published books, co-founder of the Society of Independent Southern Historians and producer and host of 80 television shows.

About the Book Cover for Rebirthing Lincoln, a Biography.

Scant confirming evidence exists to substantiate Abraham Lincoln's claimed month, day and year of his birth, his place of birth or the name of the man he claimed to have been his biological father.

On the other hand, there is persuasive evidence that he was born in western North Carolina, the son of a prominent and successful man named Abraham Enloe, and born years before his mother, Nancy Hanks, moved from North Carolina to Kentucky and met and married a fellow named Thomas Lincoln, who, although not the baby's father, did help Nancy raise little Abe to adulthood.

The book front cover is a campaign photo taken in Abraham Lincoln's home town of Springfield, Illinois on June 3, 1860, about two weeks after he was nominated in Chicago to be the Northern States Republican Party's candidate for President of the United States of America. Lincoln never grew a beard prior to leaving Springfield for Washington. Since *Rebirthing Lincoln, a Biography* focuses on his life prior to taking the Office of President, this picture without a beard is most appropriate.

The book back cover presents pictures of two sons fathered by Abraham Enloe in North Carolina:

> On the left is Wesley Enloe, a legitimate son of Abraham Enloe and his wife, Sarah.

> On the right is Abraham Enloe, Jr., an illegitimate son of Wesley's father, Abraham Enloe, who was renamed Lincoln by his mother, Nancy Hanks, upon her marriage to Thomas Lincoln. This son was born in North Carolina and grew up in Kentucky and Indiana. As an adult, he moved to Illinois, where he began his career as a lawyer and politician, eventually rising to become President of the Remaining United States.

The author hired Palmetto Publishing of Charleston, SC to take his photos and text and help him create the book cover. He thanks their cover artist for helping him.

Rebirthing Lincoln, a Biography | Copyright © 2021 by Howard Ray White

Rebirthing Lincoln, a Biography is published by:

SouthernBooks, Charlotte, North Carolina

Introduction

For 160 years, biographers and historians have struggled to make sense of President Abraham Lincoln's childhood life. To make sense of his childhood, the biographer/historian must ignore, or set aside, the science of biological inheritance — the science requiring that, for baby Abe to become an exceptionally gifted man, his four biological grandparents had to have inherited and passed on genes that enabled conforming physical traits and exceptional intelligence and leadership ability.

For 160 years, biographers and historians have accepted as truthful Abraham Lincoln's story of his childhood life — his politically helpful story that his mother, Nancy Hanks, was married to Thomas Lincoln before his birth and that Thomas was his father. That was the story he, himself, had presented to the public and to men who were writing his campaign biographies in 1860. In accepting Lincoln's story of his childhood, said biographers and historians have ignored significant testimony in North Carolina and Kentucky indicating that he was lying about his birth, covering up politically embarrassing history that he was born in North Carolina and that he was the illegitimate son of Abraham Enloe.

Specifically, if an biographer or historian is an independent thinker and embraces the science of biological inheritance, then

1. He or she must ignore that birth date that Lincoln personally wrote in his Bible, and

2. He or she must ignore the Lincoln-dictated campaign biographies and, instead:

    a. He or she must figure that Lincoln was lying about his illegitimate ancestry to achieve political success.

    b. And he or she must search for historical evidence of the existence of those four biologically-true grandparents who were exceptionally capable ancestors and who passed to baby Abe their physical appearance and their exceptional genetic traits, which enabled the adult Abe to become:

        i. A very successful lawyer,

        ii. A very successful political leader, and

        iii. President of the United States.

You see, when a child is conceived in the womb:

1. At conception, the mother's egg has, in that instant, contributed the winning genetic mix from her parents — the winning genetic mix from among

the variety that had been given to her, the mother, at the time, decades earlier, of her conception.

2. At conception, the father's sperm has, in that same instant, contributed the winning genetic mix from his parents — the winning genetic mix from among the variety that had been given to him, the father, at the time, decades earlier, of his conception.

This is true for dogs, cats, cows, horses and we human beings. By this method, every child, at conception, is the product of the genetic inheritance given by his or her four grandparents.

My investigation, my search for four exceptional ancestors, is what we will be doing, together, in *Rebirthing Lincoln, a Biography*. But, we will be doing more. We will also be analyzing how Abe kept his illegitimate birth secret from Democrat newspapermen, political opponents, and the curious public.

So, what have Lincoln historians and biographers reported that is certain? They have only reported that baby Abe's mother was known as Nancy Hanks, and they seem to accept that she was illegitimate and the daughter of Lucy Hanks, who was perhaps also illegitimate. Lincoln historians and biographers make no effort to discover the name of either Nancy's biological father or Lucy's biological father.

But, in *Rebirthing Lincoln, a Biography,* we will be making those searches to identify Nancy Hanks' father and maternal grandfather because that information is a crucial part of quantifying and assessing the exceptional traits of Lincoln's four gene-donating grandparents. Lincoln claimed his mother was born in Virginia and that her father owned a successful Virginia plantation, but historians have left it at that — they have made no effort to identify the Virginian sire.

Baby Abe had four biological grandparents. Historians and/or biographers have known the identity of one biological grandparent for certain — Lucy Hanks.

Although, I, Howard Ray White, do not know **for certain** the identity and history of baby Abe's maternal grandfather, his father, his paternal grandfather and his paternal grandmother, I do know those identities and histories **reasonably well** and, as you read further, you will agree that we now know those stories **sufficiently well to embrace them as far, far more likely than the politically correct history Americans have been taught to believe for 160 years**.

Should we believe that Abraham Lincoln was lying about his illegitimate birth and ancestry to enable personal political success? Well, after a tremendous amount of study, research and analysis, I have come to accept the extreme likelihood that, yes, Abraham Lincoln was lying to enable his political career. Given that premise, the science of genetic inheritance begs that we identify Abraham Lincoln's four grandparents, get to know the history of their respective lives and evaluate their similar or dissimilar physical appearance and respective exceptionalness or ordinariness.

Rebirthing Lincoln is a complete biography. You will learn about Lincoln's life and exceptional accomplishments from his birth to his death and gain new understanding about his politically-damaging secret — that he was born illegitimately in North Carolina and was lying to the public about it to avoid killing his own political advancement.

Readers of *Rebirthing Lincoln, a Biography* may engage in discussion with other readers on a website the author has established for that purpose. To view, go to www.rebirthinglincoln.com.

The Captivating 160-year-old American Puzzle

The First Puzzle Overview — Who was Baby Abe's Father and Paternal Grandparents

During Abraham Lincoln's claimed lifetime in Kentucky, Indiana and Illinois, prior to becoming President of the shrunken United States, evidence <u>lawfully</u> (with legal certainty) proving that he had been born in Kentucky as the biological descendant of Thomas Lincoln **did not exist, and records that did exist had been created by Lincoln himself** during the years he aspired to an important political career as Illinois Senator, and later, as President.

Young adult Abe Lincoln

Although there **is no proof** that Lincoln's biological father was Abraham Enloe of far-western North Carolina, there exists a **strong body of circumstantial evidence and relevant testimony** in support of that being a truthful fact. For this knowledge, we are thankful for James Harrison Cathey. He researched Abraham Lincoln's parental history and published his findings in his book, *The Genesis of Lincoln*, in 1899. Cathey's findings and presentation of supportive evidence is very hard to deny. We are also indebted to James Caswell Coggins for his research, so well documented in his book, *The Eugenics of Lincoln*, published in 1940. Furthermore, we are indebted to Jerry A. Goodnight and Richard Eller for their assessment of evidence, as reported in their book, *The Tarheel Lincoln, North Carolina Origins of "Honest" Abe*, published in 2003. Finally, we are indebted to Don Norris for his assessment as he presented it in his book, *Abraham Enloe of Western North Carolina, The Natural Father of Abraham Lincoln*, published in 2008. And we thank the University of Illinois Press and editors, Douglas L. Wilson and Rodney O. Davis, for gathering the research collected by Abraham Lincoln's law partner, William Herndon, and publishing the entire collection of testimonies in an 827 page book titled, *Herndon's Informants: Letters, Interviews and Statements about Abraham Lincoln*, published in 1998.

Abraham Enloe was a very successful man and is seen as a suitable biological father (gene donor) both in physical appearance (Abraham Lincoln's physical appearance was most unusual; it matched Enloe's and very, very few men did) and in exceptional mental ability. Furthermore, the very strong historical evidence that baby Abe's mother lived with this very Enloe family as a household servant throughout her teenage years makes conception of a baby fathered by Abraham Enloe very logical.

So, since we now know Abraham Enloe's parents, we now have very sound evidence defining baby Abe's paternal grandfather and paternal grandmother. That evidence is very supportive of a strong genetic inheritance, which explains how Abraham Lincoln obtained the abilities he utilized in advancing his legal and political goals.

The Second Puzzle Overview — Who Was Baby Abe's Maternal Grandfather?

We know baby Abe's mother. She was Nancy Hanks, who was born illegitimately, this being affirmed by Abraham Lincoln, himself. We likewise know baby Abe's maternal grandmother, Lucy Hanks, likewise perhaps born illegitimately. Historians all agree on these two women and Nancy's illegitimacy. But that is all they agree on. So, most importantly, **we need to identify Nancy's biological father**. With little exception, historians say that father lived in Virginia and that Nancy was born there. What else have they told us?

We are thankful for the research conducted by James Caswell Coggins and presented in his book, *The Eugenics of Lincoln*, published in 1940. Coggins discovered that the Honorable Columbus Tanner had in his possession a long-secret family manuscript, which revealed that his family relative, **Michael Tanner, Junior, son of Michael Tanner, Senior, was the biological father of Nancy Hanks, delivered by her mother, Lucy Hanks.** The Tanner's had emigrated from Germany and, at the time of Nancy's birth, were living very successful lives in Virginia. And, based on Coggins' historical research, we know much more about Nancy Hanks (Tanner's) life, growing up in North Carolina. Yes, while a small girl, Nancy arrived in Rutherford County, North Carolina, arriving with her father's brother.

A Puzzle Overview — How Did Abraham Lincoln Keep Secret His Biological Ancestry During His Amazing Rise in Illinois Politics and Northern States Politics?

The author, Howard Ray White, now 82 years old, has for 30 years studied American history with a focus on the South; the rise of the Northern States Republican Party; State Secession, and Lincoln's war to conquer the Confederate States of America — composed of eleven Southern States that had **legally seceded**

prior to his becoming President — a war that caused **the unnecessary deaths of one million Americans**.

Based on his extensive knowledge, White brings to readers, *"Rebirthing Lincoln, a biography,"* which reveals how a politically ambitious Illinois lawyer managed to succeed at keeping secret from opponents in the Illinois Democratic Party the fact that he had been, for many years, lying about his parentage — lying to enable his political advancement in the Illinois Whig Party and then the Illinois Republican Party.

No question about it: Abe's Mother was Nancy Hanks, who grew up in North Carolina. Yes, Thomas Lincoln, who was born and raised in Kentucky, did marry Nancy Hanks in Kentucky, soon after she had arrived from North Carolina. But, on the day of the marriage, Nancy had already given birth to baby Abe in North Carolina prior to moving with her one-year-old child into Kentucky.

The baby's biological father was Abraham Enloe of Western North Carolina. Yes, the true father was Abraham Enloe; Kentuckian Thomas Lincoln was the baby's step-father, the husband of his mother. The mother, Nancy Hanks, had originally named the baby Abraham after his true father.

A photograph of Abraham Enloe does not exist. His youngest son, Wesley Enloe was photographed by James Harrison Cathey in about 1897. Abraham Enloe was the father of both Wesley Enloe and Abraham Lincoln. Their mothers were different ladies.

Many years earlier, in North Carolina, Nancy Hanks, a homeless illegitimate child, had worked in and lived in the Enloe home near Bostic, North Carolina, as a servant; arriving as a thirteen-year-old girl and continuing as a servant through her teenage years. A well-to-do father of a large legitimate family, Mr. Enloe had managed to get Nancy pregnant when she had become about 20 years old. Nancy was about four months pregnant when the Enloe family and half-dozen other families migrated together from Rutherford County, North Carolina to newly acquired land near the Cherokee Indians just south of the Smoky Mountains, also in North Carolina. And Nancy went with the Enloes to that land south of the Smokies, helping with the smaller children during the strenuous journey.

Embarrassed, and attempting to placate his understandably irate wife, Mr. Enloe had quickly arranged for Nancy to be removed back to the Enloe farm near Bostic, North Carolina, which he and his family he recently left and leased out to a tenant farming family. There, the family that had just begun to rent that farm agreed to receive Nancy until the birth of her baby.

Soon after Abe's birth his father arranged for Nancy and baby Abe to be returned to his new farm south of the Smokies. Shortly after her return, baby Abe's father took him and his mother to Kentucky to live with the family of her mother, Lucy.

In Kentucky, Nancy Hanks introduced Abraham Enloe to a fellow named Thomas Lincoln, 28 years old, and discovered that this man was sexually sterile and seemed unable to find a young woman to marry him and become his wife. Abraham observed that Thomas was friendly toward Nancy Hanks and baby Abe and succeeded in persuading him to marry Nancy Hanks and help raise her little boy. Abraham Enloe paid Thomas Lincoln five hundred dollars to do marry Nancy Hanks. And Thomas agreed to do it.

Wrapping Up these Puzzle Overviews

Rebirthing Lincoln, a Biography provides compelling evidence in support of baby Abe's real father, Abraham Enloe, and then presents a complete biography of Abraham Lincoln, proceeding from North Carolina into Kentucky; then into Indiana, then into Illinois where he was a state legislator for several years. Then, *Rebirthing Lincoln* continues to describe Abraham Lincoln's settling in Springfield, Illinois; to his becoming a lawyer and partnering with Billy Herndon; then spending two years as a Whig Congressman in Washington; then observing the demise of the Whig Party, then taking a leading role in founding the Illinois Republican Party, then rising in prominence across the Northern States to an amazing degree, and succeeding in winning the Northern States Republican Party's nomination for President.

Going forward the author, Howard Ray White, accepts the highly, highly likely history that the four grandparents of President Abraham Lincoln were:

1. Lucy Hanks, born in Virginia illegitimately of unknown father, subsequently living in North Carolina and then Kentucky.

2. Michael Tanner, born in Virginia of exceptional people of German ancestry, then relocating to North Carolina.

3. Abraham Enloe's father, Enock Enloe, born in August, 1741 in Baltimore County, Province of Maryland and died in 1796 in Camden District, South Carolina.

4. Abraham Enloe's mother, Agnes Sprucebanks, born on June 2, 1734 in Baltimore County, Province of Maryland and died June 1, 1790 in Swain County, North Carolina.

But there is much more: as the reader proceeds through the chapters in *Rebirthing Lincoln,* he or she learns over and over again how politician/lawyer Abraham Lincoln managed to prevent political opponents from discovering that he was of illegitimate birth and had, for a decade, persistently lied about it.

If political opponents had ever discovered Lincoln's big lie, his political career would have been over, done, kaput. But Lincoln succeeded in keeping his secret. His big lie was never figured out during his lifetime. The moniker, "Honest Abe" was in reality a cover-up of lying Abe's true ancestral background.

Rest assured, footnotes completely document the sources of the very reliable records upon which this Lincoln biography, *Rebirthing Lincoln,* is based.

Upon arriving at the last page of *Rebirthing Lincoln,* you, the reader, will have acquired a profoundly new knowledge of the life and political career of Abraham Lincoln and his War to Conquer the Confederate States of America, which consisted of eleven Legally-Seceded States. You will gain a profound knowledge of American history — a knowledge so different from your previous understanding that your subsequent personal attitudes toward that era in American history will be thoroughly shaken and forever transformed.

Dedication

This historical biography, *Rebirthing Lincoln*, is dedicated to the **one million Americans, both White and Black, who died unnecessary deaths** as a result of Abraham Lincoln's decision to forgo negotiation and, instead, pursue a four-year military invasion of the South through to the eventual total conquest of the eleven seceded states.[1]

Please remember that, in 1860, when the Northern States Republican Party succeeded in electing their candidate, Abraham Lincoln of Illinois, and many Democrat Southern States responded by seceding from beneath the Federal Government, State Secession was legal and not unconstitutional.

It is hard for us to imagine how a military fight between invading armies of the Northern States and defending armies of the Southern Seceded States could so horribly destroy so many lives and the happiness of so many families, North and South.

We pray that no political party in our country will ever again resort to extreme violence, military or police state oppression, or outright war to impose its control over the people of an opposing political party.

I also dedicate *Rebirthing Lincoln* to everyone who takes the time to read and study this book and discuss it with others. In your hands is a book that should spark a determination in your heart to never let that intensity of anger between political factions within America ever again escalate to a level of violence that results in the death of millions of our people.

You have access to a new website, www.rebirthinglincoln.com, where you can engage in discussion among other readers of this book.

---

[1] *Understanding the War Between the States*, Chapter 29, *The Cost of the War in Lives Lost and Families Shattered.* This important chapter is by the late William Cawthon of Alabama. This book was authored and published by the Society of Independent Southern Historians in 2015.

Table of Contents

Chapter 1: Thomas Lincoln is Very Sick, Early January, 1851

Long Before January 1851, Lawyer and Whig Party Politician Abraham Lincoln and his Wife and Children had long ignored the Elderly Thomas Lincoln.

Over the past 160 years, Lincoln biographers and historians have uniformly praised President Lincoln and carefully supported his claim that his biological father was Thomas Lincoln, wife of Nancy Hanks, and that he was born on February 9, 1809, 2 years and 8 months after his mother married the man he claimed to be his father. However, you will be reviewing evidence that his mother had given one-and-a-half-year-old Abe the last name "Lincoln" **after her marriage**, allowing the Enloe name to be dropped and pleasing her new husband. And young Abe would be known thereafter as "Abraham Lincoln."

Since leaving the Lincoln home on the Sangamon River in Illinois in 1831, Abe, now a young man seeking his way in life, had intentionally avoided visiting Thomas Lincoln, his second wife, Sarah Bush Johnston Lincoln or Sarah's grown children. Yes, since Abe had arrived in New Salem, Illinois he — with few exceptions, and only when he happened to be in the county where they lived and alone and on business — had not taken time to even briefly visit Thomas and his second wife, Sarah Bush Johnston Lincoln. Abe's firm decision to avoid meaningful contact with Thomas and Sarah was made twenty years prior to 1851. Neither Thomas nor wife Sarah had ever met Abe's wife or children and they never would. So, clearly, Abraham Lincoln and his wife, Mary, were strident in avoiding any meaningful contact with Thomas Lincoln, his second wife, Sarah Bush Johnston Lincoln, or the adult Johnston children.

Thomas and Sarah Bush Johnston Lincoln had long lived on forty acres of land on Goose Nest Prairie, in Coles County, Illinois. The home of Thomas and Sarah was one hundred miles east of Springfield. Abe and his law partner, Billy Herndon, were accustomed to traveling across several counties in the senior lawyer's one-horse buggy. But, over the course of 20 years, with few exceptions, a visit by Abe to Thomas and/or Sarah was, apparently, very carefully avoided. Billy would never meet them during Abraham Lincoln's lifetime.

So Abe's strident rule for avoiding meaningful contact with Thomas and Sarah was complete. A visit by Abe and Billy Herndon would have been meaningful. A visit by Abe and his wife Mary would have been very meaningful. A visit by Abe, Mary and the children would have been very, very meaningful. A visit of that magnitude would have allowed Abe's children to meet the man Abe claimed to be their grandfather. You know, "Come children, this here is your Grandpa."

Thomas Lincoln is Very Sick

But now, as the first of January 1851 dawned, Abe faced a crisis concerning his determination to distance himself from Thomas Lincoln and his second wife Sarah Bush Johnston Lincoln. Thomas was dying and Abe knew he must not expose himself to a funeral gathering in Coles County, Illinois. Chances of questions about the biological tie between 1) a very tall, lanky, famous lawyer and former Congressman, Abraham Lincoln and 2) a rather ordinary looking Thomas Lincoln, who had accomplished very, very little, would certainly beg for questions. Questions like:

1. "Why did you not bring your wife and children for a visit while Thomas lived?"

2. "Since you are so physically unlike the late Thomas Lincoln, I find it so hard to believe that he could have been your father!"

3. "A friend who came to Illinois from the area of Kentucky where you grew up has told me he has heard that a fellow named Abraham Enloe was your father."

4. A fellow saying. "I heard that Thomas Lincoln was not capable of getting a woman pregnant."

Those potential conversations were the essence of Abe's concerns after he opened letters warning that Thomas was gravely ill.

In very early January, 1851, Abe received a letter from Harriet Hanks Chapman (the daughter of Sarah Elizabeth Johnston Hanks and husband Dennis Friend Hanks) and two letters from John D. Johnston (the son of Sarah Bush Johnston Lincoln and her first husband, Daniel Johnston), all urgently reporting that Sarah Bush Johnston Lincoln's husband, Thomas Lincoln, was dying and urgently wished that Abe could travel to Coles County to visit Thomas before he passed on to his reward. Concerning the first letter from John D. Johnston, Abe seems to have read and set it aside without a reply. The second letter from John D. Johnston must have been likewise read and set aside. Then the third letter arrived, the one from Harriet Hanks Chapman. At this point Abe decided to reply by letter to John D. Johnston's earlier letter regarding the serious illness that Thomas Lincoln, now 74 years old, was suffering.

Abe's Letter to John D. Johnston:

"Springfield, Jan. 12, 1851.

"Dear Brother,

"On the day before yesterday I received a letter from Harriet, written at Greenup. She says she has just returned from your house, and that father is very low, and will hardly recover. She says that you have written me two letters, and that, although you do not expect me to come now, you wonder that I do not write. I received both your letters; and, although I have not answered them, it is not because I have forgotten them, or not been interested about them, but because it appeared to me I could write nothing which could do any good. You already know I desire that neither father nor mother shall be in want of any comfort, either in health or sickness. My business is such that I could hardly leave home now, if it were not, as it is, that my own wife is sick a-bed. (It is a case of baby sickness, and, I suppose, is not dangerous.) I sincerely hope father may yet recover his health; but, at all events, tell him to remember to call upon and confide in our great and good merciful Maker, who will not turn away from him in any extremity. He notes the fall of the sparrow, and numbers the hairs of our heads and he will not forget the dying man who puts his trust in him. Say to him, that, if we could meet now, it is doubtful whether it would not be more painful than pleasant; but that, if it be his lot to go now, he will soon have a joyous meeting with loved ones gone before, and where the rest of us, [2] through the help of God, hope ere long to join them.

Thomas Lincoln photo taken in his latter Years.

"Write me again when you receive this.

"Affectionately,

"A. Lincoln." [3]

While the above letter was making its way through the U. S. Postal service, Thomas Lincoln died. Abe's letter was dated January 12. Thomas Lincoln died on January 13, 1851.

Thomas Lincoln had died "after suffering for

_____

[2] Abraham Lincoln was never a believing Christian. He was only pretending to be a Christian as he wrote his letter.

[3] Lamon, *Life of Lincoln*, page 336.

18

many weeks from a disorder of the kidneys." Perhaps Abe had received earlier reports that Thomas was quite ill and urgings to come see him one last time. We do not know.

How would Billy Herndon handle this very strange family relationship between Abe and Thomas while writing the biography of his law partner, *Herndon's Life of Lincoln?* Herndon figured that Abe's behavior toward his claimed father strange and rather embarrassing. He was glad to drop Thomas from his biography of his late law partner at first opportunity. He would drop Thomas from the biography twenty years before his death in 1851. Yes, upon arriving at the year 1831 in his *Life of Lincoln* biography, Billy handled the subsequence absence of further mention of Thomas Lincoln with these few words:

> "As [Abe Lincoln] steps out into the broad and inviting world, we take him up for consideration as a man. At the same time, we dispense with further notice of his father, Thomas Lincoln." [4]

In exactly the same way, Ward H. Lamon in his biography, *The Life of Abraham Lincoln*, terminates coverage of Thomas Lincoln in 1831:

> "It is with great pleasure that we dismiss Tom Lincoln, with his family and fortune, from further consideration in these pages." [5]

We have to ask: were both biographers of Abraham Lincoln's life, prior to his becoming President, choosing to brush Thomas Lincoln aside at the very first opportunity, save a one-page account of his January 13, 1851 death? Lamon said "with great pleasure."

Herndon had spent many years with Lincoln in law practice. I have to believe that Herndon, in his gut, believed that there was something dreadfully embarrassing about the Thomas and Abe relationship that he should wisely leave undiscovered.

So Abe wisely stayed clear of the funeral of his claimed father, Thomas. Abe claimed he was too busy with legal work and declined to make the hundred-mile journey to Coles County. In reality, he was afraid that, if he attended, he might stumble upon one of Thomas' friends or relatives who wanted to discuss early days, 45 years ago, when Thomas married his mother Nancy Hanks in Kentucky. He feared that someone might recall, "I was at that wedding and I do remember seeing you walking around the room as a very little boy. Were you almost two years old on that wedding day?"

Of course, Abe was torn: he knew his stepmother Sarah Bush Johnston Lincoln wanted him to attend the funeral.

---

[4] Herndon, *Life of Lincoln*, page 60.
[5] Lamon, *The Life of Abraham Lincoln*, page 75.

Goodness, Abe had not visited his stepfather and stepmother except for a few occasions, when alone and on legal business in Coles County. And, like the deceased Thomas, his second wife, Sarah, had never met Mary Lincoln and the children. We do not know if Sarah knew that her husband had not fathered Abe or Abe's half-sister, also named Sarah. But there is good reason to assume she knew her husband was sterile, castrated by a severe bout with the mumps during his childhood. His physical appearance below the belt should have made it obvious to her.

Anyway, Abe had been very fond of his stepmother while growing up and feelings of affection remained.

Yes, Abe simply claimed that Thomas Lincoln's death came at an awkward time for him — a 45-year-old Springfield, Illinois lawyer and future political leader. So he chose not to travel from Springfield to Coles County to attend his mother's first husband's funeral. He decided to forego the trip to Coles County even though it was only about 100 miles east of Springfield. How could a man who was destined to ride a groundswell of moral indignation, which would be carrying him forward toward an historic presidential election victory, snub the funeral of the man he desperately wanted voters to believe to have been his true, biological father?

I do not know! But, as you will learn through reading this biography, you will almost surely accept evidence that Abe Lincoln's biological father was Abraham Enloe of North Carolina! Thomas was only his stepfather, the husband of his mother. Abe's decision to abstain from the funeral was a reasoned and intelligent one. It prevented possible entanglement over discussing his childhood years with other people attending the funeral.

Chapter 2: Abraham Lincoln Contrives a Family Bible Record designed to attest that He was Born After his Mother's Marriage.

In 1851, Illinois was a Rapidly Expanding State, Especially in its Northern Counties.

At the time of Thomas Lincoln's passing, on January 13, 1851, Abe Lincoln had become a prominent Illinois lawyer and looking forward to renewed political success — renewed because he hadn't been important in Illinois or Springfield political life since he had completed a two-year term as a Whig Party member of the U. S. House of Representatives, beginning in December, 1847 and ending in March 1849. The political power of Abe's party, the Whig Party, founded to a significant extent by Henry Clay of Kentucky, had severely declined following the 1852 election season. Democrats, led by Illinois Senator Stephen Douglas, were generally in control in Illinois and across the Northern States.

But the political tapestry of Illinois was destined to experience important change. The 1850 U. S. Census had just been completed, and, when tallied, Illinois' share of seats in the United States House of Representatives and its share of Electoral College votes was destined to substantially increase. The population of northern Illinois had been increasing rapidly and projections for a continuance seemed certain. And people moving into the State were mostly moving into the northern section and mostly arriving without preconceived political views or allegiance to past American political values — many were recent or new immigrants, recently having become citizens or soon to become citizens.

Abraham Lincoln's first Written Account of his Birth Year.

Sometime during 1848 Abe Lincoln reportedly wrote a letter to a fellow politician in which he stated, among other things, "I am now in my fortieth year." This represents the first written account of Lincoln's birth year. But it occurs well after his entry into politics and is suspect. By the way, if the letter was written after the February birthday he would later claim, and if Lincoln had been born in 1809, as he would soon allege, he would have been 39 years old, going on 40. So, there may have been a one-year error in the calculation in that letter.

Abraham Lincoln asks Sarah Bush Johnston Lincoln to help him Create a Family Bible Record.

About two years after Thomas Lincoln's death, sometime in 1852 or 1853, Abe Lincoln purchased a new Bible in Springfield, said goodbye to Mary and the children, and travelled to Coles County. He was going to call on the late Thomas Lincoln's second wife, Sarah Bush Johnston Lincoln. Abe had only visited Sarah a very few times over a span of 22 years. So Sarah was surely surprised when she opened the front door of the home she and her late husband had shared for decades, and cast her eyes upon the exceptionally tall, lanky and accomplished man who had grown up as a teenager in the southern Indiana home where she and her late husband had lived.

Sarah Bush Johnston Lincoln photographed late in her life.

Abe showed her the new Bible he carried and asked if he could come in and talk about family history. Probably almost speechless at this point, Sarah complied and invited Abe into her house. We must assume that Sarah was aware of Abe's success as a lawyer and politician, although it is likely that she was not accustomed to reading a newspaper. We do know that her late husband, Thomas, had been illiterate. After a bit of conversation and an apology for not attending her husband's funeral, Abe opened the new Bible, which he had just purchased, to the center pages, which families used to periodically record names, births, marriages and deaths as the family grew and older members passed away. Having likely brought along his own quill pen and bottle of ink, Abe was fully prepared.

About 13 years after this visit — this was after President Lincoln's death — Billy Herndon would be engaged in research needed to write his biography of his deceased law partner. He would call on Sarah Bush Johnston Lincoln, introduce himself and explain his project to write a biography. Sarah would invite him into her house and they would talk, Billy taking notes as the conversation would continue. It was at this visit that Herndon made a huge discovery — he found that the births-marriages-deaths page from the Family Bible existed — the page that Lincoln had written onto that day when he had come to visit Sarah Bush Johnston Lincoln with that new Bible, a bottle of ink and a quill pen.

Apparently, the Bible itself was elsewhere or thrown away. Colonel Augustus Chapman had retained only the births-marriages-deaths page from the Bible. Augustus was the husband of Harriet Hanks Chapman, who was the daughter of Sarah Elizabeth Johnston Hanks and Dennis Friend Hanks. Sarah Bush Johnston

Lincoln, widow of Thomas Lincoln, was Harriet's grandmother. The Chapman's lived near Sarah Bush Johnston Lincoln in Coles County. So Billy left Sarah's house to visit Col. Chapman and introduced himself. Chapman handed the Bible page to Billy Herndon and invited him to copy it.

Billy would copy from the tattered page, word for word, what Lincoln had written in the Bible that day he had visited Sarah with that bottle of ink. Yes, the total record had been written out carefully by Abraham Lincoln's hand that day, all at the same time with the same pen and same ink. Herndon reported that, when he first saw the tattered page, the Bible was lost and only the page for births, marriages and deaths remained.

Billy's recorded copy follows:

"This I copied from the Bible of Lincoln — made in his own handwriting — now in the possession of Col. Chapman — ie, the leaf of the Bible — now in fragments causing me trouble to make out — pieces small — worn it in some man's pocket."

The following words Billy Herndon copied from the "fragments" as best he could. The lines in bold face are the ones you should remember:

"Sept. 9th 1865

The following births — deaths & marriages were taken from Mrs. Lincoln's Bible, by me, Sept. 9th 1865 — which record is in A. Lincoln's hand writing and now in the possession of Col. Chapman.

Sarah Lincoln was born February 10th 1807

Abraham Lincoln — son of Thomas and Nancy Lincoln was born February 12th 1809

Sarah Bush first married to Daniel Johnston and afterwards the second wife of Thomas Lincoln

Thomas Lincoln was born Decr. 13th 1788 —

John D. Johnston — son of John and Sarah Johnston was born May the 11th married to Mary Bar Octr 13th 1834— who was born July 22d 1816

Thomas L. D. Johnston — son of John and Mary Johnston was born January 11th 1837

Abram L. D. Johnston — son of same parents was born March the 27th 1838.

Marietta Sarah Jane Johnston daughter of same parents was born January 21st, 1840 —

Squire H. Johnston son of same parents was born December 15 1841 —

23

Richard M. Johnston son of same parents was born October the 26th 1845

Dennis F. Johnston son of same parents was born December 13th 1847

Nancy J. Williams was born March 18th 1836

Abraham Lincoln — son of Thomas Lincoln was married to Mary Todd Nov 4th 1842

John D. Johnston was married to his 2d wife, Nancy Jane Williams March the 5th 1851 —

Thomas Lincoln died January 17th 1851 — aged 73 years & 11 days —

Daniel W. Johnston — son of John D. & Mary Johnston died July 15th 1846 —

Nancy Lincoln, wife of Thomas Lincoln died October the 5th 1818.

Sarah daughter of Thomas Lincoln, wife of Aaron Grigsby died January 20th 1828.

Thomas Lincoln married to Sarah Johnston Decr. 2d 1819.

Sarah Lincoln, daughter of Thomas Lincoln was married to Aaron Grigsby Aug. — 1826.

Sept 1865

W. H. Herndon [6]

So, as Sarah recalled family names, birth dates, marriage dates and death dates for her non-Lincoln Johnston family, Abe had written the record into the births, marriages and deaths pages of the Bible using his bottle of ink, inkwell and quill pen (but he may have been using a metal nib dip pen by the early 1850s). He recorded Sarah Bush Johnston's family, her first husband and their children rather completely. But Abe's family record was strangely incomplete. Births were not noted for his mother, Nancy Hanks Lincoln. But Abe, in truth born in late 1804, recorded the date he wanted people to believe to have been his own birthday — February 12, 1809!

In Ward Hill Lamon's biography, *The Life of Abraham Lincoln*, he records this same Bible recording event thusly:

---

[6] *Herndon's Informants*, page 110-111. The first entry, that of Sarah Lincoln, born February 10th, 1807, was misstated as Nancy Lincoln, perhaps because of torn fragments reassembled. I have substituted Sarah.

"The lives of [Thomas Lincoln] and his mother, and the history and character of the family before their settlement in Indiana, were topics upon which Mr. Lincoln never spoke but with great reluctance and significant reserve.

"In his family Bible he kept a register of births, marriages, and deaths, every entry being carefully made in his own handwriting. It contains the date of his sister's birth and his own (February 12, 1809); of the marriage and death of his sister; and of the death of his mother; and of the birth and death of Thomas Lincoln. The rest of the record is almost wholly devoted to the Johnston's and their numerous descendants and connections. It has not a word about the Hanks or the Sparrows. It shows the marriage of Sally Bush, first with Daniel Johnston, and then with Thomas Lincoln; but it is entirely silent as to the marriage of his own mother. It does not even give the date of her birth, but barely recognizes her existence and demise. . . ."[7]

William "Billy" Herndon, Abe Lincoln's law partner for 16 years.

The Bible perhaps began falling apart. In any event, Abe's record of births, marriages and deaths was torn from the Bible and, as of the publication of Lamon's biography of Abraham Lincoln, that page or pages was in the possession of Harriet Hanks and her husband, Col. Chapman, who remained in Coles County, Illinois.

How convenient! In one hour while sitting beside the late Thomas Lincoln's widow, Abraham Lincoln had placed on paper the original written documentation of his birth. There was no birth record for baby Abe in a county in North Carolina where he had been born. And, while he was just a little baby in arms, his mother Nancy Hanks had taken him away from his birthplace near Bostic, North Carolina. There was no birth record of baby Abe in Kentucky because he was not born in that State. But there was now a birth record on one or two pages from what remained of a brand new family Bible written at Sarah Bush Johnston Lincoln's house in Coles County, Illinois, **written during only one sitting by Abraham Lincoln, himself — after Sarah's late husband, Thomas Lincoln, had passed away and just as prospects for a renewed political career for the scribe was beginning to brighten.**

Let us review what appears to be the truth.

---

[7] Lamon, *The Life of Lincoln*, page 17.

Abe was born in the fall of 1804 to Nancy Hanks, being fathered out of wedlock by Abraham Enloe! I must suspect that the purpose of Abe's 100-mile buggy ride to visit with his stepmother a year or so after Thomas' death was to establish for posterity a written record of his birthday, or, I suppose I should say, to establish for posterity a written record of his alleged birthday.

Chapter 3: The difference in the Physical and Mental Ability of Abraham Lincoln and Thomas Lincoln Defies Logical Explanation.

A Detailed Verbal Description of Abraham Lincoln's Physical Appearance

On July 16, 1899, Professor Frank M. Vancil, who knew Abraham Lincoln in Illinois, wrote a detailed description of his physical appearance and mailed it to James Harrison Cathey. Cathey thought Vancil's was "one of the best if not the best pen portrait of Abraham Lincoln." Vancil was describing the mature Lincoln, not the youthful rail splitter. It follows:

"He was six feet and four inches in height, the length of his legs being out of all proportion to his body. When he sat on a chair he seemed no taller than the average man, measuring from the chair to the crown of his head, but his knees were high in front. He weighed about 180 pounds, but was thin through the breast and had the general appearance of a consumptive. Standing he stooped slightly forward, and sitting, he usually crossed his long legs or threw them over the arms of the chair. His head was long and tall from the base of the brain and the eyebrow; inclining backward as it rose. His ears were very large and stood out; eyebrows heavy, jutting forward over small, sunken, blue eyes; nose large, long, slightly Roman and blunt; chin projecting far and sharp, curved upward to meet a thick lower lip which hung downward; cheeks flabby and sunken, the loose skin falling in folds, a mole on one cheek, and an uncommonly large Adam's apple in his throat. His hair was dark brown, stiff and unkempt; complexion dark, skin yellow, shriveled and leathery. Every feature of the man – the hollow eyes with the dark rings beneath; the long, sallow, cadaverous face, his whole air and walk showed that he was a man of sorrow." [8]

We all know from experience that a child inherits physical appearance, physical ability and mental ability from his or her four grandparents. The egg contains a variety of inheritable characteristics from the mother's two parents and, likewise, the sperm from the father's two parents. When union of egg and sperm occur, those offerings from four grandparents, in a flash, sort out to create what would become the child.

Abraham Lincoln was a very unusual man in both physical and mental characteristics.

We know, without a doubt, that Nancy Hanks was Abraham Lincoln's mother.

---

[8] James H. Cathey, *The Genesis of Lincoln*, page146-147.

Abraham (Enloe) Lincoln, son of Abraham Enloe of North Carolina, Wesley's half brother

Wesley Enloe, son of Abraham Enloe of North Carolina, Abe's half brother

Thomas Lincoln, Nancy Hanks' husband

Within a very short time, a man can impregnate a woman without leaving a trace of his presence at the conception. However, the woman carries the child for nine months and then gives birth. We must ask ourselves, "How could Abraham Lincoln have been the biological son of Thomas Lincoln?"

The man that Lincoln claimed to have been his biological ancestor, Thomas, was five foot, ten inches high with a characteristic muscular male build. Mentally, he was probably less able than the average Kentuckian of his generation. So, it is prudent that we students of history be attentive to evidence and testimony concerning an alternate biological father.

Furthermore, Lincoln's mother, Nancy Hanks was about five feet, seven inches high and probably a bit heavy set. She had dark brown or black hair and blueish green or hazel eyes. Her complexion was pale, fair or sandy. Many in the Hanks family were red heads with freckles, but she was only described as sandy and fair. She was described as

28

amiable, charitable and affectionate. She probably was able to read the Bible some, but we know of no letters written by her. She was a Christian and church attender in Indiana. [9]

And, finally, Sarah Lincoln, daughter of Nancy Hanks Lincoln and an unknown father did not favor Abe at all. She was described as a thick-set, short built woman. Her eyes were dark gray and her hair was dark brown. She was described as kind, tender and good natured. Like her mother she was a member of the Baptist church in Indiana. She was probably able to read simple stories, but no letter from her survives. [10]

Billy Herndon, who knew his law partner better than any other man, felt it very likely that Thomas Lincoln had not fathered Abraham Lincoln. After the death of President Lincoln, Billy quickly began a huge project to learn about his late law partner's life prior to the years of their time together in the same two-man law practice, a practice begun sixteen years before the departure for Washington. All of Billy's investigative findings have been lately compiled into a book titled, *Herndon's Informants: Letters, Interviews and Statements about Abraham Lincoln*, and published in 1998 to make the records readily available to historians. I am drawing on that valuable resource.

It is likely that Billy Herndon never met, face to face, Thomas, the man his law partner claimed to be his father. Relying on other sources, Herndon presented the following description of Thomas Lincoln:

"He was, we are told, five feet ten inches high, weighed one hundred and ninety-five pounds, had a well-rounded face, dark hazel eyes, coarse black hair, and was slightly stoop-shouldered. His build was so compact that Dennis Hanks used to say that he could not find the point of separation between his ribs. He was proverbially slow of movement, mentally and physically; was careless, inert, and dull; was sinewy, and gifted with great strength; was inoffensively quiet and peaceable, but when roused to resistance a dangerous antagonist. . . . At the time of his marriage to Nancy Hanks, he could neither read nor write." [11]

We now proceed to Chapter 4 to learn about many of Herndon's findings as he had acquired them.

---

[9] See *Herndon's Informants*, reports by John Hanks, Dennis Hanks, Samuel Haycraft and Nathaniel Grigsby, pages 5, 598, 67, 113.

[10] *Herndon's Life of Lincoln*, page 17 and *Herndon's Informants*, John Hanks, page 456.

[11] Herndon's *Life of Lincoln*, by William Herndon and Jesse Weik, page 12.

Chapter 4: Billy Herndon — Lincoln's Law Partner, Political Advocate and Most Important Biographer.

Herndon's Informants

During William Herndon's search for his upcoming Lincoln biography, he obtained testimony from Kentucky stating that Thomas Lincoln was not Abraham Lincoln's father and, furthermore, Thomas Lincoln had suffered a bad case of the mumps, or something that rendered him incapable of fathering a child. Herndon had long been suspicious that Abe was withholding a politically damaging secret concerning his birth and childhood. In letters from Kentucky he was now seeing testimony detailing specifics.

In a letter from E. R. Burba to Billy Herndon, written in Hodgensville, Kentucky on March, 31, 1866, we see writtem testimony that Burba had obtained from William Cessna:

> "Thomas Lincoln was not considered all right in consequence of having mumps or something else." Explaining how he knew, Cessna stated that, "he had been with him often in bathing together in the water."

In a second letter to Herndon from E. R. Burba, dated May 25, 1866, he confirms:

> "As to your first inquiry in regard to Thomas Lincoln not being able to get a 'baby' from his first marriage, that seems to be the impression from the best information I can get." [12]

A letter from Charles Friend written to Billy Herndon in Sonora, Kentucky on July 31, 1889 reported:

> "You asked me a question: Was Thomas Lincoln castrated? I heard a cousin of my father's, Judge Jonathan Friend Cessna, say that his father, William Cessna, said that Thomas Lincoln could not have been Abe's father for

---

[12] *Herndon's Informants*, page 240.

one of Thomas' testicles was not larger than a pea or perhaps both of them were no larger than peas." [13]

Within the 721 pages of letters, interview notes and statements published in *Herndon's Informants*, 16 pages of letters from Kentucky argue that Abraham Enloe was Abraham Lincoln's biological father.

A sampling of testimony follows.

John B. Helm was born and lived his early life in Elizabethtown, Hardin County, Kentucky until 1852, when he moved to Missouri where he practiced law. He wrote a letter to Billy Herndon from Missouri, dated August 1, 1865. He described several Enloe families (they spelled the name, Enlow):

"As far back as I can recollect, there lived in Hardin County three families of Enlow's, all said to be cousins – I think from North Carolina, but not certain.

"Isham Enlow married a widow Larue and had a family of some distinction. Governor [John Larue] Helm is of Mrs. Enlow's descendants by her first husband, Larue, and several other persons of distinction by her Larue and Enlow husbands.

"Abe Enlow, another cousin, a tall dignified looking man of fine personal appearance; very neat, silent and reserved; more of a book worm than for action; married a Vernon, one of our best families, and raised a respectable family.

"Then comes our veritable Abe Enlow who claims to be the father of the President. This Abe was a man over six feet tall; pretty much in appearance as if he might have been of the same family of the President." [14]

Here, we students of history need to think about the clue which John B. Helm gave Billy Herndon early in his biographical study, in August, 1865: "I think from North Carolina." We can be fairly sure that Billy did not want to investigate the possibility that baby Abe's alleged Enloe father lived in North Carolina. Was not Nancy Hanks in North Carolina shortly before appearing in Kentucky, where she married Thomas Lincoln and, eight months later, gave birth to a daughter, Sarah? What did Billy know about Nancy Hanks' whereabouts before arriving in Kentucky, and just when did she arrive there? Why did Billy choose not to investigate this lead? Was he reluctant because he preferred to not know the real truth about Abe's parents?

---

[13] *Herndon's Informants*, page 674.
[14] *Herndon's Informants*, page 83.

John B. Helm, in his August 1, 1865 letter to Billy Herndon, enclosed another letter, which he had received from Samuel Haycraft, dated July 5, 1865. Concerning Abraham Lincoln's biological father, Haycraft said:

"Thomas Lincoln, as the name was always spelled but pronounced Linkhorn, was a low, heavy built, clumsy, honest man; his wife was a heavy built, squatty woman (the Lord only knows, except Abe Enlow did, where Abraham Lincoln got his length and his sense)." [15]

Many other letters gathered by Billy Herndon and his writing partner, Jesse W. Weik, discussed the likelihood that a man named Abraham Enlow, or Enloe. fathered Abraham Lincoln with Nancy Hanks. One Kentucky fellow, named Abe Enlow, apparently hearing the Abe Enlow story often, even bragged that he was the father of Abraham Lincoln. But on close examination that Abe Enlow fellow was only 15 years old when baby Abe was born (based on the birth year recorded on the Bible page Lincoln created with Sarah Bush Johnston Lincoln) or 10 years old (based on a birth date in North Carolina). This misleading claim, easily proven false, helped historians discard the whole body of evidence in support of the illegitimate fatherhood of President Abraham Lincoln.

Early on, in his biographical investigations, Herndon seemed scared about probing too deep into a search for his former law partner's biological father. Yes, he had many reasons to doubt that Thomas Lincoln begot Abraham Lincoln. But how could a person successfully publish a biography of the late President Lincoln who was glorified, thought of almost as a saint. Publishing houses would refuse to publish a biography that mentioned an illegitimate birth of the biographed man. Too many soldiers had died in Lincoln's war to conquer the seceded states. So Herndon did not dig deep. He never travelled to Kentucky and he never travelled to North Carolina, the former Seceded State, which had been the home of more deceased Confederate soldiers than had any other Southern State.

By September 1867, Herndon had accumulated letters, interviews and statements that filled 571 pages of the book, *Herndon's Informants*, which I am referring to while writing *Rebirthing Lincoln*. Only 164 pages of letters, interviews and statements filled the remainder of that book, many of them collected by Jesse Weik, who eventually helped Herndon write his biography, *Herndon's Life of Lincoln*, written and published 21 years later. What happened? Why did Herndon lose interest in following through with writing the Lincoln biography for which his research had occupied so much of his time from mid-1865 to late 1867, a little over two years?

---

[15] *Herndon's Informants*, page 84.

We need to step back to the summer of 1861 to reflect on that question.

Herndon's first wife and mother of his first six children, Mary Maxcy Herndon, had died on August 19, 1861 about six months after his law partner had departed Springfield to become President. Billy and Mary had been married 21 years. Mary had long suffered from tuberculosis and her body finally gave out. Realizing his six children needed the care of a mother, Billy went looking for a second wife. He thought he had found her while courting Anna Miles, a beautiful lady 18 years younger than he. Members of her family were Democrats and Herndon needed President Lincoln's help in winning her over.

Apparently, Anna's sister was married to a Mr. Charles W. Chatterton, who hoped for a Federal appointment. Figuring that getting the brother-in-law a Federal appointment would win Anna's heart, Billy packed his bags and rode the train to Washington, D. C., where he called on the President. Historian David Herbert Donald, in his biography of Herndon, would describe the event in these words:

> "The President rose from his chair and said, 'Let's go down to the Indian affairs department and see Dole.' The commissioner of Indian affairs, W. P. Dole, was an old friend from Paris, Illinois, and at the personal request of the President he did not find it difficult to locate 'one of [former President James] Buchanan's appointees who could be spared from the service.' A commission was issued shortly afterward, and Chatterton was made agent for the Cherokee Indians at a salary of $1,500 a year." [16]

Delighted, Billy was now a hero in the Miles family and, on July 30, 1862, Billy and Anna married. In 1860, Herndon's personal property had been valued at $11,000 and, until 1862, he was still earning $1,000 per year as a state banking commissioner. According to biographer David Herbert Donald's biography of Herndon:

> "The new wife brought to the Herndon home a whirlwind of energy. The house was renovated, an adjoining lot was purchased, and the grounds were landscaped for a flower garden. The Herndon house became a showplace in Springfield and visitors at the St. Nicholas Hotel used to stroll by in the evenings to see Herndon's roses."

But the good times were not to last very long for William H. Herndon.

Five months after Abraham Lincoln departed for Washington, in July 1861, Herndon brought a young man, Charles S. Zane, into a law partnership as a junior law lawyer. Born in New Jersey and apparently a "vociferous and radical

---

[16] Lincoln's Herndon, by David Herbert Donald, page 152.

Republican," the Herndon and Zane partnership operated out of the old Lincoln and Herndon office on the public square.

But Herndon would be slowly losing interest in the practice of law.

After Lincoln's death in 1865, Herndon spent over two years on biographical research. When 1866 dawned, Herndon lost the $1,000 per year income earned for serving as a state banking commissioner. By the end of 1867, his Lincoln biography research was deemed completed and Herndon had finished paying a copyist to make an accurate copy, organize the resulting tall stack of copied papers, and have them professionally bound into book form. Then he stored away the original pages in the back of the law office.

Herndon's father, Archer Gray Herndon, died on January 3, 1867. Shortly before passing, he deeded to his oldest son, Billy, a beautiful farm of almost 600 acres along the Sangamon River, six miles north of Springfield, along the road that led to Petersburg, Illinois, where his wife, Anna, had grown up. Herndon biographer, David Herbert Donald, would describe this farm in lovely detail:

> "The farmhouse stood on the steep bluff called Chinkapin Hill and looked out across flat, rich bottom lands along the meandering river. Herndon called his place 'Fairview,' for he had a grand sweep of the countryside – the dusty road that wound from Springfield toward Petersburg, the gray of the cypress trees along the river, an occasional dull glint of sunlight reflected in the sluggish stream, the level fields of corn, green-black under an August sun," [17]

After Billy's inheritance of the family farm, farming and the beauty of the land also became a diversion. He started out big. In 1867-1868, Herndon purchased 60 blooded cattle, 12 horses and 100 hogs. He also planted 500 grape vines and 400 fruit trees (apple, peaches, plum and cherry). He surely had hired farm workers, too. By this time Billy had invested all of his life's savings in the farm that he had inherited from his late father.

By 1868, Zane wanted out of the partnership, and it was terminated.

Yet, Herndon somehow lacked the drive to carry on and write the biography of his late law partner who had become President of those United States that had not seceded. Unable to pay for college educations for his three sons, he strove to teach them to be farmers. But Herndon had paid high prices for farm machinery blooded cattle, horses, hogs, grape vines and fruit trees when farm products brought high prices, only to suffer horribly when the agricultural depression hit

---

[17] *Lincoln's Herndon*, by David Herbert Donald, page 247.

and low farm prices followed in the late 1860's and early 1870's. For example, between 1868 and 1872, the price of corn fell 50 percent.

Ward Hill Lamon Buys the Bound Copy of Hendon's Research and Writes a Lincoln Biography.

Financially, Herndon was ruined. Desperately, he sought money. He even gave up his library, which he adored. He rented out part of his Springfield home to help pay the mortgage. Then, in early 1869 — it was January or February — Ward Hill Lamon visited Herndon in Springfield to discuss buying the before-mentioned copy of Herndon's Lincoln biography records, so nicely bound in three book volumes.

In later pages of *Rebirthing Lincoln*, you will hear more about Ward Hill Lamon. You will read of him during the 1860 Northern States Republican Convention, during President-elect Lincoln's travels to Washington and during his years as President. But, for now, our attention is directed at the Lincoln biography that Lamon would get accomplished author Chauncey F. Black to ghost-write for him.

Ward Hill Lamon bought the copies.

Herndon and Lamon dickered back and forth. Eventually, on September 17, 1869, Herndon agreed to give Lamon possession of the copies of his records that he had paid to be copied and bound. Lamon paid Herndon $2,000 cash and gave him a note for an additional $2,000, which, three months later, Herndon used as collateral to underwrite a $2,000 loan. Herndon retained the original papers that had been used to make the copies that Lamon purchased.

Meanwhile, while Chauncey Black poured over the three bound volumes of Lincoln records, their creator, Billy Herndon, was sinking deeper in debt. The bank foreclosed on the mortgage on Herndon's home and adjacent rose garden in Springfield, and, in early 1871, he and his family moved out to the inherited farm on Chinkapin Hill, which overlooked the Sangamon River. The Herndon family was no longer residents of Springfield.

Ward Hill Lamon's 547 page biography, *Life of Abraham Lincoln: From His Birth to His Inauguration as President,"* was published in June 1872. Herndon biographer, David Herbert Donald, would describe how Black and Lamon deleted important sections of their original biography manuscript in response to demands by the publisher — deleted significant segments from the original manuscript that Chauncey Black had ghost-written using Herndon's three bound volumes of records:

Prior to acceptance for publication by James R. Osgood & Company, giving in to pressure from Lamon and the publisher, "Black deleted some of his more extreme statements about Lincoln's personal history, but the final chapter of his book remained a venomous indictment of Republican policies during the secession winter of 1860-1861." But those deletions were insufficient. So, "however it came about, in early 1872, Lamon, without asking the consent of his collaborator, agreed to revise many small matters and to suppress the entire last chapter of Black's manuscript.

Concerning Lamon's book, David Herbert Donald, in his biography, *Lincoln's Herndon*, would explain:

"It was a sensation. After all the deletions and revisions, this was probably the most harshly critical biography that had appeared in America. It combined ruthless revelation and flippant cynicism to give a devastating caricature of Lincoln. At the time of Abraham's birth, the biography began, his parents 'are supposed to have been married about three years,' but for this belief, there exists no evidence but that of mutual acknowledgment and cohabitation.' [18] This was but the start. For the first time, the stories about which Herndon had been gossiping for years in his 'indirect language' were now revealed in their ugly nakedness – the illegitimacy of Lincoln's mother, Lincoln's 'infidel book,' the jilting of Mary Todd, domestic difficulties in the Lincoln household, Lincoln's 'shrewd game' in deceiving preachers by pretending to be a Christian. Throughout, the emphasis was on Lincoln the schemer and the politician, cunning, ambitious, unprincipled. Black had charity for none." [19]

Jesse Weik and Herndon's *Life of Lincoln: The True Story of a Great Life*

We now advance our story of Billy Herndon to the five-year span, from 1876 through 1881. This, too, is a sad story; a story of loneliness, excessive drinking and illness. Eventually Billy turned his life around and, in October, 1881, began corresponding with Jesse William Weik a twenty-four year old son of a German immigrant and a graduate of Indiana Asbury University (later DePaul). A year later, in November, 1882, Weik was given a job in the Federal Government's Department of Interior, which involved handling disability claims submitted by war veterans, and was told to establish his office in Springfield, Illinois.

---

[18] Several years later a record of the marriage would be discovered in Kentucky.
[19] *Lincoln's Herndon*, David Herbert Donald, page 267-269.

After obtaining a hotel room, Jesse located Herndon and, together, they went to the back room of the old Lincoln and Herndon office where Billy had been storing his original copies of his Lincoln record over the past 15 years (I am amazed someone had not thrown them away during those 15 yars). Of these few hours, Herndon biographer David Herbert Donald would say:

> "Herndon had not looked at them for so long they were almost as new to him as to his visitor. Delightedly they rummaged through the boxes, and each new bundle of papers brought new stories and reminiscences to Herndon's mind."

Two years and four months later, March, 1885, there is evidence that Herndon and Weik were together (an entry in Weik's diary). The diary reports that Weik "spent an hour or two at the office of W. H. Herndon and listened to him telling stories about Lincoln." As it turns out, Jesse Weik was about to resign from his job with the veteran pension service and begin a writing career. He was considerably overweight and thought his health needed such a career change.

Soon afterward, Weik proposed to write an article about Lincoln for *Harper's Monthly* and invited Herndon to help with supplying content. "If I can help you in any way," Herndon submitted, "I will do so at all times willingly." That was the beginning of a cooperative Lincoln biographical project, a project that would grow far beyond *Harper's Monthly*, and become *Herndon's Life of Lincoln: The True Story of a Great Life*, a full length book by William H. Herndon and Jesse W. Weik.

By the fall of 1885, Herndon got busy — writing long letters about Lincoln, drawing on his personal experiences and his Lincoln Records. Between October, 1885 and January 1886, he wrote and sent to Jesse 35 such long letters. By late January, 1886, Herndon nudged Jesse with these encouraging words: "It seems to me that I have written to you enough matter to make a respectable Life of Lincoln. . . . Had you better change your plans and issue a little Life of Lincoln yourself?" Herndon kept writing material for Jesse Weik's use going forward until his death on March 18, 1891.

William Herndon and his wife and children had never experienced any social get-togethers with Abe, Mary and their children over the long span of 16 years when the two lawyers had worked together in their two-man office in Springfield. They had worked intimately toward victory in legal cases and toward the political advancement of the senior partner. But Billy had never spent time with Mary Lincoln and her husband socially. It was said that Mary never invited Herndon or his family to dinner at the Lincoln home. It is said that Mary did not like Billy Herndon. Perhaps Mary and her husband wanted a firm social separation, believing that policy would best keep secret certain embarrassing aspects of Abe's parentage.

And that policy in the Lincoln home was most wise. Billy Herndon was smart and studious. If given a clue, Billy just might have sought out supportive evidence.

Herndon was plenty suspicious anyway. In his Lincoln biography, *Herndon's Life of Lincoln,* he wrote:

"On the subject of his ancestry and origin, I only remember one time when Mr. Lincoln ever referred to it. It was about 1850, when he and I were driving in his one-horse buggy to the court in Menard County, Illinois. The suit we were going to try was one in which we were likely, either directly or collaterally, to touch upon the subject of hereditary traits. During the ride he spoke, for the first time in my hearing, of his mother, dwelling on her characteristics, and mentioning and enumerating what qualities he inherited from her. He said, among other things, that she was the illegitimate daughter of Lucy Hanks and a well-bred Virginia farmer or planter; and he argued that from this last source came his power of analysis, his logic, his mental activity, his ambition, and all the qualities that distinguished him from the other members and descendants of the Hanks family."

In March, 1887, Jesse Weik did what Billy Herndon had always been reluctant to do: travel to Lincoln's childhood region of Kentucky and personally search for the true story of his paternity. If Herndon had made the Kentucky trip in 1866, could he have found that Nancy Hanks had come from western North Carolina? Could he have made sense of the often-told story of Abraham Enlow or Enloe and where the Enloe clan had lived before immigrating into Kentucky? How many Abram, or Abraham Enloe's could he have identified? Weik arrived in Kentucky 21 years later. The trail was then very cold. Jesse made less sense of these questions than Herndon had already uncovered.

Jesse William Weik, Herdon's biography writing partner

For a full month, from August 1 to September 5, 1887, Herndon was at Jesse's home in Greencastle, Indiana, sitting with him working full time on the joint Lincoln biography project. For Herndon, the work was quite tiring. After a month, he apologized and took the train back to Springfield, Illinois, walking on to his farm.

By July, 1888, Jesse and Billy had completed their manuscript to their satisfaction and begun seeking a publisher. This proved very difficult. It took a courageous publishing house to produce a Lincoln biography that revealed so much unflattering personal life and upbringing. Eventually, a small time New York publisher, Belford, Clarke & Company, showed interest. Terms were agreed to. In September, Herndon and Weik shipped the manuscript to this publisher. But Belford, Clark & Company was deeply in debt, on the verge of bankruptcy. *Herndon's Lincoln* was published in June, 1889, only 1,500 books being printed initially, the quantity that matched the contract rule, which stipulated that all profits would be retained by the publisher. In late September, 1889, Belford Clark & Company went into bankruptcy. A second edition of 1,500 books was produced and distributed in the spring of 1890. That was the end of Belford Clark & Company's effort.

Charles Scribner's Sons, a major publishing house, considered printing a third edition during the winter of 1890 and most of 1891. But, when the late President' son, Robert Lincoln, complained, Scribner's gave in to political correctness pressures and informed Jesse Weik of their decision to withdraw from the project in a letter dated October 1. 1891.

Billy Herndon had passed away six months earlier, on March 18, 1891, still hoping for another book publication run and receiving some royalty money for his family. While alive, he had received no royalties from his efforts in partnership with Jesse Weik.

Although Charles Scribner's Sons declined to publish a new edition of *Herndon's Lincoln*, today, reprint copies of the book are readily available on Amazon.

William H. Herndon was an important person in American history. His work toward promoting the political advancement of his law partner was very meaningful; perhaps without it, history would have been different. One might reason that, had Herndon not been Lincoln's law partner, history would have taken a very different turn and another, perhaps William Seward of New York, would have been nominated for President by the Northern States Republican Party. Once elected President, history suggests that President Seward might well have chosen negotiation with President Davis instead of the war of conquest actually chosen by President Lincoln.

I close this chapter concerning Billy Herndon by quoting from David Herbert Donald's biography:

"Seventy-two years old, fragile as a sheet of yellowed paper, he was 'sick pretty much all winter with the grippe.' His condition was not considered serious, but in March he was confined to his bed. Mrs. Herndon was more worried about her son than her husband. Willie Herndon, a fine boy of twenty-one, suffered from 'an attack of catarral-fever which resulted in pneumonia'. His father too was uneasy about him. 'I am afraid Willie will be taken from us,' he told Anna Herndon.

"Early in the morning of March 18, 1891, Willie died. Though the news was carefully kept from his father, Herndon seemed to know that his son was gone. He suffered an abrupt relapse. Before noon Mrs. Herndon was hoarsely called to her husband's bed. 'Anna,' he whispered, 'the summons has called. I am an overripe sheaf. I go and take the weak [meaning his son] with me and leave you the strong. All I ask is that you do not weep. Do not forget my first wife's children and tell them goodbye'.

"Two days later, with a winter wind whipping about the hearse, the funeral procession plodded through muddy roads to Springfield's Oak Ridge Cemetery. A small group of old friends gathered for a moment on the slope opposite Lincoln's tomb. The preacher said simply: 'We will leave his record with his Maker'." [20]

---

[20] Lincoln's Herndon, by David Herbert Donald, pages 340-341.

Chapter 5: James H. Cathey's North Carolina Informants

The List of Fourteen

James Harrison Cathey of Sylva, North Carolina, published a book in 1899 titled, *Truth is Stranger than Fiction: True Genesis of a Wonderful Man* (I am using a reprint titled *The Genesis of Lincoln*), in which he detailed numerous witnesses in support of the likelihood that Abraham Lincoln was born to Nancy Hanks in western North Carolina about one-and-a-half to two years before she married Thomas Lincoln in central Kentucky. Between 1895 and 1898, Cathey recorded testimony from fourteen important and believable witnesses. He had considerable help from the person whom his informants identified as Abraham Lincoln's half-brother, Wesley M. Enloe. By 1895, Abraham Lincoln would have been 90 years old. James Cathey and Wesley Enloe knew that very, very little time remained to visit and record testimony from the few witnesses of Lincoln's birth who were still alive during the span from 1895 through 1898. The list of the 14 most relevant people that Cathey was able to interview, and/or communicate with by letter, follows:

Wesley's nephew, Captain William A. Enloe.

Dr. Issac N. Enloe of Illinois.

Mr. Sam G. Inloe of Missouri.

Wesley's son, Mr. J. Frank Enloe of North Carolina.

Wesley's niece, Mrs. Floyd, of Texas.

Mr. H. J. Beck of Ocona Lufta, North Carolina.

C. A. Ragland, Esq. of Stockton, Missouri.

Mr. Joseph A. Collins, of Clyde, North Carolina.

Captain E. Everett of Bryson City, North Carolina.

Mr. D. K. Collins, also of Bryson City North Carolina.

Mr. Philip Dills, of Dillsboro, North Carolina.

Honorable William Dills, also of Dillsboro, North Carolina.

Mr. Sion T. Early, also of Dillsboro, North Carolina.

Captain James W. Terrell, of Webster, North Carolina. [21]

---

[21] *The Genesis of Lincoln*, James Harrison Cathey, page 22.

For the sake of brevity, I will now present a sampling of several of James Cathy's informant's testimonies pertaining to Abram (Abraham) Enloe, likely biological father of Abraham Lincoln.

Philip Dills

"Mr. Dills was born in Rutherford County, N. C., January 10, 1808. His father emigrated to the mountains of Western North Carolina almost contemporaneously with Abraham Enloe. . . .   He said, 'I knew Abraham Enloe personally and intimately. I lived on the road which he frequently traveled in his trips south, and he made my house a stopping place. He was a large man, tall, with dark complexion, and coarse, black hair. He was a splendid looking man, and a man of fine sense. His judgment was taken as a guide, and he was respected and looked up to in his time.

"I do not know when I first heard of his relation with Nancy Hanks, but it was . . . while I was a very young man. The circumstance was related in my hearing by the generation older than myself, and I heard it talked over time and again. I have no doubt that Abraham Enloe was the father of Abraham Lincoln." [22]

Walker Battle

"Mr. Battle was born February 12, 1809, in Haywood County. His father was one of the three men who came to Ocona Lufta with Abraham Enloe. He was a highly respected citizen of Swain County. The following statement was received from him in 1895. He has since died."

The following statement is from his son, Milton Battle, of Bryson City, North Carolina:

"My father was one of the first settlers of this country. He came here with Abraham Enloe. I have lived here my entire life, and I knew Abraham Enloe and his family almost as well as I knew my own.

"The incident occurred, of course, before my day, but I distinctly remember hearing my own family tell of the trouble between Abraham Enloe and Nancy Hanks when I was a boy. I recall, as if it were yesterday, hearing them speak of Nancy's removal to Kentucky and that she married there a fellow by the name of Lincoln; that Abraham Enloe had some kind of correspondence with the woman after he sent her to Kentucky – sent her something – and that he had to be very cautious to keep his wife from finding it out.

---

[22] *The Genesis of Lincoln*, James Harrison Cathey, page 39.

"There is no doubt as to Nancy Hanks having once lived in the family of Abraham Enloe, and there is no doubt that she was the mother of a child by him." [23]

Joseph Collins, concerning Judge Gilmore's testimony

"Mr. Collins is fifty-six years old and resides in the town of Clyde, in Haywood county. . . He is now proprietor of a hardware store in his home town. He is well known over the entire western part of the state as a gentleman of the most unquestionable integrity. He said:

"'The first I knew of any tradition being connected with Abraham Lincoln's origin on his father's side was in 1867. At that time I was in Texas, and while there I made the acquaintance of Judge Gilmore, an old gentleman who lived three miles from Fort Worth.

"'He told me he knew Nancy Hanks before she was married, and that she then had a child she called Abraham. While the child was yet small,' said Judge Gilmore, 'she married a man by the name of Lincoln, a whisky distiller. Lincoln,' he said, 'was a very poor man, and they lived in a small log house.'

"'After Nancy Hanks was married to the man Lincoln,' said Gilmore, 'the boy was known by the name of Abraham Lincoln.' He said that, 'Abraham's mother, when the boy was about eight years old, died.'"

"'Judge Gilmore said he himself was five or six years older than Abraham Lincoln; that he knew him well; attended the same school with him. He said Lincoln was a bright boy and learned very rapidly; was the best boy to work he had ever known.

"He said he knew Lincoln until he was almost grown, when he, Gilmore, moved to Texas."

Joseph Collins concerning Phillis Wells' testimony

"Years ago, I was traveling for a house in Knoxville. On Turkey Creek, in Buncombe county, N. C., I met an old gentleman whose name was Phillis Wells. He told me that he knew Abraham Lincoln was the son of Abraham Enloe, who lived on Ocona Lufta.

"Wells said he was then ninety years of age. When he was a young man he traveled over the country and sold tinware and bought furs, feathers and ginseng for William Johnston, of Waynesville. He said he often stopped with Abraham Enloe. On one occasion, he called to stay overnight, as was his custom, when Abraham

---

[23] *The Genesis of Lincoln*, James Harrison Cathey, page 40-42.

Enloe came out and went with him to the barn to put up his horse, and while there Enloe said:

"'My wife is mad; about to tear up the place; she has not spoken to me in two weeks, and I wanted to tell you about it before you went into the house.' Then, remarked Wells, 'I said, what is the matter?' And Abraham Enloe replied: 'The trouble is about Nancy Hanks, a hired girl we have living with us.' Wells said he staid all night, and that Mrs. Enloe did not speak to her husband while he was there. He said he saw Nancy Hanks there; that she was a good-looking girl, and seemed to be smart for business.' Wells said before he got back there on his next trip that Abraham Enloe had sent Nancy Hanks to Jonathan's Creek and hired a family there to take care of her; that later a child was born to Nancy Hanks, and she named him 'Abraham.'

"Meantime the trouble in Abraham Enloe's family had not abated. As soon as Nancy Hanks was able to travel, Abraham Enloe hired a man to take her and her child out of the country, in order to restore quiet and peace at home. He said he sent her to some of his relatives near the State line between Tennessee and Kentucky. He said Nancy and the child were cared for by Enloe's relatives until she married a fellow by the name of Lincoln.

"I asked the old gentleman if he really believed Abraham Lincoln was the son of Abraham Enloe, and he replied: 'I know it, and if I did not know it I would not tell it'."

"I made special inquiry about the character of Wells, and every one said that he was an honest and truthful man and a good citizen." [24]

H. J. Beck

"Mr. Beck was born and reared and has all his life lived on Ocona Lufta. He was one of Abraham Enloe's neighbors, as was his father before him. He is now an octogenarian. He is well-to-do, intelligent and of upright character. He said:

"'I have heard my father and mother often speak of the episode of Abraham Enloe and Nancy Hanks. They said Abraham Enloe moved from Rutherford County here, bringing with his family a hired girl named Nancy Hanks. Sometime after they settled here, Nancy Hanks was found to be with child, and Enloe procured Hon. Felix Walker to take her away. Walker was gone two or three weeks.

---

[24] *The Genesis of Lincoln*, James Harrison Cathey, page 55-57. In *Rebirthing Lincoln*, I have chosen to not rely on "Jonathan's Creek" and "his relatives near the line between Tennessee and Kentucky."

"As to Abraham Enloe, he was a very large man, weighing between two and three hundred pounds. He was justice of the peace." [25]

Capt. William A. Enloe

"Captain Enloe was born in Haywood (now Jackson) County, and is sixty-six years of age. He is a successful merchant and businessman. [During the war] he was Captain of Company F, 29th N. C. Regiment. . . He has represented his county in the General Assembly. He is a grandson of Abraham Enloe. He said:

"'There is a tradition come down through the family that Nancy Hanks, the mother of President Lincoln, once lived at my grandfather's, and while there became the mother of a child said to be my grandfather Abraham Enloe's.

"'One Mr. Thompson married my aunt Nancy, daughter of Abraham Enloe, contrary to the will of my grandfather; to conceal the matter from my grandfather's knowledge, Thompson stole her away and went to Kentucky; on the trip they were married. Hearing of the marriage, my grandfather reflected and decided to invite them back home. On their return they were informed of the tumult in my grandfather's household because of Nancy Hanks, who had given birth to a child; and when my uncle and aunt, Thompson and wife, returned to their Kentucky home, they took with them Nancy Hanks and her child. This is the family story as near as I can reproduce it from memory'." [26]

Wesley M. Enloe

"Mr. Enloe was born in 1811, in Haywood county, N. C., and is the ninth and only surviving son of Abraham Enloe. He resides on the same farm and in the same house in which his father lived when Nancy Hanks was banished from the household. . . He said:

"'I was born after the incident between father and Nancy Hanks. I have, however, a vivid recollection of hearing the name Nancy Hanks frequently mentioned in the family while I was a boy. . . .

"'Nancy Hanks lived in my father's family. I have no doubt the cause of my father's sending her to Kentucky is the one generally alleged. The occurrence as

---

[25] *The Genesis of Lincoln*, James Harrison Cathey, pages 57-58. I have relied on testimony: "Hon. Felix Walker to take her away."
[26] *The Genesis of Lincoln*, James Harrison Cathey, pages 59-61. The story that the Thompson's took baby Abe to Kentucky is in error because Nancy Enloe was still a child when Nancy Hanks was taken to Kentucky with baby Abe. I am unable to adapt this story to my telling of *Rebirthing Lincoln*.

understood by my generation and given to them by that of my father, I have no doubt is essentially true'." [27]

C. A. Ragland, Esq.

"Mr. Ragland is a citizen of Missouri and a leading attorney in the town of Stockton. He wrote:

"' . . . About twelve years ago I called on Col. T. G. C. Davis at his office in St. Louis, Missouri. . . Col. Davis, having once resided for a long time in Illinois, the conversation naturally turned upon her times and men. He said he was personally acquainted with President Lincoln. . . . He said that he knew the mother of Lincoln; that he was raised in the same neighborhood in Kentucky, and that it was generally understood, without question, in that neighborhood, that Lincoln, the man that married the President's mother, was not the father of the President, but that his father was Enloe'." [28]

An 1983 Article in the, then well-respected, newspaper, the Charlotte *Observer*, Sunday, September 17th, 1893, page 2

On the previous Sunday, September 10th, 1893, this newspaper had presented an article which alleged that Thomas Lincoln was not the true father of President Lincoln. This prompted a person, calling himself "A Student of History," to pen an extensive, long article on the President's father, Abraham Enloe, and evidence supporting the claim that Enloe had fathered Abraham Lincoln. Quoting a small part of this article is appropriate. The writer is relating his experience talking to Col. Davidson of Asheville N. C., the father of North Carolina's late Attorney General. Col. Davidson said:

"Abram Enloe lived in Rutherford County. He had in his family a girl named Nancy Hanks, about ten or twelve years of age. He moved from Rutherford to Buncombe and settled on a branch of the Ocona, in what was afterwards Swain County. At the end of eight years he moved to the house at the foot of the smoky mountains, the . . . present home of Wesley Enloe.

"Soon after Abram moved, his own daughter, Nancy Enloe, against his wish, ran away and married a Kentucky gentleman named Thompson, from Hardin County in that state.

"In the meantime, during the absence of Mrs. Nancy Enloe Thompson in Kentucky, at the home of Abram Enloe, a son was born to Nancy Hanks, then

---

[27] *The Genesis of Lincoln*, James Harrison Cathey, pages 62-63.
[28] *The Genesis of Lincoln*, James Harrison Cathey, pages 77-78.

about twenty or twenty-one years of age. The relations between Mrs. Enloe and her husband became, as a matter of course, unpleasant.

"There is a lady now living, says Colonel Davidson, who, as a girl, was visiting Abram Enloe. This lady says that Nancy Enloe Thompson, having become reconciled with her parents, had returned from Kentucky to North Carolina. They were to start to Kentucky again in a few days, and she remembered hearing a neighbor say, 'I am glad Nancy Hanks and her boy are going to Kentucky with Mrs. Thompson. Mrs. Enloe will be happy again'.

"I married into the Enloe family myself. I settled Abram Enloe's estate, and have frequently heard this tradition during my life, and have no doubt of its truth."

The Charlotte Observer newspaper article closed with the story of President Lincoln's gift to Nancy Enloe Thompson's son:

"'I am a lawyer. I was seated in my office, since the war and soon after its close. A gentleman called, introduced himself as Thompson and stated he learned that I was the man who settled Abram Enloe's estate; that he was a son of Nancy Enloe Thompson. He stated, among other things, that he was a Democrat, and had been an Indian agent during the Lincoln administration.

"'I asked . . . how Lincoln, who was a Republican, appointed him, a Democrat, an Indian agent?

"'Thompson replied that Lincoln was under some great obligation to his (Thompson's) mother, and expressed a desire to aid her, if possible, in some substantial way. She finally consented that he might do something for her son, and this is the way I got my appointment'." [29]

That concludes a sampling of testimony collected by James Cathey. James Cathey conducted extensive research in western North Carolina between 1895 and 1898, gathering testimony concerning Abram (or Abraham) Enloe and his connection to Nancy Hanks, mother of Abraham Lincoln. This research was of highest quality and Cathey published the testimonies in his 1899 book, *Truth is Stranger than Fiction: The True Genesis of a Wonderful Man* (I am using a reprint titled, *The Genesis of Lincoln*).

All subsequent studies of Lincoln's parentage and birth, to a great extent, draw on the revelations in four fundamental historical resources:

---

[29] *The Genesis of Lincoln*, James Harrison Cathey, pages 72-74. Again, Nancy Enloe Thompson was still a child when Nancy Hanks and baby Abe were taken to Kentucky. So this story cannot be used in writing *Rebirthing Lincoln*.

1. The most convenient source of Herndon's records concerning the early life of his law partner are contained in the 827-page book, *Herndon's Informants: Letters, Interviews, and Statements*, edited by Douglas L. Wilson and Rodney O. Davis, supported by grants from the Abraham Lincoln Association, the New Salem Lincoln League and the Illinois State Historical Society and published in 1998 by the University of Illinois Press. Using the above records of Herndon's informants, Ward Hill Lamon, with considerable help from ghost writer, Chauncey F. Black, published, in 1872, a biography titled, *Life of Abraham Lincoln, from his Birth to His Inauguration as President*. Also using the above records, near the end of Herndon's life, he, with help from young Jesse Weik, compiled a biography, titled, *Abraham Lincoln: The True Story of a Great Life*, which was published in early 1889. I am using a reprint titled, *Herndon's Life of Lincoln*. My *Rebirthing Lincoln* was drawn from these resources.

2. James Caswell Coggins' book, *The Eugenics of Lincoln*, published in 1940. Here Coggins focuses on the genetic principle of traits inherited from a baby's four grandparents and digs deeper into the search for Abraham Lincoln's parents and grandparents, adding new testimony concerning Lincoln's maternal grandfather.

3. *The Tarheel Lincoln, North Carolina Origins of "Honest" Abe*, by Jerry A. Goodnight and Richard Eller; published in 2003 by Westmoreland Printers, Shelby, North Carolina.

4. *Abraham Enloe of Western North Carolina, the Natural Father of Abraham Lincoln*, by Don Norris, printed by Vantage Press in 2008.

James Caswell Coggings, in the first edition of his book, titled *Abraham Lincoln, a North Carolinian*, summarized his disbelief of the Kentucky tradition of the birth of baby Abe thusly:

"The very fact that the Kentucky tradition has as many as eleven birthplaces designated as the very spots where Abraham Lincoln was born, four in one county, is sufficient to create very grave doubts as to there being any real fact to support the Kentucky claim at all, other than simply the fact of residence or of being seen at these places mentioned." [30]

As the author of the book that you are now reading, *Rebirthing Lincoln*, I should reveal that it is not my goal to add to past fundamental knowledge of Abraham Lincoln from birth to leaving Springfield, Illinois to be sworn in as President. You see, my purpose is to accept existing historical knowledge and ask you to believe

---

[30] *Abraham Lincoln, a North Carolinian*. James Caswell Coggins, published in 1927, page 38.

that, most likely, Abraham Enloe of North Carolina fathered the future Northern States Republican Party's presidential candidate. Furthermore, in later chapters, year by year, from 1851 to 1861, *Rebirthing Lincoln* will help you understand how Springfield Lawyer Abraham Lincoln, yes "Honest Abe" himself, kept secret, from inquiring newspapermen and political opponents, that Thomas Lincoln was not his biological father and that he was born in North Carolina, not Kentucky as he claimed.

Rebirthing Lincoln now goes back to Nancy Hanks in North Carolina and moves forward, presenting the biography from the beginning of Abraham Lincoln's mother's birth and childhood. And here we identify baby Abe's maternal grandmother and maternal grandfather.

Chapter 6: 1803, Virginia, Nancy Hanks (Tanner) is born illegitimately; Lucy Hanks is mother; Michael Tanner is father.

Nancy Hanks (Tanner) was Illegitimately Born in Virginia; Her Mother was Lucy Hanks, also probably Illegitimately born; Her Biological Father was Michael Tanner

Yes that is right. Just like Abraham Lincoln should have been known as Abraham Enloe, Junior, Nancy Hanks should have been known as Nancy Hanks Tanner. In the late 1930's James Caswell Coggins discovered evidence revealing that Michael Tanner was Nancy Hanks' biological father. That completes the quartet of grandparents needed to understand the ancestry of baby Abe. In his book, *The Eugenics of Lincoln*, published in 1941 and copyrighted in 1940, Coggins describes the key discovery:

"The recent discovery of an old manuscript has brought to light a very profound family secret in regard to the birth and ancestry of Nancy Hanks, the mother of Abraham Lincoln. It shows a close correspondence to Lincoln's statement to his law partner, that his, Lincoln's, 'mother was an illegitimate daughter of Lucy Hanks and a Virginian of fine blood.' And members of this high-class family 'of good German blood' have laid claim to a close kindship to Lincoln, known only among themselves for over a hundred years, until recently discovered.

"This secret was preserved for many years in manuscript form, having been written for the family only, and showing the family relationship to Abraham Lincoln through Nancy Hanks, the daughter of Lucy Hanks, and a member of this prominent German family.

"I made this discovery while sitting in a lawyer's office at Forest City, North Carolina, getting the material for my second edition of the book, *Abraham Lincoln, a North Carolinian*. [31] This lawyer was a grandson of the old Judge who had written the matter for the family; and I not only secured the lawyer's affidavit that he had seen and read the secret manuscript, but also that he had heard his grandfather relate the same a number of times." [32]

On a subsequent visit, some few years later, Coggins made another confirming discovery. While sitting in that same lawyer's office, he learned that a second family manuscript had been written by a family member in Texas long ago, giving more

---

[31] I am using a reprint, *The Eugenics of Lincoln*.
[32] *The Eugenics of Lincoln*, by James Caswell Coggins, pages 79-80.

details. Combining the family history in these two manuscripts, Coggins revealed, in his 1940 book, Lincoln's ancestry on his mother's side in satisfying detail.

Nancy Hanks' father was Michael Tanner, Junior. His father was Michael Tanner, Senior, who had immigrated to America from Germany in 1750 or thereabouts and settled in Virginia. Michael, Senior was of an aristocratic German family and clearly an intelligent and capable man. He settled in Amelia County, Virginia and raised a family, including sons Michael, Junior and Daniel.

Lucy Hanks, a young woman of, most likely, illegitimate birth, was in Amelia County, Virginia, in about the year 1783, when she became pregnant by Michael Tanner, Junior. Lucy gave birth, delivering a baby girl she named Nancy. But Lucy seemed disinterested in raising baby Nancy and Michael, embarrassed, sought help from his brother's family. Agreeing to be helpful, Michael, Junior's brother, Daniel, took baby Nancy into his young family, intending that he and his wife would raise her along with their small legitimate children. To save face concerning Lucy Hanks and Michael's relationship, which had produced Nancy, the brothers would later tell family members that Michael, Junior's first wife — that being a fictional woman — had died giving birth to Nancy, so Daniel and his wife took the baby into their family.

In 1805, Daniel Tanner's Family Migrates to North Carolina, bringing young Nancy with them

While Nancy was still a very small girl, about two years old, Daniel Tanner and his wife took his brother's little girl and their children on a journey south. They were going to Rutherford County, North Carolina, where Daniel intended to settle down and raise his young family, and perhaps for a while, Nancy, too. Brother Michael Tanner also joined Daniel in the resettlement journey. Of course, young Nancy, now old enough to perceive it herself, considered Daniel her father. Daniel's family would expand to eleven children and include William A. Tanner, the oldest son and Martha Tanner, the youngest child.

Lucy Hanks may have also travelled to Rutherford County with the Tanner party — if not then, we know she came to North Carolina later. Eventually, the true father, Michael Tanner, Junior, would marry a Miss Panter. We have now left the Virginia story concerning Nancy Hanks Tanner. We are now situated in mid-state North Carolina.

Our history regarding Nancy's mother, Lucy Hanks, is fuzzy, but we do have solid evidence that she had moved on to Mercer County, Kentucky, sometime prior to late 1789 because, in November 24, 1789, a grand jury in that Kentucky county had indicted Lucy Hanks on a fornication charge. At the time of the fornication charge against Lucy, Nancy, then about 6 years old, was living in North Carolina with her uncle, Dicky Hanks.

Chapter 7: In 1787, Nancy Hanks (Tanner) grows up as an Orphan in North Carolina.

In 1787, Nancy Hanks (Tanner) goes to Live with Uncle Dicky Hanks on the Catawba River near Belmont, North Carolina.

Richard (Dicky) Hanks, came to North Carolina from Virginia about the same time that the Tanners had migrated to Rutherford County. Dicky Hanks travelled further southeast to a hill above the Catawba River, in southeastern Lincoln County, now Gaston County, near present-day Belmont, a 55 mile eastward journey from the Tanner's emerging farm. There, above the Catawba River, Dicky Hanks built a log cabin. When young Nancy Hanks, was perhaps 4 years old, her mother, Lucy, perhaps in response to Michael Tanner's brother's urgings, picked up young Nancy from Daniel Tanner's home in Rutherford County home and both of them traveled to Uncle Dicky's log cabin above the Catawba River to enable Nancy to live with his family.

By the way, many decades later, the cabin site land was within the property of C. T. Stowe, head of a prominent Gaston County family.

The boulder pictured here was erected by C. T. Stowe's son, Samuel Pinckney Stowe, soon after he took possession of the land. The large bronze plate is mounted to a massive granite boulder positioned near where the cabin once stood. C. T. Stowe personally remembered the cabin and often pointed out this site as the home of Nancy and Dicky Hanks. Old photos of the cabin exist. Also, a monument was erected at the site. The monument states:

President Lincoln's birth marker at Bostic, North Carolina.

> "This stone marks the site of the log cabin home of Dicky Hanks, an Uncle of Nancy Hanks, Mother of Abraham Lincoln. Nancy spent much of her childhood here with her uncle. Erected in 1902 by descendants of C. T. Stowe."

For more information see, *History of Gaston County* by Minnie Stowe Puett, published in 1939.

Dicky Hanks is important to our Abe Lincoln biography because the future president's mother, little Nancy Hanks Tanner, lived with her "Uncle Dicky" for much of her childhood. It is likely that little Nancy lived with Dicky from about 1787, when she was about 4 years old, to 1796, when she was about 13 years old. [33]

Uncle Dicky had married Phebe Hayes in October 1785 and their first child, John, was about one year old when Nancy arrived. Not far away lived the family of another uncle, James Abraham Hanks, Dicky's brother. There is considerable local historical testimony by witnesses who lived in the area while Nancy was a young girl living with her Uncle Dicky, which supports the likelihood that young Nancy lived in this cabin above the Catawba River near present-day Belmont.

Within a year or two, Nancy's mother, Lucy, left Uncle Dicky's cabin for Kentucky. She was surely in Kentucky in 1789, when she suffered a "fornication" charge by a Kentucky court.

After Nancy had been with Uncle Dicky's family about two years, a new baby entered the log cabin. That was Joshua Hanks, born in May 1789. Baby Martha Hanks arrived in September 1791, when Nancy was about 8 years old and now able to help with the children. Another son, Thomas Hanks was born in 1797, when Nancy was about 14 years old. But, she never knew baby Thomas, for the previous year, at age 13, she had struck out to make he own way. [34]

In 1896, thirteen-year-old Nancy Hanks Departs Uncle Dicky's log cabin in search of Daniel Tanner's Rutherford County home; but ends up at the Abraham Enloe Household, near Bostic, North Carolina, Working as a Child Servant.

Yes, at age 13. In those days teenage girls were considered capable of earning their keep, within a household that needed domestic help. The log cabin was feeling too crowded. Uncle Dicky and his wife Phebe felt it was time for the teenage orphan to leave. For whatever reason, one day, Nancy left Uncle Dickie in hopes of reaching the home of the brother of her father, Daniel Tanner, in Rutherford County, about 55 miles westward. According to a report in the Southern Historical Collection in the library of The University of North Carolina at Chapel Hill, in a file called the "Enloe Papers," Marvin Ritch reported:

> "Nancy was then about twelve or thirteen years of age when she went to the new Rutherford County Court House. A deputy sheriff found her sitting on a bench. He questioned Nancy, who told him she was looking for a job tending children and helping out in someone's home. The deputy contacted the Public Surveyor, Abraham Enloe, and Nancy moved in with them and their children."

---

[33] *Abraham Lincoln, a North Carolinian*, James Caswell Coggins, pages 53-59.
[34] See http://freepages,genealogy.rootsweb.com, "The Descendants of John Hanks."

This was during the year 1896. Abraham Enloe, 26, and his wife, Sarah "Sally" Edgerton Enloe, 24, had only been married a little over one year and their household only contained one child, a baby girl named Nancy P., age about one year or a few months short of one year.

It seems that historians, biographers and genealogists have persistently steered clear of any Hanks family relationships that supported evidence that Abraham Lincoln was not the legitimate son of Nancy Hanks and Thomas Lincoln, born in Kentucky on the day and year he had recorded in the Bible he had purchased and taken along on that trip to Sarah Bush Johnston Lincoln's home in Coles County, complete with his ink and pen, on that fateful day as his political aspirations were rising. Perhaps, widespread efforts to cover-up Lincoln's illegitimacy has prevented me from discovering the details of how Richard (Dicky) Hanks was Lucy Hanks' brother. But our biography must proceed without knowledge of that detail.

Abraham Enloe, Junior and wife Sarah "Sally" Egerton Enloe lived along puzzle creek, near Bostic, North Carolina in Rutherford County.

Abraham Enloe, Junior had been born in 1770 at Fells Point, Baltimore County, Maryland. His father, Abraham Enloe, Senior, was exceptionally talented and became quite wealthy, but died un-expectantly when Abraham Enloe, Junior was in his late teens. Don Norris, in his book, *Abraham Enloe of Western North Carolina* describes the senior Enloe's death, the will and Abraham, Junior's migration to Rutherford County, North Carolina, arriving with an impressive family inheritance:

"Then the unexpected happened. Abraham Enloe [senior] died prematurely, leaving [his fortune to] his children in his will. Shortly after the demise of Abraham Enloe [senior], the inheritances of [the oldest two children, brothers Abraham Enloe, Junior and Anthony Enloe was purchased by their brother] Joshua. Shortly after selling their inheritances, Abraham, Junior and Anthony migrated to Rutherford County, North Carolina" arriving with considerable money to apply to buying land and slaves.

In October 1790, Abraham Junior, hereafter called simply Abraham, purchased 300 acres of farmland in Rutherford County, that being the first written documentation of the brothers arrival in North Carolina. Twenty-year-old Abraham Enloe and slightly younger brother, Anthony, were unusually talented young men. Their late father had earned a fortune in Baltimore County, Maryland. He had been successful in real estate dealings, was adept at legal issues, understood the mercantile business and was so adept at ocean and ship skills that he held classes teaching others. In fact, between ages 13 and 19, son Abraham helped in teaching classes on ocean and ship skills, as well. Anthony helped and taught classes, too. Without a doubt, Abraham Enloe was intelligent, gifted, skillful and an unusually wealthy twenty year old man when he arrived in North Carolina.

55

The following year Abraham Enloe married Sarah "Sally" Egerton. Her parents were Scroop Egerton and Nancy Battle Egerton, recognized as a very successful family in the region. They had married on January 1, 1795. The first baby, Asaph was born the following year. The Enloe family would eventually grow to 9 boys and 7 girls. The 6 Enloe children that Nancy Hanks would help raise, prior to her departure, follow:

> Born about 1796: a boy, Asaph T.
> Born about 1797: a boy, Jesse.
> Born October 25, 1798: a boy, Scroop William.
> Born about 1799: a girl, Elizabeth L.
> Born about 1800: a girl, Nancy P.
> Born April 15, 1804: a girl, Margaret Mary (Polly).

In 1792, Abraham Enloe constructed a sizable house, constructed of logs and located on a hill above Puzzle creek. It would prove to be big enough for his family of six children and the servant girl, Nancy Hanks. Abraham Enloe was unusually tall and of an imposing physic, which helped the community recognize his leadership ability. He became Justice of the Peace. He helped illiterate members in the county with writing letters and reading letters and documents.

Nancy Hanks pitched in and earned her keep in the Enloe home, helping with chores and raising the small children. Furthermore, she was exposed to Abraham Enloe's exceptional literate abilities and to Sally's capable skills. Concerning skills, Sally taught Nancy to sew; to modify clothing a child had outgrown and resize it for a younger child; to salvage rags from worn out clothing; to take patches from unusable garments and sew them onto torn clothing; to help make quilts for the bed using pieces from worn out clothing, and to make all-new clothing and bedding from new cloth. By the time Nancy reached 19 years of age, she was a rather good seamstress and made and repaired a few items for neighbors. She was also exposed to Sally's teaching of reading and writing to the older boys, Asaph and Jesse. She surely picked up some reading and writing skills, at least to a small extent, but there would be no record in future years of Nancy Hanks writing letters to friends or family, suggesting that her reading and writing skills were rather limited. [35]

---

[35] *Abraham Enloe, the Natural Father of Abraham Lincoln*, Don Norris, pages 7-14.

Chapter 8: June 1804. Nancy Hanks, about Three Months Pregnant, goes With Abraham Enloe and Family as they Migrate to Land Just South of the Smoky Mountains.

The Group Migration to Land Near the Cherokee Indians

On April 15, 1804, Sally Enloe gave birth to her sixth child, which she and Abraham named Margaret Mary (Polly) Enloe. The baby was fine and Abraham redoubled efforts to lead a migration to land along Sono Creek and the Oconaluftee River, just below the Smoky Mountains, in present-day Swain County, next to the small Eastern Cherokee tribe that had held on to a little land there. So, during May 1804 Abraham Enloe finishing his project to gathering up nine covered wagons and 18 oxen to enable the envisioned sizable migration of Rutherford County relatives and friends to land on the southern edge of the Smoky Mountains, which Cherokees had recently ceded to the United States to permit settlement by White pioneers.

A large party would be migrating:

Abraham and Sally Enloe, six children and servant Nancy Hanks.
Abraham Enloe's brother Anthony and his family.
Abraham Enloe's sister Margaret (Polly) and her family.
Felix Walker and his family (In 1816 Felix would be elected to the U. S. House of
    Representatives and be re-elected twice).
Sarah Enloe's brother, Mr. Battle.
Mr. Walker, probably a relative of Felix.
Mr. Kennedy and his family.
John Plott and his family.
Probably some slaves and other family servants.

To transport such a large party westward, over a gap in the Blue Ridge Mountains, across creeks and rivers and up and down seemingly countless hills would be a major effort. Under Abraham Enloe's direction and to some extent with his financial help, the migration group had acquired nine rugged covered wagons and eighteen oxen to pull them. Most of the wagons would carry people. The remainder would carry furniture, tools, personal belongings, farming equipment, and such. The group departed westward from near Puzzle Creek in Rutherford County on or near June 1, 1804. They planned to cross over the Blue Ridge Mountains via Chimney Rock Gorge, which took them up to Hickory Nut Gap, where they began their descent. I could not find records of the exact route thereafter. As the crow flies, their destination was 95 miles from where they had begun. Abraham

Enloe had found a couple to lease the farm and house on Puzzle Creek and that family was ready to move in as soon as the migration got underway.

Weeks before Nancy Hanks had climbed aboard a covered wagon to begin the trip and help care for the newborn baby, Polly, she had felt different, especially in the mornings — not quite right. Her monthly period was way late. She had already missed three, maybe four. She felt fullness in her body. Sally and several friends had observed and asked about the little bulge, but she had laughed and assured that her periods were normal. Perhaps she put chicken blood on a rag and washed it out in a bucket of water when others were nearby — a sneaky way to convince the Enloe's that she just had her period. Yet, Sally Enloe was suspicious. But she felt further inquiry ought to await everyone's arrival at their destination next to the Cherokee people.

Less than one month after departing the Puzzle Creek area, the migrators entered land that the Cherokee people were monitoring. That's when they were confronted by a band of Cherokee warriors seeking to block further advances. Abraham Enloe walked toward the Cherokee giving evidence that he wanted to parley. In his book, *Abraham Enloe of Western North Carolina*, author Don Norris wrote:

> "This was an occasion demanding exceedingly tactful diplomacy, and Abraham Enloe , a man of superior tact and intelligence, talked with the old Chief and others for some time and persuaded them that the Whites were not their enemies. Terms of peace were agreed upon that were never broken on either side."

Essentially, Abraham Enloe assured the Cherokee leaders that his party would not encroach on the established

Abraham Enloe would later sell a large tract of his land to the Smoky Mountains National Park. Here is an image of his barn, which still stands near the park entrance and visitors center.

Cherokee southern boundary and would restrict their settlement to land along Soco

Creek. The two Cherokee Chiefs over the Eastern band were Yonaguskah and Sawinookih. Throughout Abraham Enloe's life near the Cherokees, he would sustain warm relations with both Chiefs.

Members of the migration now selected land to claim. Abraham Enloe marked off one square mile of land that spanned Soco Creek from where it discharged into the Oconaluftee River to the appropriate spot upstream. Felix Walker chose land upstream just below Soco Gap. The other members of the migrating party chose land closer to Abraham Enloe.

Abraham Enloe had just begun staking the corners of his new home near Soco Creek when Sally accused her husband of impregnating Nancy Hanks. It was obvious that the 20-year-old girl was pregnant. Abraham, always honest in family relations, realized his only honorable choice was to admit that he had secretly engaged in sexual relations with the household servant, Nancy Hanks. Sally went into a rage and was nowhere near settling down. She demanded that Nancy Hanks be driven away from the region, away from the land south of the Smoky Mountains.

Abraham Enloe knew he had no choice but to comply honestly with his wife's demand. He quickly sought help from Felix Walker who was just laying out his new home further up Soco Creek. He rode up to Felix's home-site and the too discussed alternatives. Two options seemed reasonable — take Nancy back to Rutherford County and 1) asked her father, Michael Tanner, to care for her until her baby was born, or 2) ask the couple leasing the Puzzle Creek farm, Jane Martin and her family, to care for her until the baby was born. Abraham complained that his wife would become double-angry if he personally left for Rutherford County with Nancy. Felix understood, and offered to take Nancy back to either the Tanner home or to the Puzzle Creek home. [36]

Nancy Hanks Returns to Puzzle Creek Farm to Give Birth

The next day or soon after that meeting, Felix Walker rode his horse down to Abraham Enloe's home-site. Nancy Hanks packed her things, mounted one of the Enloe horses and followed Felix all the way back to Rutherford County. They arrived back in Rutherford County about six days later. As it turned out, Michael Tanner's wife stood opposed to helping a woman that her husband, 20 years ago, had illegitimately fathered. But the couple who was leasing the Puzzle Creek farm agreed to take Nancy in. Upon his return, Felix told Abraham that Michael Tanner had promised to bring Nancy and her baby back to Soco Creek after the birth. Abraham thanked Felix for his successful effort and told him he would start thinking

---

[36] *Abraham Enloe of Western North Carolina, the Natural Father of Abraham Lincoln*, Don Norris, pages 21-30.

about arranging a new life for Nancy and the baby northward, somewhere north of the Smoky Mountains, in Eastern Tennessee or Kentucky.

Living again, back in the house where Nancy had spent all of her teenage years, was comforting. She resumed ties with a few old friends in the area, including Nancy Hollifield and Polly Price. And she attended Concord Baptist Church, which she had long attended with the Enloe family. There is no truthful record of her baby's birth day. Based on all available evidence, Nancy Hanks probably gave birth to baby Abraham sometime around October-November 1804. For subsequent age calculations in the remainder of this biography, *Rebirthing Lincoln*, I will be calculating from an assumed November 1, 1804 date. Yes, Nancy Hanks Tanner had decided to name her baby "Abraham," after the boy's father. [37]

Nancy's Father, Michael Tanner Takes Nancy and Baby Abe Back to Abraham Enloe's New Home

About two or three weeks after the birth, Michael Tanner arrived at the Puzzle Creek farm to escort his daughter, Nancy, and baby Abe in a long, two-horse buggy ride to Soco Creek, south of the Smoky Mountains. It was a light, but stout, wide-wheel buggy, capable of taking them the full distance with proper care. It was a good trip, arriving about eight days after departing.

Stone marking Lincoln Hill, near Bostic, where Nancy Hanks gave birth to baby Abe.

Abraham Enloe looked at the new baby and, comparing the child's exceptionally long legs and his long slender body, probably exclaimed, "No question about it; that's my boy!" [38]

Michael realized that Abraham had to send Nancy and her baby far away to regain peace in his family. Michael Tanner told Abraham Enloe that, soon after he had learned about his daughter's pregnancy, he wrote to the postmaster in Kentucky in Mercer County, where he had remembered Lucy Hanks once living and asked for his help in locating her (Lucy). He further told Abraham that he had subsequently

---

[37] *Abraham Enloe of Western North Carolina, the Natural Father of Abraham Lincoln*, Don Norris, pages 30-33.
[38] *Abraham Enloe of Western North Carolina, the Natural Father of Abraham Lincoln*, Don Norris, page 37.

received a letter from the postmaster in reply, stating that a Lucy Hanks, now married to a Henry Sparrow did live in Mercer County, Kentucky (now Louden County) and she had many children. Michael showed Abraham the postmaster's reply letter. It said that Lucy Hanks Sparrow was Nancy's mother and Henry Sparrow's wife and that Henry told him that he and Lucy would assist Nancy in getting settled in Mercer County with her baby if someone would help them travel to the Sparrow home in Mercer County. Michael explained that, except for Nancy and another illegitimate daughter, the latter children were all Henry Sparrow's sons and daughters. He confirmed that Nancy was Lucy's oldest child. Then Michael encouraged Abraham to believe that Lucy and Henry Sparrow would help Nancy and baby Abe get settled in Mercer County, perhaps even in their home or nearby.

And Michael advised Abraham that Lucy was no longer a wandering woman: she had married Henry Sparrow long ago and they had half a dozen children, or thereabouts. Since Lucy is Nancy's only family, Michael recommended, that he, Abraham, ought to take Nancy and baby Abe across the Smoky Mountains, through Tennessee and into Kentucky. With this letter as a guide, Michael told Abraham that he would easily locate the Sparrow home. Then, you should discuss the issues with them, Michael advised, and make the best possible arrangement in Kentucky for Nancy and your son, whether it be in the Sparrow home, or nearby. Agreeing with Michael Tanner's advice, Abraham reasoned that, after he gets Nancy and baby Abe well situated, and since the Soco community needed more horses, he would purchase as many as a dozen and hire someone to help him drive them back south to the south side of the Smoky Mountains thereby killing two birds with one stone, as the story goes.

Abraham Enloe realized that he could not delegate the delicate task to anyone else — the delegate task of finding a place for Nancy and little Abe to live, near or with her family, and, hopefully, find a husband to live with. Abraham explained to Sally the necessity that he, and he alone, take Nancy and her baby north and make every effort toward enabling a future reasonable future life for both. He assured his wife that, if she went along with his plan, both of them could return to a normal married life and he would never again give into a young sexual temptress. Sally concurred and Abraham began planning for the difficult trip.

But a December horseback journey over the Smoky Mountains, across the Tennessee River Valley, over the Cumberland Plateau and further north through the hills and knobs of Central Kentucky with Nancy and her baby would be too dangerous. That's when Felix Walker stepped in and volunteered to take Nancy and her little boy into his home until spring came and the snow atop the Smoky Mountains melted.

Two days after Easter, 1805, the pass at Newfound Gap was clear and Abraham decided that it was time to pick up Nancy and little Abe at the Walker's home and take them north, over the Smoky Mountains, across Tennessee and all the way to Mercer County, Kentucky. And, since he had the money, he would buy horses and bring them back for the community. [39]

Abraham Enloe takes Nancy Hanks and his Son to Mercer County, Kentucky

Abraham Enloe would travel north into Tennessee and Kentucky many times in future years on trips trading horses and slaves, but this trip with Nancy was his first across New Found Gap and down into Tennessee. So, he hired an experienced Cherokee guide to accompany them and lead them over the mountain and into Tennessee. Abraham was atop his best horse and Nancy was atop his most trusted horse with baby Abe in a papoose-like sling across her breast. They rode up the path alongside the Oconaluftee River toward Newfound Gap, elevation 5,048 feet, and then down the mountain into Tennessee. They continued down the Little Pigeon River Valley to where the Little Pigeon flowed into the French Broad River. At this point they were near Knoxville. They crossed the French Broad and headed northwest and crossed the Tennessee River by ferry. They continued northwest up and across the Cumberland Plateau, and down into the Cumberland River Valley. Turning north, they ascended the Cumberland River Valley and then up its tributary, the Fishing River Valley. Going a little farther, they were in Mercer County, Kentucky.

After questioning several area residents, Abraham Enloe succeeded in leading Nancy to the home of Henry Sparrow and his wife, Lucy. Nancy had not seen her mother since she was about 6 years old. Remembering what Lucy looked like was a struggle, but she was happy to see her. The Sparrow's were welcoming. Nancy introduced Abraham Enloe and her baby Abe. In turn, Lucy introduced her husband Henry Sparrow and their children.

Abraham Enloe remained at the Sparrow home overnight, making sure that Lucy and Henry were able and willing to help Nancy get settled in the community. Then,

---

[39] Our biography is consistent with available testimony prior to this point. Michael Tanner probably was the person who took Nancy and her baby to Abraham Enloe's Soco Creek home. There are records of Nancy Hanks being with or near her mother and Henry Sparrow for a while before she married Thomas Lincoln. However, there is no believable testimony describing who took Nancy and her baby from south of the Smoky Mountains to Mercer County, Kentucky. Therefore, I have created a logical story, involving Michael Tanner, the postmaster and Abraham Enloe, describing how that might have happened.

late the next afternoon, he shook hands with Lucy and Henry, hugged Nancy, kissed baby Abe and rode away in search of excellent horses to purchase and drive south. [40]

Upon returning home at Soco, Abraham found his wife Sally far more loving. Abraham hoped for restored relations and more children. A baby, Isabelle, would be born a year or two later (exact month and year unknown). Nine more children would follow.

---

[40] I have extensively searched for reasonable historical testimony of who brought Nancy Hanks and baby Abe to Kentucky and where she initially resided. Therefore, I have chosen to present the story as you have just read it. This is a missing link that left me no choice but to logically construct a reasonable biographical sketch.

Chapter 9: Thomas Lincoln growing up in Kentucky

Captain Abraham Lincoln of Virginia

Captain Abraham Lincoln, a Revolutionary War veteran, married Bathsheba Herring (Also spelled Bersheba) in June 1770. In July he purchased 200 acres of "colony land" on Linville Creek in Augusta County, Virginia Colony where their five children would be born. When first married, he was 26 and she was 28. First born was Mordecai, in about 1771; the second was Josiah, born in about 1773; the third was Mary, born in about 1775. About the time that Mary was born, the American Revolution began. The fourth child was a boy named Thomas, who was born January 6, 1778, midway through the war. The fifth and last child, Nancy, was born in 1780, the year prior to the October 19, 1781 victory at Yorktown, Virginia. At this time Abraham and Bathsheba were living on a 210 acre tract of land along Linville creek in Rockingham County, Virginia.

Captain Abraham Lincoln wanted to use a grant for Kentucky land that he had received from the State of Virginia. So he began to arrange to migrate west with his family. In February 1780 Abraham and Bathsheba contracted to sell their Virginia farm, now 252 acres, for 5,000 pounds sterling (at that time British currency was the basis for recording land purchases). They had sold their farm, but the buyer was allowing the family to remain there until Abraham selected his Kentucky land. In March 1780 Abraham used that 5,000 pounds sterling to purchase land warrants for 1,200 acres in the central part of Virginia's District of Kentucky. The fifth child, Mary must have been born in early 1780, for in April of that year, Abraham left for Central Kentucky to select his 1,200 acres of land. He chose 800 acres, were a cabin had been built; it was near Logan's Station in Lincoln County in South-Central Kentucky, near the headwaters of the Green River, six miles downstream of Green River Lick. The Green River flowed west into the Ohio River. He also chose 400 acres, which had no cabin; it was on Floyd's Fork of Long Run Creek adjacent to Hughes's Station in Jefferson County. He was back home by late spring, 1781.

The following spring of 1782, the Lincoln family left the Virginia farm and headed to Central Kentucky. Using one riding horse and four pack horses, they would travel 430 miles to the 800 acre Green River land at Logan's Station. Thomas was four years old. They were lucky to have avoided Indian trouble during the trip. At the time they were in the western district of the Commonwealth of Virginia, for the Treaty of Paris had proclaimed each of the thirteen colonies to be independent states.

There was worrisome Indian trouble during the two years spent at their 800 acre Green River land in south-central Kentucky, prompting Abraham to relocate to the north to his 400 acres adjacent to Hughes's Station, in Jefferson County, about 20 miles southeast of Louisville. Although much closer to the Ohio River this area was better protected against Indian attacks.

The Lincoln cabin was in the Hughes's Station cluster on Floyd's Fork. Because Native Americans from north of the Ohio River often raided new Kentucky settlements, new settlers liked to group their log cabins in defensive clusters to protect against such attacks. Life was good for the Lincoln family for about four years.

Then, in May 1786 a very sad thing happened. While working in one of his fields, an Indian in a raiding party shot Abraham dead. The oldest son, Mordecai, grabbed a rifle and killed the Indian before he could kill Josiah or Thomas, both of them in the field at the time. Bathsheba, with the daughters in their nearby Hughes's Station cabin at the time, was instantly a widow with five children to raise. [41]

Prior to his death, Abraham Lincoln had accumulated a total of 5,544 acres of Kentucky land. So, the oldest son, Mordecai, 15, would inherit those 5,544 acres of land, marry, raise fine horses and be among the wealthiest of the region. Thomas, 8, would grow up in a subsistence environment with his mother and three siblings.

Sometime in 1786, Bathsheba and her children moved in with Hananiah Lincoln at Beech Fork in Hardin County. Hananaih was a cousin to Bathsheba's late husband. In 1787 he was 31 years old. Like the late Abraham Lincoln, he fought in the Revolution, but for Pennsylvania Colony, not Virginia. Like Abraham, he rose to the level of

Mordecai Lincoln house near Springfield, Kentucky. Mordecai, the oldest son of Abraham Lincoln, Sr., inherited everything.

Captain. In 1787 he had one child who was 7. His first wife had died and he had just married Sarah Jane Jefferies. Hananiah and Sarah Jane would have 6 children. Unfortunately, Sarah Jane would die in 1800. Hananiah Lincoln would marry Lucy

---

[41] *The Life of Abraham Lincoln*, Ward Hill Lamon, pages 3-8.

Wilson in 1801. His oldest would be grown, but Lucy would surely be a big help in raising his five young children, who ranged in age from 4 to 16 years old.

As a widow, Bathsheba Lincoln would successfully raise her children with some probable help from Hananiah. Mordecai, 21, the oldest and the inheritor of Abraham Lincoln's estate, would marry Mary Mudd, a Roman Catholic, in 1792 and leave Hananiah's Beech Fork home to live with Mary on a nearby farm. The other children remained with Bathsheba and Hananiah for several more years. Josiah, two years younger than Mordecai, would soon grow to manhood, but would not marry until age 30. Mary, five years younger than Mordecai, would remain with her mother until marrying in 1801, as would her younger sister, Nancy, who would marry the same year. [42]

Thomas, seven years younger than Mordecai, would reach 18 years age in 1796. He believed he would never marry because of a dreadful illness that had struck him when young. It was probably an unusually difficult case of the mumps. A few pages later you will learn more about this physical handicap that so clouded Thomas Lincolns' future expectations.

Perhaps, Thomas Lincoln thought, he should become a carpenter and help construct buildings. But that idea worried him considerably. One of his eyes was in bad shape. Some witnesses reported that Thomas was even blind in one eye. Perhaps that was an exaggeration; perhaps his eyesight was very weak in that eye. In any event, his perception of distance was probably poor. A carpenter with poor eyesight and poor depth perception would find his career frustrating. [43]

By 1798, Thomas, 20, left the Beech Fork home of Bathsheba and Hananiah's family to live with his uncle, Isaac Lincoln, who owned a successful farm on the upper part of the Watauga River in far-northeast Tennessee. The Hananiah Lincoln home had become quite crowded, now being occupied by his mother, two sisters, Hananiah, his wife and their five young children. Furthermore, Thomas probably wanted to experience working as an adult on a large prosperous farm. Could Uncle Isaac teach him to love farming as a lifelong career? Within a year Thomas got his answer: he did not like the hard work on a farm and Uncle Isaac thought his nephew was too lazy to be a farmer. [44]

---

[42] "Lincoln's Lincoln Grandmother," by Charles H. Coleman, Journal of the Illinois State Historical Society, Volume 52, Number 1, Lincoln Sesquicentennial, Spring 1959, pages 59-90.
[43] *Herndon's Informants*, pages 125-127.
[44] "Lincoln's Lincoln Grandmother," by Charles H. Coleman, page 87.

Chapter 10: 1805 — Beechland and Elizabethtown, Kentucky — Nancy Hanks, the Sparrows and the Berrys

Nancy Hanks' mother, Lucy, left Uncle Dicky's log cabin on the Catawba River, near Belmont, North Carolina while Nancy was still a little girl. We do not know exactly when she left Uncle Dicky's, but there is a firm record in Mercer County, Kentucky of her being charged with fornication in that court on November 24, 1789. So she was in Mercer County, Kentucky Territory, probably by 1786 or early 1787. [45]

Apparently her lover was an unmarried man named Henry Sparrow, who had just turned 24. To encourage the court to set aside the fornication charge, Henry decided to marry Lucy. This marriage would last forever and many children would come from it. They married on April 30, 1790. The Mercer County Court discontinued hearings on the fornication charge on May 25, 1790. [46]

The illegitimate baby cited in the Mercer County Court fornication charge was a girl that Lucy named Mary "Polly" Sparrow. Polly would grow up in the Sparrow home and marry Benjamin Whitehouse on July 9, 1809. After marriage, Lucy Hanks Sparrow would give birth in Mercer County to seven more children, all growing up to become adults: James, Elizabeth, Peggy, Thomas, Henry Junior, George and Lucinda.

Henry Sparrow was the son of James Wright Sparrow and his wife Mary. He was born in Mecklenburg County, Virginia on October 9, 1765, the oldest son of James and Mary Sparrow. Mecklenburg is located southwest of Richmond, bordering on North Carolina. In about 1785, when Henry was 19, the Sparrow family moved to Bedford County, Virginia where James leased 100 acres of farmland. Bedford County spanned the Blue Ridge Mountains between Lynchburg and Roanoke. In Bedford County, the Sparrow family came in contact with the Hanks families and the Berry families. The Hanks' and the Berry's would be migrating to Kentucky Territory along with the Sparrows.

Four years after coming to Bedford County in 1789, James Sparrow and his family migrated to Mercer County, Kentucky Territory to occupy a 400 acres tract he had purchased. Others in Bedford County joined them in the migration, including the family of John Berry and his wife Ann Mitchel Berry. Some Hanks family members also joined them in the migration. Unfortunately, James Sparrow passed away soon after arriving in Mercer County. By his will, his Mercer County land,

---

[45] Mercer County, Kentucky Court, Book 1, page 415.
[46] Mercer County, Kentucky Court, Book 1, page 516.

consisting of 400 acres was given as follows: 100 acres to his oldest son, Henry, and 300 acres divided among his other four sons. The will was probated in the Mercer County Court House on October 27, 1789.

Prior to 1781, Richard Berry, Senior and his wife, Rachel Shipley Berry had preceded them to Kentucky Territory, settling in the Beechland region of Washington County, which bordered Mercer County to the west. Beechland, north of Springfield. was a piece of land created by a horseshoe bend in the Beech Fork River.

In 1781 or 1782, Richard Berry, Senior sold 100 acres of his Beechland property to Abraham Lincoln, Bathsheba Lincoln's husband. This 100 acre tract was along a creek later named "Lincoln Run."

The pioneering Berry couple had seven children: Joanna, Sarah, Rachel, Richard Junior, Francis, Jane and Edward. Richard, Junior was the oldest son. Richard Berry, Senior passed away in 1798, and his widow, Rachel, passed away in about 1804. This background is very important because of the Berry's close relations with both Thomas Lincoln and Nancy Hanks in the Beechland community.

Richard Berry, Junior, the oldest son, married Mary Polly Ewing on October 10, 1794 in Washington County, Kentucky Territory. After his father, Richard, Senior, passed away, Richard, Junior and Mary lived in the original Berry home. Mary Polly Ewing was born in Bedford, Virginia in 1774. They had 13 children born between 1795 and 1818. Nancy Hanks and young son, Abe were living in Richard and Mary Berry's home in the Beechland community in late 1805 to early 1806. At that time, Richard and Mary Polly had eight children, ranging in age from 11 years old to little baby Margaret Mitchell. Mary Polly Ewing was a friend of Lucy Hanks Sparrow in adjacent Mercer County and, apparently, Lucy or a Mercer County friend or relative had suggested that Nancy go to the Berry Beechland home with her young son, Abe, and help in the home and earn money as a seamstress.

Francis Berry, the second son, married Elizabeth Brazelton on November 25, 1799 in Washington County, Kentucky Territory. They lived on a tract of land within a portion of the old Berry plantation. Elizabeth was born on April 17, 1779 in Frederick, Maryland. In latter 1805 and early 1806, Francis and Elizabeth had three children, ages 5 to 3. A fourth child, Isaac Nelson, was born on May 17, 1806, during the time Nancy Hanks and Thomas Lincoln were just beginning to plan for their wedding in the home of Richard Berry, Junior and his wife Mary Polly. [47]

---

[47] See several internet sources on WikiTree, including "The Berry and Nancy Hanks; Richard Berry, Jr. (1769-1843)"; "Francis Berry (abt. 1771-1835)", and "Elizabeth (Brazelson) Berry (1779-1848)". Also see Indiana Magazine of History, volume 30, number 3, Septemer,1934, "The Romance of Thomas Lincoln and Nancy Hanks."

Kentucky Territory would become the State of Kentucky on June 1, 1792.

By the way, when Thomas Lincoln would marry Nancy Hanks in 1806, John Berry's brother, Richard Berry, would be recorded as the guardian of Nancy Hanks, since she had no family history in Kentucky, having then recently arrived from North Carolina.

On October 17, 1796, Thomas Sparrow, Henry's brother, married Elizabeth Hanks in Mercer County, Kentucky. Thomas and Elizabeth Sparrow are important people in this biography of Abraham Lincoln because they would adopt Dennis Friend Hanks, born in 1799, the illegitimate son of her sister, also named Nancy Hanks. Later in this biography, you will learn that, in 1809, Elizabeth and Thomas Sparrow and Dennis Friend Hanks lived about two miles from the Lincoln cabin on Noland Creek and Elizabeth was present when Nancy Hanks Lincoln gave birth to a son, Thomas, who died soon after he was born. Thomas Sparrow and his wife Elizabeth Hanks Sparrow and their adopted boy, Dennis Friend Hanks, would follow Thomas and Nancy Lincoln and their young children, Abe and Sarah, to Indiana Territory soon after the Lincoln migration from Kentucky. Sadly, in Indiana, the "milk sick" would cause the premature deaths of Thomas Sparrow, Elizabeth Sparrow and Abraham Lincoln's mother, Nancy Hanks Lincoln. Lincoln's law partner, William H. Herndon, would find Dennis Friend Hanks an important source of the history of Abraham Lincoln's life growing up in the State of Kentucky and Indiana Territory. [48]

According to Troy Cowan, Nancy Hanks worked for Francis and Elizabeth Berry. In addition to sewing for them and others in the community, she also helped take of the couple's three children. During this period of time, Thomas Lincoln was picking up work from the Sparrow, Berry and Bush families. According to Dan Davenport, Nancy Hanks was living at the Francis Berry home when she was courting Thomas Lincoln.

---

[48] Using the internet, Google "Sparrow Family of Mercer County, Kentucky."

Chapter 11: Nancy Hanks Marries Thomas Lincoln in Kentucky, Thomas Uses Enloe Gift to Buy a Farm and the Family Expands

Thomas Lincoln is Now a Grown Man in Elizabethtown, Kentucky

Thomas Lincoln's oldest brother, Mordecai, seven years older, had inherited their father's sizable and productive farm, married in 1792 and Bathsheba and the other children removed to another far more modest farm at Beech Fork, Beechland Community, in Washington County, Kentucky. And, up until 1801, Thomas had lived with his mother, Bathsheba, older brother, Josiah, older sister, Mary and younger sister Nancy at the family farm at Beech Fork. This farm was the 100 acre tract that Abraham Lincoln had, prior to suffering death by that Indian scalp-hunter, purchased from Richard Berry, Senior, who was raising his large family in Beechland.

During 1801, both of Thomas' sisters, Mary and Nancy, married and left home. Two years later, in 1803, his brother, Josiah, married and left home. And Bathsheba left home, too, so to speak, for she went to live with her daughter, Nancy and husband William Brumfield. Nancy and William Brumfield's farm was in the Mill Creek neighborhood of Hardin County, eight miles north of Elizabethtown. So, except for Thomas, all of Bathsheba's children were grown and on their own. At that time Thomas left, too. It was probably in 1802 that he left to live in the town of Elizabethtown to work as a carpenter and at other jobs.

Surprisingly, on September 2, 1803, Thomas Lincoln is on record for purchasing a 238-acre farm on Mill Creek, at a purchase price of 118 pounds sterling (about 500 dollars U. S.). It was near his sister, Nancy, who had married William Brumfield and where his mother Bathsheba was living. The seller was Dr. John Tom Stater. Terms of payment must have been generous. The oldest brother, Mordicai would probably make the payments. Thomas would never live there, work the land and raise crops there. Apparently Thomas loaned the 238 farmland to share croppers, expecting to receive part of the crops and meat grown on the land without personally working it. [49]

---

[49] "The Lincolns in Kentucky", by Kent Masterson Brown, presented to the Kentucky Bar Association Annual Convention, June 13-15, 2018.

Abraham Enloe Visits Nancy and young Abe in Beechland, Kentucky

During April and May 1806, Abraham Enloe was in Kentucky to buy good quality horses and visit Nancy Hanks, his son and some Enloe relatives. Through some mail correspondence he had learned that Nancy and young Abe were working for Francis and Elizabeth Berry in their home in the Beechland neighborhood north of Springfield in Washington County. When Abraham arrived at the Berry house in mid-April he found Nancy and little Abe were doing well. She was earning a living for herself and her little boy, but opportunities for a better life had not brightened. She was earning some money sewing for other people outside the home and had access to a loom where she had made some fabrics. Regarding marriage, she told her son's father that men in Kentucky were looking for young women who had not yet given birth, or, if they did have a child, they wanted legitimate widows. Furthermore, little Abe looked so different from other little boys that were one-and-a-half-years old. Men would look at him and ask, "What's wrong with the boy. He is too skinny. Are those long legs the result of some kind of disease?"

Abraham Enloe asked Nancy if she had met a young single man her age that she was fond of. She mentioned one fellow who she liked well enough, and he seemed to like her. Nancy told Abraham that the fellow thought little Abe looked strange, but that odd appearance did not seem to bother him all that much. Nancy mentioned that, for some reason she could not understand, the fellow seemed disinterested in marriage at present. She said that the fellow, for several years, had courted a young girl, but she had rejected him — a girl named Sarah Bush — and she had married Daniel Johnston two months ago. Abraham asked, "What's this fellow's name, dear?" "Thomas Lincoln," was the reply. Then she explained that Thomas had left Kentucky in early March on a flat boat trip to deliver goods to New Orleans for the Bleakley & Montgomery store in Elizabethtown, but was expected back any day now. [50]

Sarah Bush Johnston

Let's take a moment to learn more about Sarah Bush Johnston:

Sarah Bush was born on December 13, 1788 in Elizabethtown. She had been Thomas Lincoln's sweetheart, but she had rejected him for Daniel Johnston. So, Sarah, 17, and Daniel, 23, were married in Elizabethtown on March 13, 1806.

---

[50] I am beginning the Lincoln biographical sketch where I place Abraham Enloe in and around Elizabethtown and Beechland, Kentucky, hoping to buy horses and find a husband for Nancy Hanks. After extensive research on how Abraham Enloe arranged the Hanks-Lincoln marriage, I have resorted to constructing it as you will see in subsequent pages. I have no references to this exact construction.

Thomas was perhaps heart-broken, but he understood. Like all young women in Kentucky, Sarah wanted a husband who could father and help raise many children. Being "castrated" [51] by that tough case of the mumps, Thomas could not fulfill that manly role. He understood, but losing Sarah Bush depressed him. He wanted to get away for a while. So he agreed to take goods to New Orleans for the Bleakley & Montgomery store in Elizabethtown. Of course, Thomas had no way of foreseeing the future. He did not know that Daniel Johnston would die of cholera during an epidemic in 1816 and that he, Thomas, would marry the widow Sarah Bush Johnston in Elizabethtown on December 2, 1819, move her family and furnishings to her husband's Indiana log cabin and help raise her three children while she, in turn, helped raise his late wife's young children.

Abraham Enloe Pays Thomas Lincoln to Marry Nancy Hanks and Help Raise his Son

Abraham Enloe spent several days in central Kentucky selecting horses to purchase and visiting an Enloe relative. He was back in Elizabethtown in mid-May. Then he again visited Nancy and young Abe. He inquired about her friend, Thomas. Yes, he was back in town.

Thomas Lincoln was back from the flatboat trip, returning to Elizabethtown by May 1. He had earned about $150 American money for his successful trip to New Orleans for Bleakly and Montgomery. On May 16 he would receive 30 pounds, 24 shillings and 7-1/2 pence as pay for the trip, an amount equivalent to about 150 Dollars. [52]

During the second week of May, Abraham Enloe located Thomas and arranged a meeting that evening between all four of them: himself, Nancy, little Abe and Thomas. No one else was present; it was a private conversation. Abraham congratulated Thomas on a successful trip to New Orleans and back, and asked about his experiences during the trip. They chatted about the trip, man to man, for a quarter hour. Also, Abraham expressed to Thomas his sorrow over losing Sarah Bush to Daniel Johnston and asked how he was feeling now about that romantic loss, after the flatboat trip to New Orleans. Thomas said the New Orleans trip and all the sites he saw had helped him get over Sarah Bush somewhat.

Then Abraham Enloe asked a very personal question: "Why did Sarah Bush reject you?" Thomas squirmed and then he fessed up. "My family and several friends know my problem," Thomas explained. "I was castrated when a boy. Mumps we figure. Girls don't want me for their husband. Sarah and I were close for

---

[51] Details on the "castrated" story will soon appear.

[52] *Indiana Magazine of History*, Volume XXX, September, 1934, Number 3, The Romance of Thomas Lincoln and Nancy Hanks, by Louis A. Warren, page 217.

several years, but she made the reasonable decision and chose Daniel Johnston and a childbearing future."

The following testimony explains evidence to substantiate Thomas' inability to father children:

It is important to know that Thomas Lincoln was not looking for a wife. He had long believed that a young woman would never accept him because, sadly, he was sterile ("castrated") from an earlier bout with the mumps, and would never father children. Two letters from E. R. Burba to President Lincoln's law partner and biographer, William Herndon, explain:

In a letter to Herndon from Hodginville, Kentucky, dated May 25, 1866, E. R. Burba wrote, "As to your first inquiry in regard to Thomas Lincoln not being able to get a baby from his first marriage, that seems to be the impression from the best information I can get." [53]

In a letter to Herndon from Hodginville, Kentucky, dated March 31, 1866, E. R. Burba wrote: "[William Cessna] further says that Thomas Lincoln was not considered all right in consequence of having the mumps or something else, that he has been with him often in bathing together in the water. Mr. Cessna is considered a very reliable man. I know him well." [54]

In a letter to Herndon from Charles Friend in 1889, two years before William H. Herndon's death, he received confirmation that Thomas Lincoln was unable to impregnate a woman. Writing from Sonora, Kentucky on July 31, 1889, Charles Friend wrote: "You asked me a question, 'Was he, Thomas Lincoln, castrated?' I heard a cousin of my father's, Judge Jonathan Friend Cessna, say that his father, William Cessna, said that Thomas Lincoln could not have been Abe's father for one of Thomas' testicles was not larger than a pea or, perhaps both of them were not larger than peas." [55]

That being the available historical testimony concerning Thomas' physical inability, we now return to the conversation between Abraham Enloe, Thomas Lincoln and Nancy Hanks.

Then Abraham said, "Little Abe beside us is my son, as you might imagine from his thin, tall body and long legs. I have been married a long time in North Carolina, have a large family and regret having had relations with Nancy, who had lived in our home since she was thirteen — staying with us as an orphaned servant." Abraham took a deep breath and continued, "But I feel responsible for making sure that

---

[53] *Herndon's Informants*, page 256.
[54] *Herndon's Informants*, page 240.
[55] *Herndon's Informants*, pages 673-674.

Nancy and my little boy have a good life. Nancy needs a husband to help her and to help raise little Abe."

"Are you suggesting that I become her husband," Thomas asked?

"Only if Nancy would like that," Abraham answered as he turned to little Abe's mother hoping for a response.

After a reflecting pause, Nancy said, "Yes, Abraham, I do believe that I would like that, but are we not asking a lot from Thomas here?"

Abraham agreed: "Yes, we are asking a lot of Thomas, but I am prepared to help." Turning to Thomas, Abraham asked, "How much help do you need, Thomas?"

Thomas proceeded to tell a story. "On the second day of September, 1803, my brother Mordecai arranged for Dr. John F. Stater to sell me 238 acres of farmland on Mill Creek for 118 pounds sterling. The land is located near where my sister, her husband and my mother live in Hardin County. You see, my sister and her husband live near that land and my mother lives with them. They wanted me to have land near them. Dr. Stater was willing to offer generous terms and Mordecai, who, being the oldest male, had inherited our father's estate, agreed to help make the payments to Dr. Stater. A family is presently on the land on a share-crop arrangement because I am not ready to work the land full time presently. Mr. Enloe, I would consider the marriage you suggest if you gave me enough money to pay off what I owe Dr. Stater for those 238 acres of land." [56]

Abraham calculated in his head, converting 118 British pounds sterling to United States dollars. He figured 500 dollars would cover almost all of that debt. So, Abraham Enloe offered, "I will pay you $500 dollars if you marry Nancy and help her raise little Abe." Then, realizing that Thomas needed a horse and wagon to transport his future family about, and wanting to make sure his son would be properly cared for, added to his offer: "Thomas, I will also give you by tomorrow a horse and wagon to properly take Nancy and little Abe about." But, it was understood among the parties that Thomas Lincoln would not receive the $500 payment until after the wedding ceremony.

And that is how it came to pass that Thomas Lincoln agreed to marry Nancy Hanks and help raise Abraham Enloe's son. [57]

---

[56] *The Lincolns in Kentucky*, by Kent Masterson Brown, of Lexington, Kentucky, as presented to the Kentucky Bar Association Annual Convention, June 13-15, 2018.

[57] The conversation in quotes is not verifiable history. There are several witness testimonies reporting that a man named Enloe paid Thomas Lincoln to marry Nancy Hanks. Some testimony reported $500 was paid, and other testimony reported compensation in horses, mules and or a

The Hanks-Lincoln Wedding

Thomas was soon busy preparing for the marriage. On May 16th he received his pay from Bleakly and Montgomery for the flatboat trip to New Orleans: 16 pounds 2 shillings in British money plus 13 pounds, 14 shillings and 7 and 1/2 pence in gold, an amount approximating 150 dollars, U. S. Then he and Nancy got busy buying fabric, thread, etc. to enable her to make more money sewing clothing, etc. for her customers. Nancy chose 20 yards of a variety of cloth, 13 skeins of a variety of thread, 15 dozen buttons of various types and 2 yards of tape. The sewing supplies bill totaled 14 pounds 14 shillings, which Thomas paid on May 16 and May 20. Thomas wanted his future wife to be well supplied with materials to sew clothing and other fabric goods to help the family earn money. [58]

Nancy Hanks was busy getting ready for the wedding, too. She wanted another child to play with young Abe and make a more complete family. So, without telling little Abe's father or Thomas Lincoln, she started in earnest trying to get pregnant. We do not know the name of the man who impregnated Nancy Hanks a few weeks prior to the wedding day. But we are safe in assuming that she was pregnant when she married Thomas Lincoln. Yes, eight months after the wedding, Nancy Hanks Lincoln gave birth to a baby girl. Apparently, Thomas would be accepting of the event and would proudly name "his daughter" Sarah Lincoln. [59]

Thomas Lincoln's mother, his brothers and their wives, and his sisters and their husbands were terribly upset with Thomas for agreeing to marry Nancy Hanks. All of them had been told that Nancy Hanks was illegitimate and they had no idea concerning the name of her father. Someone had told them that Nancy's mother was charged with bastardy in Mercer County, Kentucky some 17 years previously. And they had heard that Nancy's little boy, about a year and a half old, was also illegitimate and the little boy's father was a man named Enloe. They felt like disowning brother Thomas for so gravely tarnishing the Lincoln family reputation. In their view, Thomas was giving away the normal loving family relationship, which he had known since his birth, by agreeing to marry Nancy Hanks. And that was, by far, not the worst of it! His Lincoln family members were horrified to learn that brother Thomas had received a lot of money as payment for agreeing to marry that illegitimate Nancy — whatever her last name should have been — and for taking on the raising of her little bastard boy. I suspect that no member of Thomas Lincoln's family was present at his wedding and I have found no reliable report that any did

---

wagon. I have selected the $500 compensation because that explains how Thomas Lincoln paid Dr. John F. Stater for the 238 acres of land.

[58] Indiana Magazine of History, Volume XXX, September, 1934, Number 3, The Romance of Thomas and Nancy Hanks, by Louis A. Warren, pages 213-222.

[59] All historians agree that Nancy's daughter, Sarah, was born 8 months after the day of the wedding.

attend. It is likely that, right away, Bathsheba Lincoln and her other children had begun to exclude — shun — Thomas and his bride-to-be. [60]

On June 12, 1806, Thomas Lincoln, 29, married Nancy Hanks, about 23, in Richard and Rachel Shipley Berry's cabin. Nancy had stayed with both Berry brothers — Richard and Francis, mostly with Francis — but Richard's house, the original Berry family home was far grander that the cabin where Francis lived. So the wedding took place at the home of Richard and Rachel Berry, in Beechland, near the town of Springfield, Washington County, Kentucky. Jesse Head, a Methodist Episcopal Church minister in Springfield, had come to Beechland to perform the ceremony.

Richard Berry home where Hanks-Lincoln wedding ceremony was held.

Richard Berry had signed the marriage bond, pledging family consent, because Lucy and Henry Sparrow were not present and Nancy, a North Carolinian, had no proof of her age, which was about 23, and Kentucky law required family or guardian consent for any woman under 21 years of age to marry.

Except for members of the Berry families, I have not found significant and reliable testimony reporting the names of persons attending the wedding ceremony. I suspect few attended. But, of course, little Abraham Enloe, afterward called Abraham Lincoln, was present, now walking rather well on his own and "running around in the room."

Concerning residents of Beechland at the time of the wedding, there are stories that "the old people said that 'Nancy's child, called Abraham, was known to be in that County before she and Tom were married'." There also exists an old story by the people who were present at the wedding confirming that "Nancy's boy sat between Tom and Nancy as they rode home in the wagon." That would be the team of horses and the wagon that Abraham Enloe gave Thomas as a "wedding present."[61]

---

[60] I have no testimony supporting a family decision to "shun" Thomas, but subsequent Lincoln behavior suggests a deterioration in normal family relations throughout his stay in Kentucky.
[61] *The Tarheel Lincoln, North Carolina Origins of "Honest Abe"*, by Jerry A. Goodnight and Richard Eller, page 43.

The most validated story from the Lincoln-Hanks wedding comes from Preacher Jesse Head himself. This story is reported by a prominent Kentucky lawyer and court judge, known simply as Judge Peters. In sworn testimony, Judge Peters reported that the story of Abraham being a little boy at the time of the Lincoln-Hanks wedding is widely circulated and most importantly he declared: "Jesse Head, when a resident of Harroldsburg, Kentucky, told an eminent lawyer that Abraham Lincoln was born and old enough to be running around at the time when he married Thomas Lincoln to Nancy Hanks." [62]

The Future President, Abraham Lincoln, one and a half years old and "running around" in the room that day was mistaken when he prepared biographical material in support of his efforts to get the presidential nomination of the Northern States Republican Party — he had guessed Thomas and Nancy were married in Hardin County. Historians would search in vain for evidence of the marriage in Hardin County. Finally, in 1878, thirteen years after Abraham Lincoln's death, R. M. Thompson followed a lead from an old Washington County settler and, in the court house in the county seat, Springfield, he found the record validating the Hanks-Lincoln wedding.

Thomas Lincoln, Nancy Hanks Lincoln and young Abe Lincoln began their family life together in a modest cabin in Elizabethtown. Abraham Enloe stopped by that evening, gave Thomas Lincoln $500, shook his hand, hugged Nancy, picked up his son, kissed him and bid the new couple goodbye.

So, at this point, Abraham Enloe leaves the pages of *Rebirthing Lincoln, a Biography.*

Abe's Baby Half-Sister Sarah

Eight months after the marriage, on February 10, 1807, Nancy gave birth to a healthy baby girl whom the couple named Sarah. [63] Thomas, Nancy, Abe and baby Sarah would live in the littlecabin in Elizabethtown until the spring of 1808. Since Thomas was sterile ("castrated") from an earlier bout with the mumps, baby Sarah's father would have been someone else. Apparently, Nancy wanted more children and had become pregnant just before her wedding.

A Little Boy in Elizabethtown.

Many years later Judge Helm would tell of when, during this time, he and Abe would frequent a store in Elizabethtown together and eat brown sugar. [64] And Samuel Haycraft, "the historian," would later tell of remembering seeing Abe about

---

[62] *The Eugenics of Lincoln* by James Caswell Coggins, page 228.
[63] *Herndon's Informants*, page 110.
[64] Herndon's Informants, page 48.

Elizabethtown during this time walking around town with his mother. [65]   Those recollections would have been before May, 1808, when little Abe was about 3-1/2 years old.

Sinking Spring Farm

In or near August 1808, Thomas and Nancy Lincoln left the cabin on the leased lot in Elizabethtown to settle on a 300 acre tract of land they called their Sinking Spring Farm.   It was 2-1/2 miles south of Hodgen's Mill, along the South Fork of Nolin River, in Hardin County, now LaRue County. Thomas had not purchased the farm. Instead it was agreed that he and his family could live there for free while, hopefully, they gathered money to buy the place. Abe was almost four and Sarah was a year and a half. This location put the Lincolns only two miles from the cabin where Nancy's relatives, Thomas and Elizabeth "Betsy" Sparrow and their adopted son, Dennis Friend Hanks, 9, lived. Also living not far away was Jesse Friend and his wife Polly Hanks Friend and their children. This move from Elizabethtown seemed to have been made to allow Thomas and Nancy to associate with her people and become more distant toward his Lincoln family members. In Elizabethtown, Thomas had earned money as a carpenter and Nancy had earned money as a seamstress where there was a good market for both of their skills. Now, Thomas was returning to subsistence farming. Because of soured family relations with his Lincoln relatives, he was continuing to let sharecroppers live on his 238 acre Mill Creek farm.

Thomas Lincoln did not buy the Sinking Spring land. He was leasing the land from David Vance who was in a slow, drawn-out process of paying Richard Mather for the land. Thomas would never be rewarded for improvements he would make to the cabin and for clearing more of the acreage. [66]

Nancy Gives Birth to a Baby Boy She Names "Thomas"

On February 12, 1809, Nancy gave birth to a baby boy she named Thomas to honor her husband. The name of the father is unknown. Betsy Sparrow was present during or soon after the birth. The baby had difficulty right away and Nancy and Betsy were unable to save him. Thomas built a casket and buried the baby near the cabin while his children and the Sparrow's comforted Nancy. Thomas fashioned a triangular limestone headstone and carve initials "T. L." on it. [67] Nancy would never give birth again. Remember this date. Why?

---

[65] Herndon's Informants, page 67.

[66] "More than a Lawyer, The Lincoln's in Kentucky," the Kentucky Bar Association Annual Conference, June 13-15, 2018, by Kent Masterson Brown, page 10.

[67] See The Abraham Lincoln Research Site at rogerjnorton.com.

Because Abe Lincoln would later claim in his family bible entry, in 1852 or 1853, that this day, February 12, 1809, was the day that he, Abe, was born.

Young Abe Lincoln was almost six years old at this point in our biography. He would intentionally omit the birth and death of baby Thomas when writing up the family bible with Sarah Bush Johnston Lincoln a year or two after Thomas Lincoln died. But, more importantly, he would claim that he, the future President Lincoln, was born on that day, February 12, 1809. It would be difficult to explain, while Abe grew up through adolescence and into and through his teenage years, how he was so big and mature for the age he would claim to have been in Kentucky, Indiana and those first years in Illinois. But, as you read further into *Rebirthing Lincoln*, you will learn more about how lawyer and political leader "Honest" Abe Lincoln kept secret his true date of birth and his origins in North Carolina.

Tommy Lincoln's Gravestone, discovered in 1933 by Work Progress Administration workers in the old Redmond Family cemetary.

Knob Creek Farm

In the spring of 1811, Thomas Lincoln moved his family about 9 miles northeastward to 30 acres of bottom land that he would call his Knob Creek Farm. Richard Mather was forcing David Vance to finish paying for the Sinking Creek Farm or give up his purchase deal. Unable to complete the purchase, Vance had forced the Lincoln family to leave. On December 19, 1816, a court judgement would award Thomas Lincoln $87.74 in compensation for his Sinking Creek Farm lease payments.

George Lindsey owned 230 acres along Knob Creek at the foot of Muldraugh's Hill. The farm, much of it in timber, was 7 miles north of Hodgen's Mill, still in Hardin County. Thomas Lincoln only arranged to lease the best part: 30 acres of bottom land along Knob Creek. By the way, most Lincoln biographers erroneously claim that Thomas Lincoln purchased those 30 acres. Thomas Lincoln and family lived in a little one-room log cabin on that bottomland. Elizabethtown, the Hardin County Seat, was 19 miles away.

Nancy did not want to leave the buried casket containing the remains of her deceased baby, Thomas, at the Sinking Creek Farm. So, Thomas unearthed the casket and headstone and brought both to a small family graveyard of a Knob Creek neighbor, George Redmon. The casket was reburied in the Redmon family graveyard on the brow of Muldraugh's Hill. And the triangular limestone headstone, bearing the initials "T. L." was properly placed. [68]

Young Abe Lincoln was about 7-1/2 years old when the family arrived at the Knob Creek Farm. He and Sarah would attend a basic "A. B. C." school while living at Knob Creek.

Thomas Lincoln's Knob Creek landlord, George Lindsey, became a defendant in a land-ownership lawsuit brought by the heirs of Thomas Middleton of Philadelphia, Pennsylvania. Once again, Thomas was forced to vacate the leased farmland on which he had settled his small family. He decided to migrate north, across the Ohio River into Southern Indiana Territory. This time, he and Nancy would leave baby Thomas' grave undisturbed, a remembrance of their married years in Kentucky. [69]

Thomas Lincoln Sells the Farm located near Nancy Brumfield and his Mother, Bathsheba

On October 2, 1814, Thomas Lincoln sold 200 acres of the 238 tract of land on Mill Creek for 100 pounds sterling, which was near the farm where Nancy Lincoln Brumfield and her husband lived and where his mother, Bathsheba, was living. Thomas had held the land, originally 238 acres, for 11 years. And we figure he had applied to that purchase, when converted to British Pounds, about 85 percent of the $500 that Abraham Enloe had paid him to marry Nancy Hanks and to help raise his son, Abe. Thomas had never lived on the 238 acre spread. Apparently, share croppers had lived on it. This is a strange and rather obscure history. This is further evidence that Thomas Lincoln's mother, brothers and sisters were shunning him. After marriage, Thomas Lincoln would never be close with his mother, brothers or sisters — instead, Thomas Lincoln had chosen to associate with Nancy Hank's people. The other 28 acres went to someone else, probably a Lincoln relative. Charles Melton purchased the 200 acres for 100 pounds sterling, about the same price per acre as when Thomas had bought the larger, 238 acre spread. [70]

---

[68] www.rogerjnorton.com and Abraham Lincoln Research site.

[69] "More than a Lawyer, The Lincoln's in Kentucky," the Kentucky Bar Association Annual Conference, June 13-15, 2018, by Kent Masterson Brown, pages 18-22.

[70] "More than a Lawyer, The Lincoln's in Kentucky," the Kentucky Bar Association Annual Conference, June 13-15, 2018, by Kent Masterson Brown, pages 5-7.

Chapter 12: The Lincoln's Leave Kentucky and Migrate to Indiana Territory; But, Sadly, Nancy Hanks Soon Dies

Thomas Lincoln Makes Plans to Immigrate to Indiana Territory.

By the fall of 1816, Thomas Lincoln decided to relocate his family to Southern Indiana Territory near the Ohio River.

We ask ourselves why Thomas Lincoln wanted to leave his home state of Kentucky and migrate across the Ohio River into Southern Indiana Territory. We have to sympathize with Thomas. Sadly, when a boy, he had been castrated by disease, probably the mumps. His girlfriend during his teen years, Sarah Bush, had rejected him for another, Daniel Johnston, and, with him, she had given birth to three children. Thomas Lincoln now had a wife and two children that he had not conceived. By leaving central Kentucky he was leaving behind rumors that he had not fathered those children. Perhaps, to poor Thomas Lincoln — the castrated man Sarah Bush and likely other women had refused to marry — leaving Kentucky behind, now with a wife and children, was exactly what his emotions were directing him to do.

He had been preparing to leave Kentucky for Indiana Territory for a couple of years. In October 1814, he had sold the 200 acres on Mill Creek, raising 100 pounds sterling.

He decided to first leave Nancy, Abe and Sarah at his Kentucky home and go to Southern Indiana Territory, look over the land and stake out a claim.

Thomas the Whiskey Distiller

We assume that Thomas Lincoln did not want to relocate his family to southern Indiana and leave his whiskey behind in Kentucky. He had made a lot of mash and distilled a lot of raw whisky, called "white lightning." Based on extensive interviews in Indiana, Billy Herndon in his Lincoln biography wrote:

> "Having determined on immigrating to Indiana, [Thomas] began preparations for removal in the fall of 1816 by building for his use a flatboat. Loading it with his tools and other personal effects, including in the invoice, as we are told, four hundred gallons of whiskey, he launched his "crazy craft" on a tributary of Salt Creek known as the Rolling Fork. Along with the current he floated down to the Ohio River, but his rudely-made vessel, either from the want of experience in the navigator, or because of the ill adaptation to withstand the

force and caprices of the currents in the great river, capsized one day, and boat and cargo went to the bottom."

Most likely the raft capsized near the river bank, perhaps becoming entangled in fallen trees, for Herndon reported a successful salvaging:

"The luckless boatman set to work, however, and by dint of great patience and labor, succeeded in recovering tools and the bulk of the whiskey. Righting his boat, he continued down the river, landing at a point called Thompson's Ferry, in Perry County, on the Indiana side. Here, he disposed of his vessel and, placing his goods in the care of a settler named Posey, he struck out through the interior in search of a location for his new home. Sixteen miles back from the river, he found land that pleased his fancy, and he marked it off for himself . . . by blazing the trees and piling brush at the corners."

Like many who planned to settle in Southern Indiana Territory, Thomas figured he would travel to Vincennes to register his claim of the land and pay for it later at $2.00 per acre.

". . . Having secured a place for his home, he trudged back to Kentucky — walking all the way — for his family." [71]

Thomas Lincoln and Family Migrate to Indiana Territory.

Soon after his return from Indiana, early in October, 1816, Thomas Lincoln, having sold his Kentucky farm, headed north with Nancy, Abe, Sarah, two horses and the personal possessions they were able to bring along. After taking a ferry across the Ohio River and arriving at the marked claim on the banks of the Little Pigeon River, they all set about digging a well and building a 14-foot-by-14-foot, three-sided log shelter of unhewn logs to get them through the upcoming winter. Of course, being open on one side, it contained no door, no window and just a dirt floor.

Much time was being spent cutting trees to clear land for crops. And 12-year-old Abe was useful in the lighter chores related to building the cabin. And Abe helped his half-sister, Sarah, 8, with chores, such as fetching water and taking grain to the gristmill. Perhaps fetching water was the biggest job, because the children had to walk one mile to get spring water. The wells that Thomas had dug were all dry. [72]

---

[71] *Herndon's Life of Lincoln*, page 20.
[72] *Herndon's Life of Lincoln*, page 21.

Thomas and Elizabeth "Betsy" Sparrow and Dennis Friend Hanks also Migrate to Indiana Territory.

The following year, 1817, Nancy Hanks's relatives, Thomas and Betsy Sparrow, previously mentioned a few pages back, left their Kentucky home and crossed the Ohio River into Southern Indiana Territory. The Sparrow's had also lived near the Lincolns in Kentucky. By this time, Thomas and Abe Lincoln had built a larger 18 foot by 18 foot, four-sided log cabin of hewed logs that was tall enough to provide crude overhead sleeping space for Abe and another fellow. So, Thomas Lincoln had invited the Sparrow's to move into the three-sided shelter that the Lincoln's had hastily built upon their arrival in Indiana. Elizabeth (Betsy) Hanks Sparrow was Nancy Hanks Lincoln's aunt and Abe's great aunt.

The Sparrows brought another relative, an adopted illegitimate nephew named Dennis Friend Hanks, 19 years old, also previously mentioned. The Sparrows had adopted Dennis when he was young. He was a first cousin to Abe's mother, Nancy Hanks Lincoln. Dennis Friend Hanks was born in Hardin, Kentucky on May 15, 1799.

Game abounded and provided a portion of the family's meat. They acquired sheep, hogs, chickens and calves and milk cows. It was the milk cows that produced the great tragedy for the two families. [73]

Nancy Hanks (Tanner) Lincoln Dies of the Milk-Sick

Billy Herndon recorded this tragedy in his Life of Lincoln:

"In the fall of 1818, the scantily settled region in the vicinity of [Little Pigeon River Community] [74] — where the Lincoln's were then living — suffered a visitation of that dreaded disease common in the West in early days, and known in the vernacular of the frontier as "the milk-sick."

Later, medical science would learn that this "milk-sick" was caused by letting cows run wild in the woods where they were prone to eat the poisonous White Snakeroot plant, also known as White Sanicle or Tall Boneset.

Herndon continued:

---

[73] *Herndon's Life of Lincoln*, page 21.
[74] Herndon called the community "Pigeon Creek".

"When the disease broke out in the Pigeon Creek region, it not only took off the people, but it made havoc among the cattle. . . Early in October of the year 1818, Thomas and Betsy Sparrow fell ill of the disease and died within a few days of each other. Thomas Lincoln . . . nailed together the crude coffins . . . and the bodies were borne to a scantily cleared knoll in the midst of the forest, and there, without ceremony, quietly let down into the grave.

"Meanwhile, Abe's mother had also fallen a victim of the insidious disease. Her sufferings, however, were destined to be of brief duration. Within a week, she too rested from her labors. 'She struggled on, day by day,' says one of the household, 'a good Christian woman, and died on the seventh day after she was taken sick.'

> White snake root, also known as White Sanicle or Tall Boneset, is a highly poisonous plant, native to North America. Their flowers are white and, after blooming, small fluffy seeds blow away with the wind. This plant has a high percent of the toxin tremetol, which is not known for killing humans directly, but indirectly. When the plant is eaten by cattle, the toxin is absorbed into their milk and meat. When humans then, in turn, eat the meat or drink the milk, the toxin enters the body and causes something called milk sickness, which is highly fatal. Thousands of ignorant European settlers died from milk sickness in America in the early 19th century.

"Abe and his sister Sarah waited on their mother, and did the little jobs and errands required of them. There was no physician nearer than 35 miles. The mother knew she was going to die, and called the children to her bedside. She was very weak and the children leaned over while she gave them her last message. Placing her feeble hand on little Abe's head, she told him to be kind and good to his father and sister; to both she said, 'Be good to one another,' expressing her hope that they might live, as they had been taught by her, to love their kindred and worship God." [75]

Nancy Hanks (Turner) Lincoln died on October 5, 1818. Sixty-one years later someone would enclose the grave in a little iron fence and set up a simple headstone bearing the inscription:

"Nancy Hanks Lincoln, Mother of President Lincoln, Died October 5, 1818, Aged 35 years. Erected by a friend of her martyred son, 1879."

---

[75] *Herndon's Life of Lincoln*, pages 25-27.

Herndon's description, "placed her feeble hand on his little head," was his adaptation to the birth date Lincoln would record in his stepmother's Bible a year or so after Thomas Lincoln's death: "February 12, 1809." Based on that record, Abe would have been 9 years old when his mother died. As we all know, a boy experiences a big growth spirt between 9 and 14. But, in the 1860's and beyond, the Hank's family members and Abe's stepmother were sustaining the birth date of their famous relative — the date that Abe himself had written in the Bible he brought to the widow Sarah Bush Johnston Lincoln's home a year or two after the death of Thomas. We might suspect that Abe was older than Sarah because it should have been to the older child that the dying mother gave final instructions. We can also wonder if the dying mother might have told Abe, in private, that her husband was not his father, but to please do the right thing going forward and obey and respect Thomas.

The above gravestone was erected many years after Nancy Hanks Lincoln died. The grounds are presently in the Lincoln Boyhood National Memorial grounds near Lincoln City, Indiana. Thomas and Betsy Sparrow are buried nearby.

The tombstone says, "Nancy Hanks Lincoln, Mother of President Lincoln, died Oct. 5 A. D. 1818, Age 35 years."

Chapter 13: Little Abe's Four Grandparents and the Science of Genetic Inheritance

For 160 years, historians and biographers have struggled to make sense of President Abraham Lincoln's childhood life:

If an historian and/or biographer accepts Abraham Lincoln's story of his childhood life, which he, himself, had presented to the public and to men who were writing his campaign biographies in 1860, then he or she is ignoring, or setting aside, the science of biological inheritance — the science requiring that, for a baby boy to become an exceptionally gifted man, his four biological grandparents had to have inherited and then passed on genes that enabled exceptional intelligence and leadership ability.

If an historian and/or biographer is an independent thinker and embraces the science of biological inheritance, then

1.   He or she has to ignore the birth date that Lincoln personally wrote in his Bible, and

2.   He or she has to ignore the Lincoln-dictated campaign biographies and, instead:

    a.   He or she must suspect that Lincoln was lying about his illegitimate ancestry to achieve political success.

    b.   And he or she must search for historical evidence of the existence of those four biologically-true grandparents who were exceptionally capable ancestors and who passed to baby Abe their exceptional genetic traits, which enabled the adult Abe to become:

        i.   A very successful lawyer,

        ii.   A very successful political leader, and

        iii.   President of the United States.

You see, when a child is conceived in the womb:

1.   The mother's egg has, in that instant, contributed the winning genetic mix from her parents — the winning genetic mix from among the variety that had been given to her, the mother, at the time, decades earlier, of her conception.

2.   The father's sperm has, in that same instant, contributed the winning genetic mix from his parents — the winning genetic mix from among the variety that had been given to him, the father, at the time, decades earlier, of his conception.

This is true for dogs, cats, cows, horses and we human beings. By this method, every child, at conception is the product of the genetic inheritance given to he or she by his or her four grandparents.

As the researcher and author of *Rebirthing Lincoln*, I, Howard Ray White, accept the highly, highly likely history that the four grandparents of President Abraham Lincoln were:

1. Lucy Hanks, born in Virginia, probably illegitimately, of unknown father, subsequently living in North Carolina and then Kentucky.

2. Michael Tanner, born in Virginia of exceptional people of German ancestry, then relocating to North Carolina.

3. Abraham Enloe's father, Enock Enloe, who was born in August, 1741 in Baltimore County, Province of Maryland and died in 1796 in Camden District, South Carolina.

4. Abraham Enloe's mother, Agnes Sprucebanks, who was born on June 2, 1734 in Baltimore County, Province of Maryland and died June 1, 1790 in Swain County, North Carolina.

By accepting the above people as President Abraham Lincoln's four grandparents, the source of his genetic inheritance, we are able to explain the source of:

1. Abe's unusual tall, thin, long-legged physic.

2. Abe's ability to self-educate himself while growing up in an illiterate subsistence farmer's rural home.

3. Abe's political ability, without formal schooling, to, as a young man, quickly win a seat in the Illinois Legislature without prior political experience.

4. Abe's success at making important and beneficial friends while enlisted in the Black Hawk War.

5. Abe's success in reading law, passing examination and gaining certification as a licensed lawyer in Illinois.

6. Mary Todd was of a politically important Kentucky family and her sister was married to a politically important Springfield family. Because of Mary's very impressive family connections, Abe suffered a severe mental breakdown or a serious depression episode, when contemplating marriage to her because he feared it would be impossible, over the long run, to keep his illegitimate birth secret from his wife and thereby destroying her reputation as well as his future legal and political career.

The familiar diagram below presents a picture of a baby's inheritance:

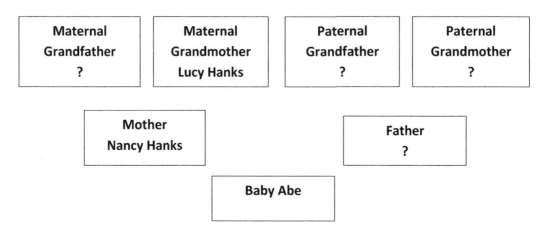

| Maternal Grandfather ? | Maternal Grandmother Lucy Hanks | Paternal Grandfather ? | Paternal Grandmother ? |

| Mother Nancy Hanks | | Father ? |

| Baby Abe |

This rational presentation regarding President Abraham Lincoln's likely grandparents is worthy of your thoughtful analysis. Our biography, *Rebirthing Lincoln*, now proceeds to the next chapter.

Chapter 14: Thomas Lincoln Marries the Widow Sarah Bush Johnston, Giving Abe a Step-mother; Abe Grows into a Young Man in Indiana.

Thomas Lincoln marries Sarah Bush Johnston

We continue this biography by quoting William Herndon's *Life of Lincoln*:

"Thomas Lincoln's widowhood was brief. He scarcely mourned the death of his first wife a year until he reappeared in Kentucky at Elizabethtown in search of another. His admiration centered, for a second time, on Sarah Bush, now the widow of Daniel Johnston, the jailer of Hardin County, who had died several years before of a disease known as the 'cold plague'."

I have already mentioned Sarah Bush, whom Thomas Lincoln had grown up with as a child and teenager, and had sought to court and marry, only to be rejected, probably because he was unable to father children. Yes, apparently, Thomas Lincoln had known Sarah Bush since both were young and living not far apart. Sarah was the daughter of Christopher Bush, an early settler of Elizabethtown, Kentucky. Perhaps, she rejected Thomas' attentions because he was sterile, castrated it was said, caused by a long-ago bought with the mumps. Anyway, that was the past; she had three children from her previous marriage, and must have been comfortable in a future life with no more births.

Herndon continues the *Life of Lincoln* biography, drawing from a letter written to him by Samuel Haycraft, dated December 7, 1866:

"He made a very short courtship. He came to see her on the first day of December, 1819, and, in a straightforward manner, told her that they had known each other from childhood. 'Miss Johnston,' said he, 'I have no wife and you have no husband. I came a-purpose to marry you. I knowed you from a gal and you knowed me from a boy. I've no time to lose; and, if you're willin' let it be done straight off.' She replied that she could not marry him right off, as she had some debts which she wanted to pay first. He replied, 'Give me a list of them.' He got the list and paid them that evening. Next morning, I issued the license, and they were married within sixty yards of my house." [76]

We suspect that the "list" was a verbal listing, not a written list on paper, for neither person was very literate.

Perhaps Thomas' Lincoln relatives — mother, brothers and sisters — had now set aside the perceived earlier shunning. Now the illegitimate woman who brother

---

[76] *Herndon's Life of Lincoln*, page 29 and *Herndon's Informants*, page 502-503.

Thomas had accepted $500 to marry was dead. His mother, brothers and sisters liked Sarah Bush Johnston and had long known her. Hearts softened. Brother Thomas was doing a good deed by marrying Sarah Bush Johnston and helping her to raise her three children. Yes, hearts softened. And, to prove it, the husband of Thomas' sister, Mary, encouraged her husband, Ralph Crume, to load his wagon with Sarah's belongings and take the newlywed couple to Thomas' log cabin in Indiana.

As Herndon continues we learn more:

"Lincoln's brother-in-law, Ralph Crume, and his four horses and spacious wagon . . . transported the newly married pair and their household effects to their home in Indiana. The new Mrs. Lincoln was accompanied by her three children, Sarah, Matilda and John."

Herndon received a description of Sarah Bush Johnston Lincoln from her granddaughter, Harriet Chapman, daughter of her child, Sarah or Matilda. When he received this letter, Sarah Bush Johnston Lincoln was still living:

"My grandmother is a very tall woman, straight as an Indian, of fair complexion, and was, when I first remember her, very handsome, sprightly, talkative, and proud. She wore her hair curled till gray; is kind-hearted and very charitable, and also very industrious."

At the time of the couple's arrival at the Lincoln log cabin in Indiana, Sarah Bush Johnston Lincoln's children ranged in age from thirteen down to nine: Sarah Elizabeth Johnston, 13, Matilda Johnston, 10, and John Johnston, 9. At this point the little 18-foot by 18-foot, one-room cabin would shelter 8 people. Abe Lincoln was 15 and his sister Sarah was 12, soon to be 13. Dennis Friend Hanks, son of the victims of the milk sickness, was 20. To avoid crowding sleeping room on the cabin floor, Abe and Dennis climbed a peg ladder driven into the wall and slept above on crude beds supported by the cabin rafters.

Sarah Bush Johnston Lincoln during her old age. This is the only existing photograph.

Sarah Bush Lincoln was illiterate, but encouraged Abe to seek an education. He would receive some schooling from Andrew Crawford around 1820, when 15 or 16, from James Swaney in 1822, when 17 or 18, and from Azel Dorsey in 1824, when 19 or 20. Abe's passion would be reading, and he would scour the region for books he might borrow. A friend, David Turnham loaned Abe a law book, *The Statutes of Indiana*, and many years later told William Herndon that "he fairly devoured the book in his eager efforts to abstract the store of knowledge that lay within the volume." [77]

Two marriages — Sarah Elizabeth Johnston weds Dennis Friend Hanks and Abe's Half-Sister, Sarah Lincoln, weds Aaron Grigsby

Apparently, a romance blossomed within the Lincoln cabin between Dennis Friend Hanks, 22, and Sarah Elizabeth Johnston, 14 going on 15, or already 15. They agreed to marry and decided to go back to Hardin County, Kentucky for the ceremony and license because she was so young. The marriage date was June 9, 1821. They soon returned to the Little Pigeon River community and made a home for themselves on part of the 80 acres that Thomas Lincoln had signed for with intent to purchase. Sarah Elizabeth may have been pregnant before the marriage, for, before the end of the following year, before December 31, 1822, Dennis and Sarah Elizabeth would have two children: Nancy Melvina Hanks and Sarah Jane Hanks, both to be blessed with long lives.

Dennis Friend Hanks about 40 years after his marriage to Sarah Elizabeth Johnston.

Thomas Lincoln, his first wife's daughter Sarah Lincoln and his second wife, Sarah Bush Johnston Lincoln, joined the Pigeon River Baptist Church during the year 1823. Her Johnston children may have also joined. I do not know. But, I do know that Abe Lincoln refused to join, although he often went along with the family to hear the preacher. At least once, Thomas Lincoln reprimanded 19-year-old Abe for standing on a tree stump, gathering a crowd of young people and repeating, or parodying, the preacher's sermon. During Herndon's research for his biography, Sarah Bush Johnston Lincoln would tell him, "Abe had no particular religion — didn't think of these questions at the time, if he ever did."

In August, 1826, Abe's half-sister, Sarah, married Aaron Grigsby, son of the leading family in nearby Gentryville, Indiana. Sarah was 19 and Aaron was 24 or 25.

---

[77] *Lincoln*, by David Herbert Donald, pages 24-32; *Abraham Lincoln*, by Carl Sandburg, page 13.

Sarah's stepmother, Sarah Bush Johnston Lincoln would later describe Abe's half-sister with these words:

> "She was short of statue and somewhat plump in build. Her hair was dark brown and her eyes were gray." [78]

As reported in detail in an earlier chapter, Professor Frank M. Vancil described Abe as:

> "Six feet four inches high, the length of his legs being out of all proportion to his body," and relatively slender, "he weighed about 180 pounds."

We should compare the physical description of Sarah to that of Nancy Hanks' other child, Abraham. That comparison strongly indicates that Nancy Hanks' two babies were fathered by different men.

Following the marriage, for some unknown reason, there was a quarrel between Abe, who had just turned 22, and Aaron Grigsby, or between Abe and the whole Grigsby family. By this time, Abe delighted himself with writing stories and rhymes. In fact, he had written an eight-stanza song, a parody on the Bible story of Adam and Eve. It seems that the Lincoln family had memorized and practiced singing the song, for together they had sung it at Sarah and Aaron's wedding. [79]

For months following the marriage, Abe spent many, many hours writing derogatory poetry and narrative belittling the Grigsby family with parodies that the community around the Little Pigeon River Community and Gentryville recognized as making fun of his half-sister's in-laws. And he loved presenting his parodies and rhymes to the fellows lounging at the Gentryville store.

The country store in Gentryville was the gathering place for storytellers and loungers, the fun fellows of the community. There Abe, by now self-absorbed in writing and speaking, was in his element. Furthermore, at the store would be found the Cincinnati, Ohio newspaper, which Abe loved reading aloud for the benefit of the fellows who happened to be there. He entertained everyone and provided the news to those who were poor readers or illiterate. It was here that Abe began building on a magnificent speaking and story-telling skill. But all was not fun and writing and storytelling. Abe was about to suffer another family tragedy.

Abe's Half-sister, Sarah Lincoln Grigsby Dies during Childbirth

Sixteen months after Sarah Lincoln married Aaron Grigsby and settled into a cabin about two miles distant from Thomas Lincoln's home, another tragic event struck Abe's family. The date was January 20, 1828. Sarah had been pregnant for

---

[78] *Herndon's Informants*, pages 106-109.
[79] *Herndon's Life of Lincoln,* page 43.

the full term or near it and was giving birth to a baby boy. Something went terribly wrong and both the mother and the baby died. It all happened so fast and unexpectedly. Aaron was heartbroken. He would never remarry. [80]

Now a Grown Man, Abe Lincoln and a Friend Float a Boatload of Grain and Meat to New Orleans

Two months after his half-sister's death, in March, 1828, when Abe was 23, going toward 24, he took a job helping pilot a boat filled with grain and cured meat from Indiana to New Orleans. Surely he remembered Thomas Lincoln's stories of his float trip to New Orleans a few months before he married his mother, Nancy. Perhaps Thomas encouraged Abe to engage in a similar adventure. Abe had been working for James Gentry for a while before the boat was launched down the Ohio River. Gentry's son, Allen Gentry, was in charge of the float trip and the dry goods aboard. Abe, at $8.00 per month, plus board, went along as the bow hand. The trip down the Ohio, and on down the Mississippi River to New Orleans was successful and Allen and Abe return on schedule. And they returned with a story to tell. William Herndon summarizes that story below:

> "The only occurrence of interest they could relate of the voyage was the encounter with a party of marauding Negroes at the plantation of Madame Duchesne, a few miles below Baton Rouge. Abe and Allen, having tied up for the night, were fast asleep on their boat when aroused by the arrival of a crowd of Negroes bent on plunder. [The crew] set to work with clubs, and not only drove off the intruders, but pursued them inland. Then, hastily returning to their quarters, they cut loose their craft and floated downstream 'till daylight." [81]

Abe's Step-mother's Daughter, Matilda Johnston, Marries Levi Hall

During this same year of 1828, Sarah Bush Johnston Lincoln's younger daughter, Matilda Johnston, married Levi Hall, who would be later known as Squire Levi Hall. At the time, Levi was 23, or near it, and Matilda was 18 or 19. A year following the marriage, the couple had a child they named John Johnston Hall.

Abe's Half-brother-in-law Aaron Grigsby Dies and is Buried beside his Late Wife and Abe's Half-sister, Sarah Lincoln Grigsby.

Sadly, Aaron Grigsby's life would be short. At some time during 1829, about three years following his marriage to Nancy Hanks Lincoln's daughter, Sarah, Aaron suffered death. Sarah had been buried beside Little Pigeon Baptist Church, the

---

[80] *Herndon's Life of Lincoln,* pages 42-44.
[81] *Herndon's Life of Lincoln*, page 54.

church to which Thomas Lincoln and his wife belonged. The widowed husband, Aaron Grigsby, was now buried beside his wife. Today, Little Pigeon Baptist Church and the Lincoln cabin site are within Lincoln State Park, Indiana.

Chapter 15: The Milk Sick Returns and the Families Migrate West to Illinois

Winter of 1829-1830 – the Returned Milk-Sick and the Move to Illinois.

During the winter of 1829, the dreaded "milk-sick" returned to cattle and people living in the Little Pigeon Creek Community and the surrounding Indiana region. This was a terrifying problem for everyone living on Thomas Lincoln's 80 acre farm. Apparently Dennis Friend Hanks took the lead in recommending an immediate migration to southern Illinois. In his biography, *Life of Lincoln*, Herndon explains:

"Dennis [Friend] Hanks, discouraged by the prospect and grieving over the loss of his stock, proposed a move further westward. Returning immigrants had brought encouraging news of the newly developed State of Illinois. Vast stretches of rich alluvial lands were to be had there on the easiest of terms.

"Beside this, Indiana no longer afforded any inducements to the poor man. The proposition of Dennis met with the general assent of the Lincoln family, and especially suited the roving and migratory spirit of Thomas Lincoln. . . He had moved four times since his first marriage and in point of worldly goods was not better off than when he started in life. . . Like many of his neighbors, he was ready for another change."

So, rather quickly, Thomas Lincoln sold his 80 acres to the Grigsby family, of which Aaron, the widower of his late wife's deceased daughter, Sarah Lincoln, belonged. The sale was a loss for Thomas Lincoln. Thomas had contracted to pay $2.00 per acre for the raw land, but sold is as developed land for $1.56 per acre. And young David Turnham bought his grain and livestock. The move would involve thirteen people: [82]

Thomas Lincoln and wife Sarah Bush Johnston Lincoln.

Abraham Lincoln

Dennis Friend Hanks and wife Sarah Elizabeth Johnston Hanks and their small children.

Levi Hall and wife Matilda Johnston Hall and their baby John Johnston Hall.

John Johnston.

---

[82] *Herndon's Life of Lincoln*, page 57.

So, the men managed to acquire or build a substantial wagon to be pulled by two yoke of oxen, a wagon that was capable of transporting everyone's household goods. By March, 1830, the party was ready to head west. Herndon continues the story:

> "The journey was a long and tedious one; the streams were swollen and the roads were muddy almost to the point of impassability. The crude, heavy wagon, with its primitive wheels, creaked and groaned as it crawled through the woods and now and then stalled in the road. Many were the delays, but none ever disturbed the equanimity" among the travelers. . . .

> "After a fortnight of rough and fatiguing travel. The . . . Indiana emigrants reached a point in Illinois five miles north-west of the town of Decatur in Macon County. John Hanks, son of Joseph Hanks, in whose shop at Elizabethtown, Kentucky, Thomas Lincoln had learned what he knew of the carpenter's trade, met and sheltered them until they were safely housed on a piece of land which he had selected for them five miles further westward." [83]

John Hanks had immigrated to his Illinois land more than one year earlier. Familiar with the region, he had selected land for the Lincoln extended family "on a bluff overlooking the Sangamon River. . . . Well supplied with timber, it was a charming and picturesque site." Right away, the men — Dennis, Abe, Levi, John and Thomas, as best he could — set out felling trees, hewing timbers and erecting a new log cabin.

Abe, now 26 years old, remained at the new Lincoln home place on the bluff of the Sangamon River for the remainder of 1830 and much of 1831.

Three miles distant was the land of Major Warwick. During 1830 and 1831, Abe worked for Warwick, producing fencing rails to enclose his pastures and fields. The Major must have owned a lot of land. Making his fencing rails was a massive job of felling trees, cutting the trunks the proper length and, with wedges and a mall, splitting the logs into fencing rails, each log yielding normally 4 to 8 rails. Abe worked at making fencing rails for many months. He was not finished until he had produced three thousand fencing rails. Later in this book, you will read how John Hanks and those fencing rails influenced American political history.

_____

[83] *Herndon's Life of Lincoln*, page 59.

Chapter 16: Abe, 26 Years Old and Approaching 27, Leaves Home to Make His Own Way

Abe Lincoln Makes a Second Float Trip to New Orleans; this Trip was with Denton Offutt, John Hanks and John Johnston

In February, 1831, John Hanks was approached by Denton Offutt, "a brisk and venturesome businessman, whose operations extended up and down the Sangamon River." Offutt wanted to hire Hanks to gather a crew, build a large floating boat and take to New Orleans a load of salted pork in barrels, live hogs and corn. Eventually, a deal was struck. The boat-builders/boatmen would consist of John Hanks, Abe Lincoln, John Johnston and their employer, Denton Offutt. The Hanks and Lincoln cut timber off of land known as "Congress Land," sawed it into planks at Kirkpatrick's mill, built their very large float boat, 18 feet wide by 80 feet long, and sealed it with pitch — a job requiring a full four weeks. Folk's, this was a very big float boat, and a four-man crew was needed!

Mr. Offutt's pork, corn and hogs were loaded aboard the new drift boat and he, Hanks, Lincoln and Johnston pushed off at Sangamo Town, headed for New Orleans. It was mid-April, 1831. They expected to reach New Orleans in early May. But, right away, they suffered a crisis when the boat hung up on Rutledge's mill dam. The bow went over, but the boat midsection stuck on top of the dam, leaving the bow suspended above the water below. Solving this problem took many hours. Another boat was brought alongside and the hogs and corn were transferred. But most of the barrels of pork were left on the stranded boat. At this point, Abe took charge. He rolled the barrels forward till the boat was balanced and water which had leaked into the boat during this mishap ran forward. To remove the water, Abe drilled a hole near the bow to let the water pour out, rolling the barrels as needed for balance. Abe then plugged the hole, the barrels were moved substantially toward the bow and the boat tilted and slid forward over the dam, free of restraints. The hogs and corn were then reloaded and the four boatmen proceeded down the river. At Blue Banks, Offutt purchased more hogs from Squire Godbey and they loaded those aboard the drift boat as well. Benefitting from the strong spring current, the four boatmen reached their destination in two or three weeks.

Offutt sold his goods in New Orleans and also sold the boat itself for the lumber content. Before departing, all four visited the city as tourists. In June, all four boarded a steamboat bound for St. Louis. There, Hanks, Lincoln and Johnston bid Offutt goodbye, crossed the Mississippi River and walked across Illinois to their respective destinations: John Hanks to Springfield and Lincoln and John Johnston to the Lincoln homestead on the bluff overlooking the Sangamon River, the latter two arriving in August, 1831. They had been away for five to six months. [84]

Abe Lincoln's Early Days as a New Salem Resident and as an Illinois State Legislator

At this time, Abe Lincoln, now 27 years old, left the home of Thomas Lincoln and Sarah Bush Johnston Lincoln for good. He decided to live in New Salem and help Denton Offutt construct and operate a new general store. They built the store of logs and stocked it with goods that Denton bought. Denton financed the inventory; Abe was the main clerk. Within a few months, almost everyone in the community knew Abraham Lincoln, including Bowling Green, the Justice of the Peace and James Rutledge, President of the local debating society. Green and Rutledge encouraged Lincoln to run for the Illinois State Legislature. On March 9, 1832, Lincoln agreed to throw his hat in the ring. He campaigned around the New Salem area and won over its local voters, but he was running in a large district that was served by four legislators. New Salem was a tiny piece of it.

Offutt's general store soon went under — perhaps Abe talked too much with customers and paid too little attention to making money for the boss. Abe needed another job.

Abe Lincoln Joins the Illinois State Militia in its War to Force Black Hawk's Tribe Out of the State.

On April 21, 1832, Lincoln joined the Illinois State Militia to participate in the state's fight to drive a small tribe of Native Americans back to the west side of the Mississippi River. It seems like the leader of that tribe of the Sac Nation, Black Hawk, had signed a treaty to leave Illinois the previous year, but had temporarily moved back into an edge of the state near where the Iowa River flowed into the Mississippi. The land remained good for another crop of corn and Black Hawk and the 2,000 Natives under his leadership wanted to raise a new

Sac Nation Chief Black Hawk.

---

[84] *Herndon's Life of Lincoln*, pages 61-64.

crop to feed their families. In response, the people of Illinois went to war to drive the 2,000 Natives back across the Mississippi River.

Since he was again jobless, Lincoln figured he would sign up and, for a few months, safely make a little money. Perhaps, he may have figured that military service would look good on a politician's resume as well. On July 10, 1832, Lincoln mustered out. He had spent 80 days in militia service. He had never seen a native of the Sac Nation.

During those 80 days of waiting for military action, Lincoln had made a friend of several men who would later help further his career. He had made friends with Orville Browning, a future Quincy lawyer who would become one of his most influential and important friends. Furthermore, and of more immediate benefit, he had become friends with John Todd Stuart, a cousin of Mary Todd of Kentucky and destined to become a Springfield Lawyer. Stuart would help Lincoln launch a career as an Illinois lawyer in Springfield. Mary Todd, of a politically influential Kentucky family, would help Lincoln advance his Illinois political career as well. In my book, *Bloodstains*, Volume 1, I wrote:

> "The pleasant military experience undoubtedly served to glamorize Abe Lincoln's view of military life. When, 29 years later, as Federal President, Abe Lincoln would blockade Confederate ports, and command Federal troops to invade the Confederacy, surely memory of his brief and pleasant experience with the Illinois militia was contributing to his naïve expectation that the war he was launching would be concluded with little bloodshed." [85]

Lincoln would arrive back at New Salem in time to campaign for about 18 days before the August 6 election. Of the 11 candidates, Lincoln came in eighth. But the politician bug had bit and Abe had found a calling. But he soon needed another job.

Lieutenant Jefferson Davis and the Black Hawk War

Meanwhile, Lieutenant Jefferson Finis Davis of Mississippi, a West Point graduate serving in the United States Army, was placed in charge of transferring captured Sac leaders — Chief Black Hawk and some other Sac warriors from Fort Crawford — down the Mississippi, to Jefferson Barracks, located below St. Louis. Eventually, Black Hawk would be transferred and imprisoned at Fortress Monroe, in Virginia.

After being released from Fortress Monroe and, with the help of a writer, Black Hawk would dictate his biography. Published in 1834 and titled, *Life of Ma-ka-tai-me-she-kia-kiak or Black Hawk*, the author would say the following of Lieutenant Jefferson Davis, described as a "brave young war chief":

---

[85] *Bloodstains*, Volume 1, pages 294-297.

"We started for Jefferson Barracks in a steamboat under the charge of a young war chief who treated us all with much kindness. He is a good and brave young chief whose conduct I was very much pleased. . . On our way down we called at Galena and remained a short time. The people crowded to the boat to see us, but the war chief would not permit them to enter the apartment where we were — knowing, from what his feelings would have been if he had been placed in a similar situation, that we did not wish a gapping crowd around us."

Black Hawk's book would close with the following message:

Jefferson Davis as a younger man.

"The path to glory is tough, and many gloomy hours obscure it. May the Great Spirit shed light on yours — and that you may never experience the humility that the power of the American Government has reduced me to, is the wish of him, who, in his native forests, was once as proud and bold as yourself.

"Black Hawk

"10th Moon, 1833." [86]

As a New Salem Resident, Lincoln and William F. Berry Operate a Store while Abe Runs for the Illinois Legislature

Following Lincoln's rewarding experience in the Illinois militia in search of Black Hawk, he returned to New Salem and agreed to partner with William F. Berry in purchasing one of the three general stores in the town and the inventory from another. Abe and William launched the enterprise in the mid-summer of 1832 and soon discovered substantial difficulty in making a success of the venture. In early 1833, Berry applied for a liquor license. That did not help. They closed the store and Lincoln worried how the pay off his accumulated debt. The Lincoln and Berry general store had experienced very little business, giving Lincoln lots of time to read and study, which had become an important aspect of Lincoln's life. Now 28 years old, Abe was looking for a more promising future than splitting fence rails, clerking

---

[86] *Bloodstains*, Volume 1, pages 297-298.

a store and delivering goods down the Mississippi River. He was now digging deeper into both self-education and developing a wide network of helpful friends. But, he had to figure out how to pay off the sizable debt he had acquired in the joint venture with Berry.

Two part-time jobs came his way. Friends helped him win an appointment, by the Andrew Jackson administration, to be the postmaster for the New Salem post office. He would hold this appointed job for three years, 1833-1835, and there was just a little money in it, but it gave him some status in the small New Salem town. The other job was more fruitful. John Calhoun, the official surveyor for the county, needed an assistant and a friend of Lincoln arranged for Abe to get the job. He dove into it, reading books on surveying, recording land surveys and how to make trigonometric calculations.

Lincoln had been a loser in his bid to win election to the Illinois legislature in 1832. Now, in 1834, he decided to try again, this time as a member of the Whig Party. The strongest Whig candidate was John Todd Stuart, now a successful lawyer. Lincoln and Stuart had served in the same company in the Illinois militia's war to oust Black Hawk's people and the two had become good friends. This time, Lincoln, a Whig candidate, also received some Democrat support. Of the eleven men running for the four legislative seats in the district, both Lincoln and Stuart came up winners. Remember the name John Todd Stuart, he and Todd relatives will be important people in this biography.

Abe Lincoln and Ann Rutledge

Abe was experiencing difficulties in his love life. He had grown very attached to Ann Rutledge. She was the daughter of a founder of New Salem and the owner of Rutledge Tavern where, from time to time, he roomed and boarded. At five feet, three inches tall and between 120 and 130 pounds, she was pretty, but a bit plump. Lincoln liked her a lot, but she was engaged to John McNamar, who was away in New York State, helping his family get through a hard financial situation. McNamar had been away a long time and Lincoln believed the so-called engagement would never advance to marriage. So he was encouraging Ann to consider it a broken tie and consider marrying him. Then, in the summer of 1835, Illinois experience an extremely hot, rainy summer. In August, Ann became very sick. She was diagnosed with "brain fever." It was probably Typhoid Fever caused by a flood of polluted water entering into the family well. Abe spent time with Ann, who was confined to her sick bed. He was very distraught, so troubled over the fact that he could not help her recover. She passed away on August 25, 1835.

Abraham Lincoln was crushed. For a month he was so distressed that he felt unable to resume work as a surveyor. Finally, on September 24th, there is a record that he resumed work on a survey.

Many, many years later, while President of the United States, Lincoln would be discussing with old Salem friends those then-long-ago-days living in that town. The President replied, "It is true — true indeed, I did." He continued, "I loved the woman dearly and soundly: she was a handsome girl — would have made a good loving wife. . . . I did honestly and truly love the girl and think often — often of her now." [87]

Abe Lincoln is a Member of the Illinois Legislature in the State Capital, Vandalia.

On December 1, 1835, Lincoln began his legislative career at the state capital, Vandalia, a small town of 800 to 900 people in Southern Illinois. Of the 55 members of the Illinois House, 36 were, like Lincoln, first timers. The secession would conclude on February 13, 1835. At Vandalia, Lincoln roomed with John Todd Stuart, strengthening his friendship with this experienced legislator. Although a first-timer, Lincoln was helpful applying a recognized skill at drafting a few laws that his legislative friends sought.

When winter approached, Governor Joseph Duncan called a Special Session of the Illinois legislature. It was to meet during the 1835-1836 winter months. The major job for the Special Session was to take new Illinois census data and reapportion the seats in the Illinois Legislature. Obviously, the Southern counties would be the big losers, since they were settled first, mostly by people of the Southern culture, many from Kentucky. This reapportionment would significantly begin a continuing alteration of the political balance in the State, giving the Central and Northern counties, mostly settled by people from the Northeast and recent immigrants, expanding influence over the political direction of the State of Illimois. The approved reallocation increased the Central Illinois Sangamon County delegation in the Illinois House of Representatives from four to seven. And this big gain in the size of the Sangamon County delegation would be very beneficial to Abraham Lincoln's political and legal career.

Also, while convened for this winter session, Governor Duncan wanted the Legislature to help finance the construction of a canal that would link the Illinois and Chicago Rivers, thereby allowing boats to travel between Lake Michigan and the Mississippi River. The vote was very close, 28 versus 27 in favor of authorizing a loan of $500,000 to help finance the Illinois and Michigan Canal project. Lincoln cast the deciding favorable vote.

In June 1836, Lincoln announced his candidacy for re-election to the Illinois Legislature. He was running for one of the seven House seats now allocated to Sangamon County. He won big, receiving more votes than any other candidate.

---

[87] *Herndon's Lincoln*, pages 105-115 and 389.

There is an interesting story here that relates to Lincoln's unusual height. Apparently, the seven Sangamon members of the House and the two Sangamon members of the Senate were rather tall. None were short. The men became known within the Legislature and in newspaper reports as the "Long Nine."

The previous winter secession Legislature had approved a $500,000 bill to help finance the Michigan and Illinois Canal. Well, this new legislative session seemed determined to approve a $10,000,000 bill to help finance railroads and roads across the state. Four hundred thousand dollars of it was allocated to improving the navigation on five rivers. Overall, it was a massive bill. There was a lot of trading for political influence. The Long Nine strongly supported the project. The main north-south line would run from Cairo, on the Mississippi River at the southern tip of the state, northward, never far from the Mississippi River, to Galena in northwest Illinois. Several west-east lines connected the network, including the line through Springfield. Lincoln biographer, David Herbert Donald would write, "The bill gave something to everybody." The bill was approved by a large majority.

Abraham Lincoln. This is the youngest photo of Abe Lincoln.

The massive internal improvements bill was huge, but the main focus of Sangamon County's "Long Nine" was to win support for moving the Illinois State Capital from Vandalia to Springfield. The present capital, Vandalia, was a small southern Illinois town, the State House building was in shambles and, since the central and northern population growth was predominant, relocation further north seemed appropriate. But a relocation to where? The "Long Nine" were eager for Springfield to be accepted and campaigned heavily to win votes. To eliminate small towns, Lincoln drafted a bill that required the selected site to donate $50,000 and two acres of land for the new capital building. That passed. Finally, all amendments being considered, balloting for site selection began. On February 28, 1837, on the fourth ballot, Springfield received a majority vote. The selection of Springfield would change the life and political future of Abraham Lincoln more than anything he would experience prior to the formation of the Illinois Republican Party, twenty-one years later. But, of more recent concern, the financial panic was about to strike.

Biographer David Herbert Donald would describe the financial panic of 1837 and the consequent failure of the "bill that gave something to everybody:"

"The panic of 1837 put an end to these high hopes and effectively put an end to the [Illinois] internal improvements program. Very little construction was ever completed, and the state was littered with unfinished roads and partially dug canals. The state's finances, pledged to support the grandiose plan, suffered and Illinois bonds fell to 15 cents on the dollar, while annual interest charges were more than eight times the total state revenues. Inevitably there was a search for scapegoats and questions were raised about Lincoln's role in promoting such a harebrained and disastrous scheme." [88]

---

[88] *Lincoln*, by David Herbert Donald, pages 52-64.

Chapter 17: Abraham Lincoln, Still a Bachelor and State Legislator, Is Now a Lawyer — so He Leaves New Salem to Live and Work in Springfield

Abe Lincoln is Certified as an Illinois Lawyer, Relocates to Springfield and Partners with Lawyer John Todd Stewart.

Abe Lincoln received his license to practice law on March 1, 1837. He was 32 years old, still a bachelor and had not yet accumulated any wealth. But he had made important friends as a Whig state legislator — men like John Todd Stewart — and had made important friends in the Black Hawk War. Building on those friendships and useful acquaintances, Abe Lincoln was looking forward to a much brighter future.

And he intended to put Thomas Lincoln and Sarah Bush Johnston Lincoln farther and farther behind him, deep into the unmentioned past. He recognized that the less people knew about his late mother, her husband and his childhood and early life in Kentucky and Indiana the better for his personal future career. He knew he had to keep secret from the public stories revealing his true father, Abraham Enloe of North Carolina!

The next month, April, 1837, Abe rode proudly into the future State Capital, Springfield, where a lawyer and fellow Whig state legislative friend, John Todd Stuart, took him into his established law practice as an equal partner. They would jointly practice law under a new law firm organization. John Todd Stuart and Abraham Lincoln had grown to know each other during the Black Hawk war and as state legislators. Apparently, the established lawyer was happy to put the newly certified lawyer into his office. Lincoln had left declining New Salem for good. When considering from whence he had come, surely, Abe Lincoln had arrived. The partnership was called "Stuart and Lincoln." The town population was 1,400, including 11 lawyers and 18 doctors, and rapid growth in population and legal work was assured. He was now established in a career in law in the future State Capital and was recognized as a rising politician.

Short on money, Abe accepted Joshua Speed's off-hand offer to share his double bed, positioned above the general store that he partly owned and helped operate. Speed's was one of 18 Springfield stores that sold to a population of 18,000 people in the surrounding countryside. Joshua Speed would become one of Abe's few close friends. The year prior to Abe's arrival, young Billy Herndon had clerked in this very store, but was presently away at Illinois College in Jacksonville. You have already read much about William H. "Billy" Herndon.

Lincoln's Law Partner is Elected to the United States House as a Whig.

In early November, 1837, Democrats held a political convention to nominate their candidate for the Third District of the U. S. House of Representatives, which included 35 counties in central Illinois. A majority of the Delegates were supporters of the policies of President Andrew Jackson. They nominated young Stephen Douglas as their candidate, denying another term to incumbent Representative William May, a Democrat who had opposed Andrew Jackson's agenda and who exhibited Whiggish leanings. Only 24 years of age, Douglas would be old enough when the next House convened.

The Whigs of the Third Federal House District also convened. They nominated Abe Lincoln's senior law partner, John Todd Stuart, as their candidate. Stuart was a seasoned and well-known lawyer and politician. Political observers figured little Stephen Douglas would have no chance against Stuart. Referring to the fact that Douglas was quite short of height, Abe Lincoln wrote a fellow politician: "We have adopted it as part of our policy here, to never speak of Douglas at all. Isn't that the best mode of treating so small a matter?"

John Todd Stuart, Abe's law partner.

John Todd Stuart won the election over Democrat Stephen Douglas by a comfortable margin. The House District that included Springfield would remain in the control of the Whig Party for several more years.

Abe Lincoln, Billy Herndon, Joshua Speed and Speed's Store

In 1838, Joshua Speed took Billy Herndon back as a clerk in his general store. Billy had decided to forgo further college education since his father, Archer, had refused to pay for it. Abe Lincoln was still living with Speed in the large upstairs room over the store. A young clerk who worked at a nearby store was also sharing the large upstairs room. But there was perhaps a bit more room upstairs, and Billy was not all that welcome back at his parent's house, so Speed invited Billy to find himself a spot in the room over the store as well. So by this fate of circumstance, three bachelors – Abe Lincoln, Billy Herndon and Joshua Speed – were brought together as rooming friends in 1838. Abe was 33, Billy was 19, and Joshua was 25. Lincoln biographer David Donald would conclude, "From the beginning, Speed was his close companion, and he became perhaps the only intimate friend that Lincoln ever had."

Joshua Speed had grown up on a prosperous large-scale farm near Louisville, Kentucky. Called Farmington, his family's large scale agricultural enterprise provided work and support for 70 bonded African Americans. His was so unlike Thomas Lincoln's upbringing in the log cabin of a small-scale subsistence farmer. Also, Joshua Speed had attended private schools in Kentucky and had studied for 2 years at St. Joseph's College in Bardstown. Coming to Springfield seeking his fortune, young Speed had begun by taking a financial interest in the above-mentioned general store. For nearly 4 years Abe and Joshua would share a double bed above the store. Billy Herndon would also share that upstairs room. Such arrangements were not uncommon in that era – living space was at a premium, especially warm wintertime living space, and neither Abe nor Billy had significant money. It is historically important that, during those years, these young men talked a lot, particularly of political matters. Joshua was educated and was a window into southern States social life. Billy was bright, well read and imbued with the fire of Abolitionism, recently ignited at Illinois College by Edward Beecher and his faculty, which was from the northeastern States. Abe Lincoln, short on formal education, but obviously gifted at politics, was playing catch-up. He was absorbing much from his better-educated friends and shaping his opinions of American life – life in the northern States and the North's perception of life in the southern States. [89]

Legislator Abe Lincoln and the 1838-1839 Winter Legislative Secession

Abraham Lincoln was again a member of the 1838-1839 winter session of the Illinois State Legislature. Although Springfield was now the State Capitol, the legislature was meeting in Vandalia until the legislative building in Springfield would be finished. Lincoln was of the minority Whig Party, but more of a party leader than previous years. The financial panic of 1837 had taken a devastating toll on the excessively ambitious $10,000,000 state internal improvements project. Yet, Lincoln struggled to find some way to keep, a least, a small part of the project going forward. And opponents of making Springfield the state capital kept scheming to reverse the decision of the previous legislature.

Lincoln argued equally for state support of the State Bank of Illinois, which was near failure as a result of the Panic of 1837 and the devastating depreciation of issued bonds. Like most Whigs, Lincoln favored a strong Illinois state bank. But Whigs were the minority, and like most Democrats, those in the Illinois Legislature

---

[89] *Lincoln*, by David Herbert Donald, pages 64, 69-70, 73-74, and Stephen A. Douglas, by Robert W. Johannsen, pages 61-63 and *Lincoln's Herndon*, by David Herbert Donald pages 10 and 14 and *Bloodstains*, Volume 1 pages 334, 339-340, 345, 352.

supported President Andrew Jackson's dislike of the Bank of the United States, and likewise of an Illinois state bank.

Abe Lincoln and Springfield's Young Men's Lyceum

During this time, Abe Lincoln was a member of the Young Men's Lyceum in Springfield. In this group, members were engaged in debate and taking turns delivering speeches or lectures. Lincoln got his turn at delivering a lecture in January 1838. Because this lecture revealed an important characteristic of the speaker, concerning his goals for himself — according to a many-years-later analysis by his most important biographer, David Herbert Donald — I am devoting a half-page of my biography to quoting from his book, *Lincoln*. The fit between Lincoln's closing remarks in this 1838 lyceum lecture and his behavior following his 1860 election as President of the United States is truly haunting. Both David Donald and I recognize that. David Donald wrote:

> "In previous generations, [Lincoln] suggested, when the outcome of the American venture in self-government was still in doubt, 'all that sought celebrity and fame, and distinction, expected to find them in the success of that experiment.' Even now there were 'many great and good men' who aspired 'to nothing beyond a seat in Congress, a gubernatorial or presidential chair.' But, he added, in a rare moment of self-revelation, 'such belong not to the family of the lion, or the tribe of the eagle.' Such honors were not enough for 'men of ambition and talents.' These routine offices would not satisfy 'an Alexander, a Caesar, or a Napoleon,' from whom the greatest danger to popular government must be expected. 'Towering genius disdains a beaten path,' Lincoln reminded his audience. 'It seeks regions hitherto unexplored. . . . It thirsts and burns for distinction; and, if possible, it will have it, whither at the expense of emancipating slaves, or enslaving freemen'."

> "Probably most of Lincoln's listeners thought this nothing more than another rhetorical flourish at the end of a long speech. Few could have realized that he was unconsciously describing himself." [90]

Legislator Abe Lincoln in the 1840 Legislative Winter Secession

The State Bank of Illinois remained a major issue when the legislature convened in late 1840, now in the new state capital, Springfield. And it is interesting to observe that the central branch of the bank was also located in Springfield. Well, the State Bank of Illinois had been long surviving on paying obligations with paper and never with specie, or hard money. So, Democrats approved a bill that would force the bank to start paying obligations with specie the day after the adjournment of the present secession of the legislature. Desperate to postpone the inevitable, Whigs

---

[90] *Lincoln*, by David Herbert Donald, pages 80-81.

were persistently absent to prevent a quorum from being present for a vote to adjourn. It was December 1840. Day after day, Democrats were unable to count a quorum present. Then, one evening some Democrats rose from their sick bed and appeared, increasing the quorum. Seeing a likely quorum present, Abe Lincoln tried to escape the room only to find that the sergeant of arms blocked the way out. Desperate, Lincoln climbed out the window. It was a second floor window, but being very tall, he reached the ground unharmed. His escape effort was not enough because the Speaker counted him present. The vote to adjourn passed. The session was concluded "and the bank was killed." Democrat newspapers explained that Lincoln was not hurt during his escape because "his legs reached nearly from the window to the ground."

This session, 1840, was Lincoln's final year in the Illinois Legislature. He would not seek re-election. There were many reasons for his decision not to run again. First, the state was now bankrupt as a result of the overly-ambitious $10,000,000 State Internal improvements Act. Would he be paid if he returned for another legislative session? That worried him. Second, his political popularity was in free-fall — it would be far more difficult to win since he and other former legislators were responsible for the ridiculous $10,000,000 act. "The Long Nine" were now called "The Springfield junto." Third, his law partner, John Todd Stuart, had failed to win re-election to Congress. For the past two years, Stuart had spent many months in Washington, leaving Lincoln to run the practice alone. Now Stuart was back in Springfield and was expected to move beyond the partnership with Lincoln. Lincoln expected to soon be looking for a new law practice partnership and new clients. [91]

---

[91] Herndon's Lincoln, pages 159-162.

Chapter 18: Abe Lincoln Marries Mary Todd, Daughter of a Prominent Kentucky Family and Sister to the Wife of a Prominent Illinois Family

Ninian and Elizabeth Todd Edwards, a Prominent Springfield Family

In 1839, Springfield, Illinois, was a town of about 3,000 people. During the summer, the State Capital had been relocated from Vandalia to Springfield, bringing prosperity to this island within a sea of economic depression. A statehouse was under construction. The State Supreme Court and the Federal District Court had begun meeting in Springfield. Numerous lawyers with political ambitions and many opportunistic businessmen were moving to town. Business and home construction was brisk. This was the situation when, in December, 1839, the State Legislature convened for its winter session – consequently sparking the opening of the Springfield winter social season. At the top, yes, the very top, of Springfield society was lawyer and politician Ninian Wirt Edwards and his wife Elizabeth Todd Edwards.

Ninian Wirt Edwards was a lawyer, a staunch Whig and a member of the State Legislature. He was the son of former Governor Ninian Edwards, who had been born in Maryland, later moving to Kentucky, where he had been a Legislator and a Justice on the Kentucky State Supreme Court. Edwards had then been appointed Governor of Illinois Territory by President James Madison and reappointed thereafter until statehood (1809-1818). After statehood, Edwards was elected Federal Senator (1818-1825), was appointed Minister to Mexico by President James Monroe (1824), and was elected Illinois Governor (1827 to 1830). He had died six years before Springfield's rise to become the State Capital.

Elizabeth Todd Edwards.

His son, Ninian Wirt Edwards, was married to Elizabeth Todd, the daughter of Robert Todd, a prosperous banker, farmer and manufacturer in Lexington, Kentucky. Ninian had met Elizabeth while attending Transylvania University in Lexington. One of Elizabeth's cousins was John Todd Stuart, Abe Lincoln's law partner. Another of Elizabeth's cousins was John Hardin, who had been State's Attorney for the First Illinois Judicial District, one of six within Illinois. However, three years previously, through political maneuvering, Stephen Douglas had won appointment by the Illinois Legislature to assume Hardin's State's Attorney job. From that beginning, Douglas would rise to great political prominence.

Although Ninian's father had been a Democrat, Ninian and Elizabeth were Whigs. They often entertained at their luxurious and spacious home in Springfield, and it was an honor to receive an invitation to an Edwards party.

Although Ninian and Elizabeth exhibited the typical characteristics of snobbery, they had felt obligated to invite John Stuart's law partner, Abraham Lincoln. Actually, Ninian took a liking to the tall newcomer. He respected Lincoln as a fellow Whig and a member of the State Legislature, first taking a seat on December 1, 1834. Yet the men were so different, for Lincoln was a self-made man who declined to discuss his family background in detail — for Abe drew his primary political strength from the everyday farmer and laborer. It appears that Ninian often invited Abe to social gatherings because he thought the tall newcomer might be politically useful, although he found him "a mighty rough man."

Ninian and Elizabeth also occasionally invited young Stephen Douglas, even though he was a Democrat. Ninian realized that Douglas was a rising political power who was very much worthy of serious cultivation.

Edward's parties were fun for men to attend because Ninian and Elizabeth's guest list included the most attractive young women in Springfield. At previous parties Elizabeth had found a husband for her sister Frances: a local physician named William Wallace. So, it was in early 1839 that she invited another sister, Mary Todd, to come up from Lexington, Kentucky, for an extended visit. [92]

Mary Todd of Lexington, Kentucky Visits her Sister in Springfield.

Perhaps Mary Todd had decided to again visit her sister Elizabeth in Springfield partly to get away from her stepmother, Elizabeth Humphreys Todd. But, more likely, it was to enjoy Springfield society. She had turned 20 in December and was already well into marriageable age. Her father, Robert Todd, had been raised in a prominent Kentucky family. Politically, he was a Whig, and he maintained close political ties to a neighbor, Henry Clay, whom some considered the leader of America's Whig Party. Robert Todd had been a senator in the Kentucky Legislature. He was of Scottish descent, by way of the northern section of Ireland. He had Todd ancestors in both Pennsylvania and Virginia.

Robert Todd's first wife and Mary's mother, Eliza Parker Todd, had died shortly after childbirth when Mary was only 7 years old. Eliza had been raised in a well-to-do Kentucky family and was descended from Scots as well.

---

[92] *Lincoln*, by David Herbert Donald, pages 84-85; *The President's Wife, Mary Todd Lincoln*, by Ishbel Ross, pages 29-32; and *Bloodstains*, Volume 1, by Howard Ray White, pages 360-361.

Robert Todd had remarried soon after Eliza's death. John Crittenden, who would become a prominent Federal senator, had been best man. Robert's second wife, Elizabeth Humphreys Todd, was the daughter of a physician who had moved to Kentucky from Virginia. Robert had met her while she had been working for the State Legislature. She was "highly cultivated," with important family political connections. For example her uncle was a Federal Senator from Louisiana and would become Minister to France. As mentioned earlier, family members believed that Mary had always disliked her stepmother, although she is never recorded making a point of it in adult life.

Upon attaining the age of 8 years, Mary Todd had attended school at an academy run by John Ward, an Episcopal clergyman. Later, as a 13-year-old teenager, she had attended Madame Mentelle's boarding school, a finishing school for girls. She still loved to read and had been "a model student, getting top marks with ease in all her subjects." And she most enjoyed the dancing instruction, for she excelled at it. During 1832, when she was at finishing school, Mary saw Andrew Jackson during a big campaign barbeque. Already quite interested in politics, she watched intently as Jackson "rode in an open carriage while women waved hickory sticks and handkerchiefs, and horsemen, military companies, clubs and orders marched to blaring bands." But she was an admirer of neighbor Henry Clay and true to her family's allegiance to the Whig Party. Perhaps she had looked with disdain upon the hordes of less prosperous voters who were being attracted to the Democratic Party.

Mary had spent three months with Ninian and Elizabeth Edwards two years previously, then returning home after the social season was concluded. Back in Lexington that year, she had taken more classes with John Ward, the Episcopal minister whose school she had attended as a little girl. [93]

Our story now arrives at early 1839 with Mary Todd again in Springfield, a guest of her sister, Elizabeth Todd Edwards.

Bachelor Abe Lincoln Meets and Courts Mary Todd

Abe Lincoln first saw Mary in early 1839 at a party given by Ninian and Elizabeth Edwards. He admired her dancing, and ascertained that she was a "bright and brainy girl." He observed that the older men "liked to talk to her and listen to her political views," whereas the younger men "preferred to dance with her and flatter her." In contrast to the Todd's and Edwards' life style, Abe Lincoln was still living upstairs above Joshua Speed's store, and sharing a bed with him.

After getting to know Abe, Mary thought him "the most unkempt and unworldly man [she] had ever known." And her sister Elizabeth thought Abe was "cold and

---

[93] *The President's Wife, Mary Todd Lincoln*, by Ishbel Ross, pages 13-29; and *Bloodstains*, Volume 1, by Howard Ray White, page 361.

dull, as well as gauche." Elizabeth was confident that her sister's "sense of humor and her social ambitions would protect her from Lincoln."

Billy Herndon, 20 years old, was occasionally invited to these Edwards' parties, too, and he occasionally talked with and danced with Mary Todd. Although he found her "openly flirtatious," he discovered that her "agreeable qualities instantly disappeared beneath a wave of stinging satire or sarcastic bitterness," whenever she found a situation disagreeable. For example, on one occasion, after dancing with Mary, Billy had complimented her for gliding through a waltz with the "ease of a serpent." Instantly offended, Mary had replied, "Mr. Herndon, comparison to a serpent is rather severe irony, especially to a newcomer."

People who attended Ninian and Elizabeth's parties found Mary to be an entertaining conversationalist with considerable social skill – witty, cultured, graceful and dignified. Two young lawyers who were destined to play pivotal roles in American history seriously courted Mary Todd. I am speaking of Stephen Douglas and Abraham Lincoln.

Mary Todd.

Mary Todd seemed attracted to Douglas early on, but the attraction dimmed as it became more apparent to her that he was not interested in matrimony. Furthermore, Douglas was a Democrat and Mary was a dedicated Whig. Years later Mary would tell one of her relatives, "I liked him well enough, but that was all." Douglas also paid some attention to Julia Jayne, later to become the wife of Lyman Trumbull, Federal Senator, Whig and, subsequently, changing to the Republican Party. But falling in love was not in the forefront of Stephen Douglas' agenda. He was only 25 years old. At this point in his life, his love was politics. [94]

Mary Todd would spend most of the next two years in Springfield as a houseguest of her sister, Elizabeth Todd Edwards. As the months would roll by, Abe and Mary would often spend time together, enjoying their mutual interests in poetry and politics. Both were Whigs and that would make Mary comfortable with Abe's politics. And the more she would know of him the more confident she would

[94] *Lincoln*, by David Herbert Donald, pages 84-85; *The President's Wife, Mary Todd Lincoln*, by Ishbel Ross, pages 29-34; *Stephen A. Douglas*, by Robert W. Johannsen, page 73, and *Bloodstains*, Volume 1, by Howard Ray White, pages 361.

become that Abe had a gift for attracting votes from a wide spectrum of the voting public. So, motivated by her own political ambition, she would be attracted to Abe, for it seemed that her personal ambition was to share in a future husband's political success.

Although Elizabeth Edwards had originally discouraged a marriage between her sister, Mary Todd, and Abe Lincoln, she and her husband Ninian had, by late 1840, come around to favoring the thing. Around Christmas 1840 Abe and Mary were engaged. [95]

The Mystery of Abe Lincoln's Strange Mental Depression.

Then, strangely, a few weeks afterward, as 1841 dawned, Lincoln started getting depressed over the prospect of marriage. He probably felt inadequate to support a lady who had known luxury and social prominence all her life. His income was small and his voter appeal had declined as a result of Democratic Party successes. But most importantly, Abe Lincoln was a man with an unexplainable tendency to suffer depression, ranging from melancholy, to deep moodiness, to depressive illness. Within a few short weeks he totally lost his nerve, and told Mary he did not love her. As one would expect, those little words drove Mary to tears and broke the engagement.

Then Lincoln became even more depressed, and some friends feared he might commit suicide. He was sick in his room under the care of a doctor for several weeks. Lincoln's nervous collapse was the talk of the town, and Ninian and Elizabeth, who by that time stood strongly opposed to the marriage, told their friends that Lincoln was "crazy." As would be expected, law partner John Todd Stuart was also undoubtedly very upset with Lincoln for jilting his cousin. Apparently, John Stuart, for that reason, would ask Lincoln to leave the law firm in April, 1841.

Perhaps we should reflect a bit on what was making Lincoln so frightfully nervous over a marriage to such a prominent lady as Mary Todd. Remember, we have concluded that Abe Lincoln was the illegitimate son of Abraham Enloe of far western North Carolina. Most likely, Abe knew that he was Enloe's son. Perhaps he thought, "How can I keep my real parentage secrete from a wife all of my life?" And Mary Todd was no ordinary lady. Far from it: she was of extraordinary upbringing and family connections. Lincoln was sick with worry that it would be impossible to keep his parentage secret from such noble and politically connected families.

Anyway, about seven months later, giving a month or two, in the fall of 1841, Mrs. Simeon Frances, wife of the editor of the *Sangamo Journal*, invited both Abe Lincoln and Mary Todd to a social affair where she had encouraged them to "be

---

[95] *Lincoln*, by David Herbert Donald, pages 84-85, and *Bloodstains*, Volume 1, by Howard Ray White, page 369.

friends again." This renewed friendship was being kept a secret from Mary's sister, Elizabeth Edwards. Surprisingly, from that point on, Abe and Mary had resumed dating, secretly, often meeting at the Frances home. Although the renewed courtship seemed, on the surface, to be a positive activity, it would strangely lead to deadly political mischief.

At the beginning of 1842 Abe Lincoln moved from the bed above Joshua Speed's store to live with the family of William Butler, who was a good friend and the Clerk of the Sangamon County Court. Speed had sold his interest in the store in preparation for moving back to Kentucky to be married. Apparently, Butler did not charge Lincoln for boarding at his home. And Abe and Mary Todd were seeing each other again. [96]

Abe Lincoln and Mary Todd Have Political Fun Together, but James Shields Got Mad and Called for a Duel!

The above-mentioned opportunity for Abe and Mary to be involved in future mischief was made possible in February, 1842 when the State Bank of Illinois, which Lincoln had often defended in the State Legislature, was forced to close. The Bank's notes were instantly worthless, and, as a result, commerce virtually ceased throughout Illinois for a while. To protect the State treasury, State Auditor James Shields declared that the failed bank's notes would not be acceptable in payment of

taxes. It seemed folks wished to protest the politics that had contributed to the banks failure, so there was considerable sentiment to put one over on the tax collectors by paying taxes with the worthless notes. But Shields would not allow it. Abe and Mary would soon become involved in this controversy.

Illinois State Auditor James Shields.

Mary Todd knew James Shields well, for they had attended parties together, and there had been the remote possibility of a romance. Being a political buff and eager to engage in political intrigue, Mary had decided to vent her literary talent on Shields, who was, of course, a Democrat. She had targeted Shields because, as State Auditor, he had directed that tax payments to the Illinois Government had to be tendered in gold and silver coin. She had planned a cute literary game, complete with personal attacks. Abe Lincoln and Mary's friend, Julia

---

[96] *Lincoln*, by David Herbert Donald, pages 85-88, and *Bloodstains*, Volume 1, by Howard Ray White, pages 369-370 and 378.

Jayne, had agreed to help, but Mary had been the primary author. They had written a series of fictional stories for the *Sangamo Journal* that made fun of Shields. The series, called the "Township Letters," was literary fiction, but easily understood by readers to be making much fun of State Auditor Shields.

Well, State Auditor Shields got mad – real mad! In fact, Shields sent his designated friend, General John Whiteside to Tremont, Illinois, where Lincoln was working in court, to deliver a formal challenge to a duel. Lincoln reluctantly accepted the challenge. Because dueling was outlawed in Illinois, the men agreed to conduct the duel across the Mississippi River in Missouri. On September 22, 1842, accompanied by proper witnesses and seconds, the 2 duelists arrived at the dueling ground. Lincoln had chosen broadswords as the dueling weapon, believing his height and long arms would give him an advantage. He told a friend, "I didn't want the damn fellow to kill me, which I rather think he would have done if we had selected pistols." Fortunately, friends at the dueling ground persuaded both Shields and Lincoln to apologize and abandon the duel. In fact, they shook hands before departing the place.

Abe Lincoln was painfully ashamed of his and Mary's childish and unprofessional behavior, from the beginning with the first "Township Letter" to the conclusion on the dueling grounds. He and Mary "mutually agreed never to speak of it." In fact Abe made sure that Mary's involvement in writing the letters was kept secret. Very little would be said of it over the years. [97]

Congressman John Hardin.

Abe Lincoln had not permitted anyone to know that Mary Todd was a co-conspirator in writing the "Township Letters," and she loved him ever the more for his chivalrous response to Shield's challenge. For the second time, Abe and Mary were in love. The wounds from the broken engagement seemed healed.

Elizabeth Edwards' Cousin is Elected to the U. S. House

A Whig had once more won election to the Federal House seat that included Springfield and other central Illinois counties. Elizabeth Edward's cousin, John Hardin, a Jacksonville lawyer, won the seat. Jacksonville was the other city in the Federal House District that included Springfield. Hardin and Abe Lincoln

---

[97] *Lincoln*, by David Herbert Donald, pages 92 and 111; *The President's Wife, Mary Todd Lincoln*, by Ishbel Ross, page 46, and *Bloodstains*, Volume 1, by Howard Ray White, pages 381-382.

had competed for the Whig Party nomination at the District Convention, but Hardin had gained the nod. There had been a feeling among Whig Delegates that the Federal House job should be rotated and not repeatedly go to a lawyer from Springfield. This arrangement would favor a bid by Lincoln next time. Edward Baker, Lincoln's former law partner and Federal Representative for the past 2 terms, had not sought the nomination again. He had wanted to remain in Springfield and work full-time on his law business. Hardin was another of Mary Todd's relatives, a Kentuckian who had been educated at Transylvania University in Lexington.

Abe Lincoln Will Not Serve in the State Legislature Again.

1842 was the last year that Abraham Lincoln was to serve in the Illinois Legislature. He had declined to run for reelection. The Whig Party was declining and the Democratic Party was in its ascendency. His temper and interest in legislative politics had run its course. He had served four terms, from 1834 to 1842. His true parentage — discovery of Nancy Hanks' and his connection to Abraham Enloe of Western North Carolina — remained a secret from his political opponents. Perhaps he was now confident that he could aim for greater political triumphs. Anyway, at this point, Lincoln was now focused on proposing marriage to Mary Todd.

Abe Lincoln Proposes Marriage to Mary Todd.

For the second time, Abe proposed marriage. Mary accepted. It would be a quiet, almost secret wedding. Abe Lincoln and Mary Todd were married on November 4, 1842, in Springfield at the home of Mary's sister, Elizabeth Todd Edwards, and husband, Ninian Edwards. The Edwards were given just a few hours' notice that they were to host a small wedding. Abe's best man was notified about 4 hours before the wedding was to take place. It was, indeed, a very small and discrete ceremony.

Abe was 38 years old and Mary was 23 years old. For 9 months, until the birth of their first baby, the couple would room and board at the Globe Tavern hotel.

Mary Todd's marriage to Abe Lincoln

The Illinois Democratic Party Wins Big in the 1842 Elections. The Whig Party is in Steep Decline

The Illinois Democratic Party had won big on Election Day, August 7, 1842. Democrat Stephen Douglas beat his Whig opponent by the narrowest margin of any of the 7 Illinois races for Federal House seats: by 51.4% versus 48.6%. Five other Democratic Party candidates were victorious. In all, six Democrats won their races for House seats. John Hardin won the only House seat for the Whig Party – the District that included Springfield. Yet, Hardin's margin of victory was comfortable.

Abe and Mary Have a Son, Robert Todd Lincoln.

Six days prior to that Election Day, on August 1, 1842, Mary Todd Lincoln had given birth to a son, Robert Todd Lincoln. The baby was named after Mary's father. Soon after birth of their first baby the Lincoln's moved from a room in the Globe Tavern hotel to a 3-room rental house. In 1844, they would purchase a house with 3 downstairs rooms and, in a half-loft above, two bedrooms and an attic, which could be used as a maid's room. [98]

Robert Todd Lincoln as a boy.

---

[98] *Lincoln*, by David Herbert Donald, pages 94-96; *Stephen A. Douglas*, by Robert W. Johannsen, pages 122-123, and *Bloodstains*, Volume 1, by Howard Ray White, pages 382-383.

Chapter 19: The Lincoln and Herndon Law Partnership is Established

By this time, Abraham Lincoln had served as the junior partner in two Springfield law firms:

In September, 1836, Lincoln was licensed to practice law and, on April 15, 1837, he had arrived in Springfield and joined with John Todd Stuart in a new law partnership. But, during the four years of the Stuart and Lincoln law partnership, John Todd Stuart had spent many months in Washington, serving in the Congress. During those months, working alone in Springfield, Lincoln had made little money.

So, in April, 1841, Lincoln had left the partnership with John Todd Stewart and entered into a new law partnership with Stephen Logan. But, with Logan, during 1841, 1842, 1843 and most of 1844, Lincoln was still making little money.

So we now get to know Billy Herndon.

The Lincoln and Herndon Law Practice is Launched.

Billy Herndon had been studying law at the office of Logan & Lincoln for many months when, finally, on November 27, 1844, he was given a "certificate of good moral character by the Sangamon County Circuit Court" in Springfield. That was the first step. A couple of weeks later, on December 9, 1844, he was admitted to the bar. Now William H. Herndon was licensed to practice law.

Lawyer Abraham Lincoln in 1846.

Abe Lincoln and Billy Herndon had been friends for a long time, particularly during the years when both had slept over the store along with Joshua Speed. And they had worked together at Logan and Lincoln for many months. Well, soon after Billy was admitted to the Bar, Abe Lincoln decided to end the almost four-year-long partnership with Stephen Logan.

So, Lincoln asked Herndon to give up his work clerking at Stephen Logan's law office and partner with him in a new law practice. Lincoln offered Herndon a full partnership in a new firm to be called "Lincoln and Herndon." David Donald, using approximate dialogue, would describe the invitation in his Herndon biography:

"It was about this time that Lincoln, his coattails flapping behind him, came dashing up the office stairs. 'Billy,' he asked breathlessly, 'do you want to enter into partnership with me in the law business?' Herndon was flustered but he managed to stammer: 'Mr. Lincoln this is something unexpected by me – it is an undeserved honor; and yet I say I will gladly and thankfully accept the kind and generous offer.' Lincoln bypassed the speechmaking by remarking easily, 'Billy, I can trust you, if you can trust me,' and, sensing the younger man's almost hysterical gratitude, said nothing more until the partnership papers were drawn up."

Billy Herndon eagerly agreed because he liked Abe Lincoln and recognized it was indeed an honor for such a young man as he to be Lincoln's partner. At this time Lincoln was 39 years old. And Billy was almost 26 years old. Perhaps Lincoln saw a political advantage in teaming up with Billy, an advantage that would help him succeed Edward Baker to the Federal House of Representatives during the next election for Congress. Abe was well connected with the prosperous leaders of the area through his previous law partners and his marriage to Mary Todd. He already had considerable contacts with the everyday workingmen of the region.

William (Billy) Herndon while in partnership with Abraham Lincoln.

But Billy was a leader of the young populist Whigs about town, so teaming up with him strengthened those ties. Billy's father, Archer, a leader in the Democratic Party and a State Senator, believed in the policies handed down by Andrew Jackson and despised opposition politicians, who he referred to as, "Abolition, Federal, silk stocking, ruffle shirt, Whigs." But, in full defiance of his father, Billy was already an ardent and outspoken Abolitionist.

It seems like that political persuasion did not bother Lincoln. He figured it added flexibility in an age where the road to future political success was indecipherable. With Billy in the law practice, Lincoln could, at any future time, embrace Abolitionists. On the other hand, the obscure tie to Archer might someday help some Democrats view Lincoln in a more favorable light. Although Billy's college training was incomplete, he was well educated, an avid reader, and an intellectual of his day. By the way, William H. Herndon would, late in his life, create the most important biography of the then late President Lincoln that would ever be written.

Yes, Lincoln invited Herndon to be his law partner. Lincoln was most generous. He offered to give Herndon a full 50% of all future income earned by the practice.

The division of work agreed to between Abe Lincoln and Billy Herndon would put Lincoln most often traveling the circuit while Billy would most often man the office in Springfield. Lincoln continued his practice of staying on the road on weekends spending time with the local folks in whichever town would be holding court that week. Lincoln would continue to build the personal ties that would be so valuable to his future political career, making contacts that he would ride to inconceivably magnificent political prominence.

Of course, the Lincoln marriage would continue to suffer from too little togetherness, but the marriage would adapt. There would be quarrels, and Mary could unleash quite a temper. Abe could be exasperatingly moody and depressed. But from all appearances, they would remain faithful, and history records no suspicion of any unfaithfulness or extramarital affair. It appears that shared political ambition was the tie that bound Abe and Mary Todd Lincoln. [99]

On March 10, 1846, Abe and Mary were blessed with the birth of a second child, a boy. They named him Edward Baker Lincoln to honor Lincoln's friend.

---

[99] *Lincoln*, by David Herbert Donald, pages 100-109; *Lincoln's Herndon*, by David Herbert Donald, pages 13 and 18-19. *Bloodstains*, Volume 1, by Howard Ray White, page 498.

Chapter 20: Congressman Abraham Lincoln in Washington, 1846-1848

Abe Lincoln campaigned hard in the spring of 1846 to obtain the Whig Party nomination for the Federal House seat for the number 7 District, which included Springfield and Jacksonville. Former Representative John Hardin, a Whig from Jacksonville and a cousin of Elizabeth Todd Edwards, had made a pitch to return to his Federal House seat, but Lincoln had out-maneuvered him and had succeeded in winning the Whig Party nomination.

Democrat Peter Cartwright Criticizes his Opponent's Religious Beliefs

Lincoln's Democratic Party opponent was Peter Cartwright, a well-known Methodist minister. Cartwright was a Democrat who supported the policies espoused by President James K. Polk. However, he was not a shrewd politician and had failed to stir up much interest. In fact, newspapermen gave little coverage to Cartwright or Lincoln during the campaign of the summer and early fall of 1846.

The most notable event in this campaign was Peter Cartwright's success at exposing to public view his critique of Lincoln's religious beliefs. Cartwright, correctly as we students of the biography of Abe Lincoln know, accused Lincoln of pretending to be a Christian.

Lincoln was obviously reluctant to debate the accusation face to face. Instead, he carefully wrote a response and had it printed as a handbill to be passed out among the voters and newspapermen. In his little handbill, dated July 31, 1846, Lincoln summarized his belief in what he termed the "Doctrine of Necessity." In the handbill, detailed in full below, Lincoln freely admitted that he did not belong to any church and he rather "beat around the bush" to imply some feeling for some sort of religion, and he concluded with an obtuse rebuke of his political opponent — obtuse because the name of the Democrat candidate is entirely omitted:

"To the Voters of the Seventh Congressional District.

"A charge having got into circulation in some of the neighborhoods of this District, in substance that I am an open scoffer at Christianity, I have by the advice of some friends concluded to notice the subject in this form. That I am not a member of any Christian Church is true; but I have never denied the truth of the Scriptures; and I have never spoken with intentional disrespect of religion in general, or any denomination of Christians in particular. It is true that in early life I was inclined to believe in what I understand is called the "Doctrine of Necessity" – that is, that the human mind is impelled to action, or held in rest by some power, over which the mind itself has no control; and I have sometimes (with one, two or three people, but never publicly) tried to maintain this opinion in argument. The habit of arguing thus however, I have, entirely left off for more than 5 years. And I add here, I have always understood this same opinion to be held by several of the Christian denominations. The foregoing is the whole truth, briefly stated, in relation to myself, upon this subject.

"I do not think I could myself, be brought to support a man for office, whom I knew to be an open enemy of, and scoffer at, religion. Leaving the higher matter of eternal consequences, between him and his Maker, I still do not think any man has the right thus to insult the feelings, and injure the morals, or the community in which he may live. If, then, I was guilty of such conduct, I should blame no man who should condemn me for it; but I do blame those, whoever they may be, who falsely put such a charge in circulation against me.

A. Lincoln"

By the way, Lincoln's so-called "Doctrine of Necessity" is a free-thinking spiritual notion and not a tenant of any legitimate Christian church. [100]

Abe Lincoln Wins Election to the U. S. House

Lincoln's quiet campaign yielded him excellent results. An unprecedented majority elected him to the 30th Congress on August 3, 1846. He had a lot of time to prepare for his trip to Washington, D. C. The next Federal House was not scheduled to assemble until December 6, 1847, 15 months into the future. [101]

In late October, 1847, Abe and Mary stored their furniture in one upstairs room and rented out the remainder of the house for 12 months. Billy Herndon would carry on the law practice in the senior partner's absence in Washington. On October 25, the Lincoln family departed Springfield for a three week visit with Mary's family in Lexington, Kentucky. This would be Mary's first visit home since her marriage. She had sisters and cousins in Springfield, Illinois, and her father Robert Todd had visited Abe and Mary once in Springfield, but otherwise Mary's family had never met Abe or the children.

We should now reflect on why Abe had chosen this time to take his wife and children to Lexington, in Central Kentucky, the state where, 85 miles from Mary's family home, he had lived as a little boy, the State he had purposely avoided visiting

---

[100] The religious idea that our God the Father, of whom Jesus Christ spoke, sometimes "impelled to action , or held at rest by some power" is not Biblical, especially since Lincoln did not define "some power" as being either the Devil or God our Father.
[101] *Lincoln*, by David Herbert Donald, pages 113-115 and *Bloodstains*, Vol. 1, by Howard Ray White, pages 428-429

for 31 years, the State from which, when obligated to name his father and mother (he always tried to avoid that subject) he feared exposure to stories that his biological father was Abraham Enloe. We now understand why the visit to Mary's home was at this time and not some earlier time following their marriage. Abraham Lincoln was taking Mary and the children to Lexington, Kentucky at this time because he was arriving there as a new member of the United States House of Representatives. Finally, he could present himself to the Todd's in Central Kentucky as a man of accomplishment. He could easily laugh at any unlikely stray story about an Abraham Enloe, if encountered.

Abe, Mary and Children Visit the Todd's in Lexington, Kentucky

This three-week visit in Lexington in the large Todd residence was probably the most important exposure Abe Lincoln would ever have to southern States society and to servants and field workers who were slaves. Few people of African ancestry lived in Illinois. Of course, African American people, slave and free, were plentiful in Kentucky. At the Todd home, Mary relaxed as the servants took responsibility for the Lincoln children, the cooking and washing and ironing clothes.

When Henry Clay addressed a large audience at Lexington on November 13, Lincoln was present and heard this most important founder of the Whig Party argue that the War against Mexico was "unnecessary and offensive aggression." On another day, Mary's father, Robert Todd, took Abe to visit Henry Clay at his home, a time when he was still mourning the death of his son, Henry Clay, Jr., who had been killed in the War against Mexico, at the battle of Buena Vista. And the Lincoln's were guests in several other prominent Lexington homes. During the three-week visit, Abe observed several farms and a cotton mill, all worked primarily by bonded African Americans.

The Lincoln Family in Washington

After saying goodbye to the Todd's, the Lincoln family travelled on to Washington, arriving on December 2nd. Lincoln was the only Whig Representative from Illinois, for the State was heavily Democratic, except for central Illinois. And he well knew that Stephen Douglas was the most prominent Federal politician from his State. Douglas had already been a Congressman for two terms (1843 to March 1847). Now Douglas was one of Illinois' two senators. [102]

---

[102] *The President's Wife, Mary Todd Lincoln*, by Ishbel Ross, pages 65-67 and *Lincoln*, by David Herbert Donald, page 118.

As a freshman Whig Representative, Lincoln expected to have little influence on the Democratic Polk Administration, in spite of the fact that Whigs controlled the House by a slim majority of 115 versus 108 (4 other). The Senate was overwhelmingly in Democratic hands with a lopsided majority of 36 versus 21 (1 other). Lincoln was assigned to the Committee on Post Offices and Post Roads and to the Committee on Expenditures in the War Department. He would be rather attentive to his Committee duties, performing them with proper completeness.

Congressman Abraham Lincoln.

The Lincoln's arranged to live in a boardinghouse operated by Ann Sprigg, where former Representatives from his District, John Stuart and Edward Baker, had previously resided. Eight other Representatives, all of them Whigs, also boarded with Mrs. Sprigg. This produced lively debate among the boarders – debate that was to play a major role in shaping Lincoln's political attitudes and future contacts. The most influential boarder would be Representative Joshua Giddings of Ohio, a leading advocate of complete Abolition of African American bonding (slavery). The war against Mexico was essentially won, but, like many Northeasterners, Lincoln would strongly oppose forcing Mexico to give up her vast land west of Texas, which extended to the Pacific Ocean. Without a doubt his discussions at Mrs. Sprigg's boarding house would be sharpening his political attitudes, because those attitudes would be contrary to the attitudes of his constituents back home.

Tiring of Washington, Mary Leaves to Stay with her Parents in Kentucky

Abe and Mary initially found Washington City an exciting place, with its 30,000 European Americans, 8,000 independent African Americans and 2,000 bonded African Americans. However, the newness wore off by spring, and Mary concluded that the boardinghouse was far too confining – perhaps more than it ought to have been, because Mary Todd Lincoln biographer Ishbel Ross would conclude, "She made no attempt to make friends" as she busied herself alone with the two children. So, in early spring, Mary left Washington with the children and returned to Lexington, Kentucky, to stay with her father. She would remain there for about 5 months. Abe would not see Mary and the children until September, 1847. He wasn't very sad. Mary's absence would permit Abe to enjoy full-time immersion in his true love: politics. [103]

The War with Mexico was by now rather complete. The defeat of the Mexican Army at Buena Vista had completed the conquest of northern Mexico. Mexico City had been conquered by September 15, 1847. By then, Mexican land north of the present-day boundary – called Alto Californio and Nuevo Mexico – was under United States military rule and there was little doubt that this land would be seized by the victors and divided up into new territories and their subsequent States. However, negotiating a final settlement with the Government in Mexico City was not yet accomplished.

President James Polk had dispatched Nicholas Trist to Mexico City months earlier with instructions to negotiate a settlement, but Mexican leaders had refused to deal with Trist. By October, Polk realized that Trist's mission was hopeless, so he had issued orders that Trist return to Washington. This was the situation when Polk was preparing his State of the Union Message for the opening of the House and Senate in early December, 1847.

President Polk used his Annual Message to Congress to recommend a more vigorous prosecution of the War against Mexico to force officials to the negotiating table. He hinted that more Mexican land might be added to the minimum demand of Nuevo Mexico and Alto Californio, but he said he wished not "to make a permanent conquest of the Republic of Mexico, or to annihilate her separate existence as an independent nation." Polk went on to encourage the House and Senate to proceed with organizing into new National Territories the conquered Mexican land called Alto Californio and Nuevo Mexico. Polk suggested that disposition of occupied land to the south would depend on the "future progress of the war, and the course which Mexico may think proper hereafter to pursue." He was warning that Mexico would bleed further – losing even more land – if she refused to sign a treaty ceding the aforesaid land and accepting peace.

For a short while, Mexican officials held to a glimmer of hope that American northeastern States politicians, especially Whig politicians of that region, might improve Mexico's situation as a byproduct of their efforts to politically harm President Polk. After all, 1848 would be a year for electing a Federal President and at this time in American history elections for President could produce amazing shifts in American political attitudes.

During December, 1847 and January and February, 1848, Representatives in the House spent a great deal of time debating issues related to seizing Mexican land

[103] *Lincoln*, by David Herbert Donald, pages 118-121; *The President's Wife, Mary Todd Lincoln*, by Ishbel Ross, pages 65-67 and *Bloodstains,* Vol. 1, by Howard Ray White, pages 448-449.

west of Texas, and possibly south of Texas as well. Representatives opposed to the Polk Administration focused on reviewing the history of the war's justification and its prosecution, and arguing about the proper way to terminate the occupation of Mexico. To a great extent, the aim of their rhetoric was to win 1848 elections for the House, the Senate and for President. Abe Lincoln joined northeastern States Whigs in attacking Polk, that being his first notable speaking effort, and the first time he attacked the southern States on the floor of the House. This attack came in the form of a vicious and inappropriately legalistic diatribe against Democrat President Polk of Tennessee and the Federal military actions that had instigated America's War with Mexico.

Contrary to Abe Lincoln's political instincts, Illinois voters were solidly patriotic in their support of America's War with Mexico, and many Illinoisans had fought in Mexico. So Lincoln faced a major political dilemma: should he build long-range political ties to further his national political ambitions by joining with Massachusetts and neighboring States in denouncing America's War with Mexico, or should he be loyal to his constituents and be soft-spoken and mildly supportive of patriotic Illinoisans? Lincoln's decision appears to represent a major turning point in his political career, for **he chose to build political ties with politicians in the Northeastern States at the expense of his Illinois political supporters**. Perhaps fellow residents at Ann Sprigg's boardinghouse had persuaded Lincoln that the future road to major political office would result from the politics of excluding African Americans from all future National Territories and all future States.

So, Representative Abraham Lincoln attacked President James Polk on the floor of the House with what would become known as his "Spot Resolutions," which he introduced before the House on December 22, 1847, only 16 days after the start of his Congressional term. Attempting to convict the Federal Government for starting the war, Lincoln attacked Polk as if he, Lincoln, were the prosecuting attorney cross-examining Polk as a witness – as if they were before a jury in some criminal courtroom. At issue was the location of the first border skirmish on April 25, 1846, in which several American soldiers had been killed by Mexican troops. Lincoln's resolutions demanded that the President provide to the House "all the facts which go to establish whether the particular *spot* of soil on which the blood of our citizens was so shed, was, or was not, our own soil . . . whether the inhabitants of that *spot* had ever "submitted themselves to the Government or laws of [the Republic of] Texas . . . by voting in elections, or paying taxes, or serving on juries, or . . . in any other way." [104]

---

[104] On December 29, 1845, The Republic of Texas gave up being an independent nation so it could be a state within those United States. For ten years the Republic had been an independent nation as a

Lincoln went on: "Let [Polk] answer, fully, fairly, and candidly. Let him answer with facts, and not with arguments." If the President does not respond, Lincoln argued, such inaction would prove "that he is deeply conscious of being in the wrong – that he feels the blood of this war, like the blood of Abel, is crying to Heaven against him."

Beyond that point, Lincoln's fierce accusations that day entered the realm of nonsense. He accused Polk of having started the war to acquire "military glory – that attractive rainbow that rises in showers of blood – that serpent's eye that charms to destroy." But, Lincoln concluded that, in the absence of glory, "this bewildered, confounded, and miserably perplexed man," could only speak in "the half insane mumbling of a fever-dream." [105]

President James K. Polk of Tennessee

Abe Lincoln seemed quite proud of his oratory before the House that day and reportedly expressed confidence that he was making a name for himself in Washington City. However, nobody in town gave it much attention, and the House never even initiated debate over his "Spot Resolutions." Showing normal good sense, President Polk never publicly acknowledged Lincoln's inflammatory oratory. Lincoln was criticized in Illinois for not revealing during his election campaign that he opposed the War with Mexico. How could Lincoln, Illinoisans argued, show such disrespect to the predecessor in the House seat that he held — Representative John Hardin, who had resigned that seat in the House, joined the Federal Army and been subsequently killed in the battle of Buena Vista? Lincoln's political enemies would remember his demand that President Polk show him the "spot" where blood was first shed. Stephen Douglas would call him "Spotty Lincoln" during the future 1858 "Douglas-Lincoln" debates, and others would occasionally use the issue to question Lincoln's patriotism twelve years later, after he would be elected President in 1860.

---

result of the Texas revolution against rule by Mexico City. Heroes of that effort were Sam Houston and other settlers and leaders from the American South, especially from Tennessee.

[105] *Lincoln*, by David Herbert Donald, pages 122-124; *Stephen A. Douglas*, by Robert W. Johannsen, pages 212-213, and *Bloodstains*, Vol. 1, by Howard Ray White, pages 449-450.

Back in Springfield, Billy Herndon Warns of Political Damage

Meanwhile, back in Springfield, Billy Herndon was sounding public opinion and warning Lincoln that he was not in step with local sentiment regarding the War with Mexico and seizing vast lands west of Texas. Lincoln had been mailing Herndon the *Congressional Globe* ever since arriving in Washington City. Many letters passed back and forth between Herndon and Lincoln. Herndon constantly warned his partner of strong local dissatisfaction with his opposition to President Polk's handling of the War with Mexico. Lincoln countered with legal defenses of his actions.

Abe Ignores Billy's Advice

On January 3, 1848, Massachusetts Representative George Ashmun introduced a resolution before the House that declared that the war with Mexico had been "unnecessarily and unconstitutionally begun by the President of the United States." Of the Whig Representatives, 85 of the 115, including Abe Lincoln, voted for the resolution, and enough Democrats joined in to win adoption by the House. But nothing came of Ashmun's resolution in the Senate, and, in the final analysis, the House and Senate did not hamper the Polk Administration's campaign to bring the war to a conclusion favorable to America's Nation Builders. [106]

James Polk's escalation strategy worked! Contrary to his October, 1847 order that Nicholas Trist return to Washington City, the diplomat had stayed in Mexico hoping for a break. The tough stand in the Federal House and Senate had convinced Mexican leaders that politicians opposed to taking a vast amount of their land did not have the votes to deny America's Nation Builders control over Alto Californio and Nuevo Mexico. Mexican leaders became resigned to the conclusion that it was prudent to give in to United States demands for a peace treaty. The result was the Treaty of Guadalupe Hidalgo. Mexico agreed to accept the Rio Grande boundary up to near the Gila Mountains, thence along the Gila River to the Colorado River, and then westward to San Diego. The United States Government was taking about 500,000 square miles of Mexican land. In compensation for the vast tract of land defined in the Treaty of Guadalupe Hidalgo, the United States Government was agreeing to assume any debt that Mexicans owed to Americans and to pay Mexico $15,000,000. When the treaty was received in Washington City, Polk reviewed it with his Cabinet and decided to recommend its ratification. Accordingly, he presented the Treaty to the Senate in late February. There was considerable debate between Democrat senators who wanted more Mexican land, those wanting all of Mexico, and those who wanted less Mexican land.

---

[106] *Lincoln*, by David Herbert Donald, pages 123-124, *Lincoln's Herndon, a Biography*, by David Herbert Donald, pages 24-29, and *Bloodstains*, Vol. 1, by Howard Ray White, page 450.

The Treaty of Guadalupe Hidalgo was approved by the United States Senate on March 10, 1848, by a vote of 38 for, versus 14 against. Senators opposed to the Treaty included Douglas and Breeze and 5 other Democrat Senators from western States, all of them wanting more land; 7 Whigs who wanted less land. [107]

The same month that President Polk had presented the Treaty of Guadalupe Hidalgo to the Senate for ratification, gold was discovered in Alto Californio! Word of the discovery would soon propel hordes of men seeking their fortune in the new gold fields of occupied Alto Californio. Mining claim disputes, abuse toward Mexicans and Native Americans, murder and gang rule would greatly magnify the normally turbulent and ruthless behavior associated with occupying armies. [108]

Whigs Refuse to Nominate Lincoln for Second Term.

When Springfield-area Whigs convened to nominate their candidate to replace Lincoln in the Federal House, it was apparent that the party would be struggling to win again the seat that Lincoln had won by a large margin two years previously. Yes, by the spring of 1848, Whig political leaders in the district that included Springfield had turned against Congressman Lincoln. They refused to nominate him for a second term. Instead, for the seat that Lincoln had held for two years, they nominated his former law partner, Stephen Logan. Just as Billy Herndon had warned, Lincoln had lost far too much political support over his opposition to the War with Mexico. Abe Lincoln was to become a one-term Federal Representative. The Democratic candidate was Thomas Harris a wounded veteran of the battle of Cerro Gordo. Harris would successfully discredit Logan for endorsing Lincoln's "spot" resolutions and would win much support from patriotic voters in the District. Democrat Harris would win the election. Lincoln had won the district by a 1,511 votes. Harris beat Logan by 106 votes. Whigs would never again win the Federal House seat that Lincoln had held for two years. [109]

Lincoln Stays East and Works on the Whig 1848 Presidential Campaign to Elect General Zachary Taylor of Kentucky.

When Congress adjourned, Abe Lincoln decided to stay East and work to help advance the Whig Party's voter strength during the 1848 elections.

---

[107] *Stephen A. Douglas*, by Robert W. Johannsen, page 215-217, *Jefferson Davis, American Patriot, 1808-1861*, by Hudson Strode, page 197, and *Bloodstains*, Vol. 1, by Howard Ray White, page 451.
[108] Stephen A. Douglas, by Robert W. Johannsen, page 241, and Bloodstains, Vol. 1, by Howard Ray White, page 451.
[109] *Lincoln*, by David Herbert Donald, pages 124-130.

We ask why Abe stayed East? Well, he was not nominated to run for a second Congressional term. In Illinois, as an unpopular one-termer, rumors might surface concerning who was his real father -- perhaps a rumor concerning one Abraham Enloe of North Carolina. That kind of rumor would not be a problem in the East, working on the Whig Party campaign. There, he could make valuable contacts. It would prove to be a good political decision.

Lincoln was convinced that General Zachary Taylor of Kentucky would make a winning candidate for President for the Whig Party. The tie between Henry Clay and Zachary Taylor, both of Kentucky families, would strengthen Taylor's Whig credentials. Lincoln said:

General Zachary Taylor of Kentucky.

> "I am in favor of General Taylor as the Whig candidate for President," he announced, "because I am satisfied we can elect him, that he would give us a Whig Administration, and that we cannot elect any other Whig."

Furthermore, Whig politicians were attracted to a General Taylor candidacy because he had no political record, no government experience and no political agenda. While attending to his duties as a Congressman, Abe spent the spring working in the East on the Whig 1848 campaign. He attended the Whig National Convention in June and then returned to Washington. On July 27, he stood before the House and delivered a speech praising the General, a hero of the War against Mexico. Of course, the Taylor family owned about 200 slaves in Kentucky. That seemed not to bother Representative Lincoln.

After Congress adjourned on August 14, 1848, Lincoln remained East to campaign for the Whig ticket. He helped with the Whig newspaper, the *Battery*, and oversaw the distribution of thousands of campaign documents. By early September, Mary and the children were ready to leave her father in Lexington and join Abe in Washington for a family tour of New England. She and the children watched as Abe delivered speeches in Worcester, Boston, New Bedford, Lowell and other towns. It was a three way race for President: Whig Party candidate Taylor; Democrat Party candidate Cass, and Free Soil Party candidate Van Buren. On the way home to Illinois, the Lincoln family visited Niagara Falls. Whig Representative Abraham

Lincoln had made a significant first impression upon political leaders in New England and Massachusetts. [110]

Furthermore, General Zachary Taylor would win the three-man race for the presidency — the last hurrah for the Whig Party.

Lincoln Returns to Washington for the Second Year of his Congressional Term

Mary and the children did not return to Washington with Abe when he left Springfield to take his seat when the House resumed on December 4, 1847. Mary had chosen to remain at home. Preventing slaves to move into any of the National Territories would be the focus of Northern politicians during the winter of 1847-1848. For the first time, Representative Abe Lincoln sorted the issue in his mind and began taking positions on the subject. He definitely sided with the principle of "Exclusion":

Exclusionism was easy because, in 1853, only five years into the future, Illinois would exclude free people with evidence of African ancestry, down to a slightly black skin, from entering into the State to live. The vast majority of Illinois voters were in step with reserving for White people like themselves every bit of the National Territories, including that taken from Mexico. It seems strange to us today, but Abe reasoned that, if slaves were denied access to new territorial lands, the owning of slaves would eventually become unprofitable and the owners would either set them free to live in States that would permit their presence or send them as freed people to Africa or South America. Northern politicians who adopted that philosophy wanted voters to assume that freed people of African ancestry would never live in Illinois and would probably be shipped out of the country.

The South had considerable power in the Senate, so Exclusionist political advocates sought in debate in the House. The easiest target was forcing the sale of slaves that lived in the District of Columbia to buyers in Maryland or Virginia and all the way west to Texas. Abe Lincoln began contributing to that debate. Lincoln conceived of a bill that would free all D. C. slaves except household servants of Federal Government officials. The bill would obligate the Federal Government to pay each D. C. slave owner who freed a slave the "full cash value" price of each slave freed. After 1850, babies born to slave mothers would be born free. If passed by Federal legislation, this whole project would be submitted to the White male voters of the District of Columbia to approve or reject. If approved, the project would

---

[110] *Lincoln*, by David Herbert Donald, pages 123-132.

encourage the immediate sale to new Southern owners all child-bearing female slaves, for 1850 was soon to arrive.

At first Lincoln felt he had acquired considerable support for his District of Columbia slavery referendum project. But, once revealed, opposition escalated. Lincoln never submitted the bill he envisioned to the House floor. Instead of positive recognition, Lincoln was branded, "that slave hound from Illinois."

On March 4, 1849, Zachary Taylor took the oath of office and began his term as President. The 30th Congress had adjourned. So Lincoln, his term expired, headed home. [111]

Closing Comments Regarding Congressman Abraham Lincoln's Experiences in Washington City

Before closing this chapter concerning Lincoln's two-year term in Washington, we ought to reflect on and contrast his political attitudes concerning, first, the United States military's conquest of land held by the sovereign nation of Mexico and, second, his future political attitudes concerning the United States military's conquest of land held by the sovereign nation of the Confederate States of America. Don't be swayed by President Lincoln's unsubstantiated claim in 1861 that the states of the Confederacy were in rebellion — those Southerners had legally seceded and just wanted to go their own way — they did not aim to interfere with the politics of the North — and Lincoln refused to allow the Supreme Court to hear arguments concerning the legality of State Secession.

The common aspect of both events is a war of conquest. Lincoln opposed the first war -- the conquest of upper Mexico. Lincoln would instigate and oversee the second war – the conquest of 11 Seceded States. In 1861, President Lincoln would refuse to negotiate. Sadly, one million people would suffer death as a result of President Lincoln's war to conquer those legally seceded States.

---

[111] *Lincoln*, by David Herbert Donald, pages 135-138.

Chapter 21: Lincoln's Politically Down Years, the Illinois Black Code and the Politics of Bleeding Kansas

The Illinois Black Code of 1853

The Illinois Black Code of 1853 prohibited every person of noticeable African ancestry (down to one-eight) coming from outside Illinois and entering the State to stay for more than ten days. Any person who appeared to be Black or very slightly of that skin appearance, who remained in Illinois beyond the ten-day legal limit, was subject to arrest, detention, a $50 fine, or deportation to, most likely, Kentucky. [112]

The 1853 Illinois Black Code would remain on the statute books until repealed in early 1865, just prior to the surrender of Robert E. Lee's Confederate Army.

This racial exclusion law was, perhaps, the beginning of the political movement in Illinois to also deny Blacks from living in Kansas Territory and all future National Territories and States. During the 1858 debates with Illinois Senator Stephen Douglas, Abraham Lincoln would refer to the year 1853 when arguing his "A house divided against itself cannot stand" fear tactic:

> "If we could first know where we are, and whither we are tending, we could then better judge what to do, and how to do it.

> "We are now far into the **fifth year**, since a policy was initiated, with the avowed object, and confident promise, of putting an end to [agitation over what to do about bonded African Americans]."

You see, 1858 was "the fifth year."

The Nation Builders — An Amazing 241-Year Era in America's History Comes to a Close

We are coming to the conclusion of the era of America's Nation Builders — an era exceeding two centuries, ten generations of pioneering families — an epic period of 241 years, beginning with the founding of the English settlement at Jamestown, Virginia Colony in 1607, and concluding with the approval of the Treaty of Guadalupe Hidalgo, which gained to America all of the former Mexican land west of Texas. Except for later acquiring a relatively small arid strip south of the Gila River, America had been built from Canada to Mexico and from "sea to shining sea." She would add Alaska and Hawaii later, but they would be detached appendages. At this point in our history, the work of the *Nation Builders* was essentially complete – the

---

[112] "History of Slavery in Illinois," wikipedia.org and other sources.

work of John Smith, George Washington, Thomas Jefferson, Daniel Boone, Andrew Jackson, Sam Houston, James Polk, Jefferson Davis, and countless other courageous men.

But, more important than these men and other notable leaders, America had been built by courageous women – pioneering women who braved a new world to make a new life for their families and their future descendants. Women like those Englishwomen who braved conditions in early Jamestown and pioneering Scots like Elizabeth Jackson and Elizabeth Houston who ventured west across Tennessee and beyond.

Not so the French or the Spanish! Having brought with them far too few such pioneering women, Frenchmen were doomed to lose to the Nation Builders the land in North America that they had originally conquered. Although Spanish men had arrived in the Americas long before English men and Scottish men, they had brought far too few Spanish women. So Spanish men took Native wives and thereby also lost their best land to the Nation Builders.

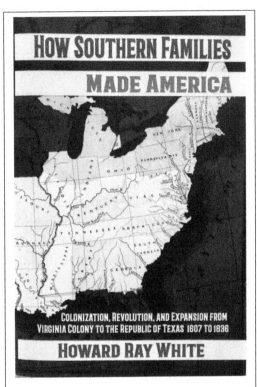

How Southern Families Made America, by Howard Ray White. Available on Amazon.

The Demagogues

We are now leaving the era of the Nation Builders and entering the era of the Political Demagogues. Going forward we will witness Political Demagogues sweeping up a gullible population – many of them rather recent immigrants – and securing their political support by demanding that bonded African Americans (slaves) be excluded from all National Territories. Exclusionist political activists would imply that they aimed to exclude both bonded African Americans and independent African Americans. All descendants of West Africans were to be excluded. Hints of deportation would calm fears that African Americans then living in the Southern States might ever become neighbors of people living in the Northern States.

And these same Exclusionist politicians were promising to drive the remaining western plains Native Americans (Indians) to extinction, or nearly to extinction.

135

We are now at the year 1850, a decisive year in American history. The 1850 census will empower the Northern States to theoretically win national elections without even one vote from the Southern States. This is so important I need to repeat it:

> "The 1850 census will empower the Northern States to theoretically win national elections without even one vote from the Southern States."

And that election math will intensify the political demagoguery and encourage the rise of the Northern States Republican Party – organized to dominate all Northern States, and also seize control of the Federal Government, without any Southern States votes.

And you will see Stephen Douglas fighting the Exclusionists from his powerful political position as Chairman of the Senate Committee on Territories and as the District of Columbia's leading Democrat from the Northern States. You will see him champion the Kansas-Nebraska Act, which he wrote, and learn how the resulting conflict among Kansas Territory settlers — those from the South versus those from the North — fueled the political demagoguery that gave birth to the Northern States Republican Party. You will live through Bleeding Kansas and the terrorism of John Brown and the like.

You will see Abraham Lincoln and Billy Herndon being swept up into the Exclusionist Movement, and you will see Lincoln rise to prominence as a Republican Party leader in Illinois, although he would not be holding any elected office at the time. But eventually you will see Stephen Douglas' personal ambition to become President force him to succumb to the overwhelming political power of the Republican Party's Exclusionist message, eventually transforming this powerful Democrat into an Exclusionist, too. And that transformation will work to destroy the national nature of the Democratic Party and assure the 1860 Republican Party triumph.

The Political Demagogues will be destroying the Federation of American States that the Nation Builders had built – a Federation built on the marvelous principle of State Rights – a Federation in which the sovereignty of each State was only limited by a carefully restricted Federal Government – a Federation of peoples who felt proud to be Pennsylvanians, Massachusettsans, Illinoisans, Mississippians, Tennesseans, Virginians, Texans, . . . et cetera . . . and spoke proudly of *these* United States! [113]

---

[113] *Bloodstains,* Volume 1, *The Nation Builders,* by Howard Ray White, 453.

The Kansas-Nebraska Act of 1854

Early Monday morning, January 23, 1854, Senator Stephen Douglas called his Senate Territories Committee together for a quick meeting prior to the opening of the day's Senate session. He showed the Committee his modified Nebraska Territory Bill. Committee Members realized that Douglas had changed the Bill drastically without consulting them, but there was insufficient time for them to read it, much less, discuss it among themselves. Committeeman Edward Everett of Massachusetts was able to give it only a hasty examination. Committeeman John Bell of Tennessee complained that he barely had time to glance over it, and told Douglas he thought he would agree with the language on striking down the 36-degrees-30-minutes boundary — slaves were to be allowed to live south of it and not north of it. But Bell warned that he reserved the right to express opposition on the Senate floor if revelations pressed him in that direction. Committeeman Robert Johnson of Arkansas was not able to make the early meeting and was forced to query Douglas on the floor about the make-up of the bill. Although Douglas was acting like the dictator of the Senate Territories Committee, which he chaired, he alleged before the Senate at large that the Bill was the Committee's recommendation. [114]

The major changes that Douglas had made to the Bill astounded the politicians who were closely following the measure. The Bill was totally unlike the Nebraska Territory Bill that had been debated for a while. The replacement Bill proposed, not a huge region to be named Nebraska Territory, but two smaller regions. The northern region was to be named Nebraska Territory and the southern region was to be named Kansas Territory. The full eastern boundary of Kansas Territory was joined with Missouri. Douglas had moved the southern boundary of Kansas Territory northward — from 36-degrees-30-minutes to 37 degrees — apparently because the strip lying south of 37 degrees was part of the land that belonged to the Cherokee Nation, and Douglas did not want Kansas Territory to include Native Americans from Southeastern North America, some of whom owned bonded African Americans. The new Bill retained language permitting either Territory Legislature

Senator Stephen Douglas of Illinois.

---

[114] *Stephen A. Douglas*, by Robert W. Johannsen, pages 415-416

(Kansas and/or Nebraska) to vote up or down to include or exclude bonded African Americans, sometime prior to application for their statehoods, but did not stipulate a population count that would qualify either to do so.

During a Sunday meeting with President Franklin Pierce, Douglas had added the language, which dealt with officially striking down the 36-degrees-30-minutes boundary agreement that Congress had established in 1820. The new bill said: "The [Federal] Constitution, and all [Federal laws] which are not locally inapplicable, shall have the same force and effect within the said Territory as elsewhere in the [Federation]."

But Douglas had tacked on an exception of his own wording: "except the eighth section of the Act preparatory to the admission of Missouri into the [Federation], approved March 6, 1820, which was superseded by the principles of the legislation of 1850 [concerning National Territories and African American bonding], and is declared inoperative."

Basically this heap of legalese declared that bonded African Americans would no longer be excluded from National Territories north of 36 degrees and 30 minutes by any Federal law. Instead, the issue would be decided by a vote of settlers, first during the National Territory stage and then upon application for statehood.

This legislation would enable an Exclusion and Abolition campaign for political control of Kansas Territory, which would quickly escalate into Terrorism and launch the politics that would produce the rise of the Northern States Republican Party, State Secession and the Federal Invasion of the Confederacy. [115]

Although Stephen Douglas' Committee had not previously acted to subdivide Nebraska Territory, there had been some discussion in and out of the Committee about splitting the region into 2 or 3 Territories. William Sebastian of Arkansas, Chairman of the Senate Committee on Indian Affairs, had recommended keeping the Cherokee Nation wholly out of the new Territory. There had been rumors of organizing present-day Oklahoma into Cherokee Territory, but several important politicians wished to not disturb the Cherokees and the four other Native American Nations from the Southeast, which had moved into that region, Indian Territory, in compliance with the 1830 Indian Removal Act.

Sentiment for breaking Nebraska into two Territories had come from several quarters. An unofficial delegation, which had been sent by early settlers in the proposed Territory, advocated two Territories. Both of Iowa's Senators favored two Territories. Missourians in the House and Senate may have encouraged the idea of two Territories, for Douglas claimed such support when he introduced his revised

---

[115] *Stephen A. Douglas*, by Robert W. Johannsen, page 415

Bill. Biographer Robert Johannsen would think it likely that Douglas "regarded two Territories as essential to the promotion of both a central and a northern Pacific railroad route."

Meanwhile Senator Salmon Chase of Ohio was leading an Exclusion and Abolition propaganda crusade to demagogue the Kansas-Nebraska Bill, to discredit mainstream Democrats and to ferment sectional hatred. He and several other Abolitionist political leaders were working on an editorial masterpiece titled, "The Appeal of the Independent Democrats in Congress to the People of the United States":

Senator Salmon Chase of Ohio.

In their "Appeal" Chase and the other writers demonized the Kansas-Nebraska Bill "as a gross violation of a sacred pledge; as a criminal betrayal of precious rights; as part and parcel of an atrocious plot to exclude from a vast unoccupied region immigrants from the Old World, and free laborers from our own States, and convert it into a dreary region of despotism, inhabited by [people from the Southern States and bonded African Americans]. . . . The blight of [African American bonding] will cover the land." The "Appeal" predicted the whole Federation would be subjugated "to the yoke of [politicians who owned bonded African Americans]." Then it asked: "Shall a plot against humanity and democracy so monstrous, and so dangerous to the interests of liberty throughout the world, be permitted to succeed?"

The polished text of the "Appeal" was completed, printed and circulated among friendly newspapers, first published on the afternoon of January 24, 1854 in Washington's exclusionist and abolitionist newspaper, the *National Era*.

Heated Senate Debate Over the Kansas-Nebraska Bill.

Debate on the Kansas-Nebraska Bill began a week later on January 30, 1854. The Senate was crowded to capacity: the galleries were packed and standing room behind the Senator's seats was overflowing. Stephen Douglas launched the debate with a furious attack on the "Appeal."

During his speech before the Senate, Douglas reminded Senators that he had successfully inserted into the 1845 joint resolution accepting Texas statehood the

36-degrees-30-minutes latitude boundary, which prohibited slavery on the North side. He had advocated extending that boundary to the Pacific in 1848 when California, Utah and New Mexico were before the Senate, but Northern States Senators had defeated the extension proposal because the North want to exclude bonded African Americans in Southern California. Douglas told Senators that the 1848 vote was the first time the principles of the boundary were ever abandoned. He then reminded the Senate that the 1848 boundary defeat was followed by the House and Senate embracing a new principle for choosing to include or exclude slavery — "a great principle of self-government, which would allow the people to do as they thought proper."

In fact, the Kansas-Nebraska uproar was almost entirely a Northern States affair. People in the Southern States were mostly puzzled about the thing, but they clearly realized it threatened State Rights as guaranteed by the Federal Constitution.

Debate on the Kansas-Nebraska Bill occupied most of the Senate calendar throughout February. Senator Stephen Douglas led those who favored the measure. Ohio Senator Salmon Chase led the effort to kill the bill. Douglas strove to maintain ambiguity over the precise meaning of the "popular sovereignty" program, which was his name for allowing settlers in a National Territory to vote to include or exclude bonded African Americans. But when could the exclusion-versus-inclusion vote be taken? Southern States Senators were encouraged to believe that settlers could not vote to include or exclude bonded African Americans in their future State Constitution until their National Territory gained sufficient population to apply for statehood. Northern States Senators were encouraged to believe a binding vote on that aspect of the future State Constitution could be authorized in the early stages of settlement. Douglas kept the bill's language purposely vague in hopes his coalition of mainline Northern States Democrats and Southern States Democrats would not falter.

The Senate Votes to Approve the Kansas-Nebraska Bill

To circumvent attacks by Chase, Douglas submitted two Amendments to the bill that were accepted. The result was a major shift in Federal policy toward a very powerful, almost independent, Territory Government — it prevented the appointed Territorial Governor from vetoing **unwise and reckless legislation passed by the Kansas Territory Legislature.** The Kansas-Nebraska Bill permitted a Territory Legislature to pass anything it wished with a two-thirds vote. The foolishness of granting such awesome power to a green and divergent legislative body, in a new Territory stirred with the passions of land disputes and politically-charged sectional conflicts, would soon become terribly apparent. This move to grant unprecedented powers to the Kansas Territory Legislature was a significant step toward engulfing Americans in the sectional hatred that would result in the rise of the Northern States Republican Party, State Secession and President Lincoln's war to conquer the Seceded States.

Seeking to impart some reasoning to the newly empowered voting population of the future Territories, Senator John Clayton won acceptance of an Amendment that required that Territory voters be United States citizens. The vote, 23 for versus 21 against, was a pure sectional vote with Senators from States where bonded African Americans lived representing the slim majority.

On March 3, Senator John Bell of Tennessee opened the day with a long speech in opposition to passage. Many other speeches followed. Finally, at 11:30 that night Douglas began his 3-hour closing speech. Douglas championed his "great principle" of "popular sovereignty." Then he expressed hope that self-government of the Territories would "destroy all sectional parties and sectional agitations."

Finally, Independent Senator Sam Houston closed debate with a more brief and final plea to resurrect the 36-degrees-30-minutes boundary agreement, which had been established in 1820 as part of the Missouri Compromise. With a wisdom that exceeded that of any other Senator, he cried out for a surrender of Kansas Territory to the Exclusionists:

> "If this [Bill becomes law] I will have seen the commencement of the agitation, but the youngest child now born, will not live to witness its termination. . . . I ask again, what benefit is to result to the [people of the southern States] from this measure? . . . Will it secure [either of] these Territories to [them]? No, sir, not at all." Instead it will supply "those in the [Northern States] who are enemies of the [Southern States] with efficient weapons."

As a teenager, Sam Houston had lived with Cherokees in East Tennessee on an island in the Tennessee River. Cherokees there called him a friend and named him "The Raven." So Houston argued again for protection of the rights of Native Americans, "a race of people whom I am not ashamed to say have called me brother." But Houston admitted he had "little hope that any appeal I can make for [them] will do any good."

As he approached his close, The Raven pointed to the eagle on the wall of the chamber, which was draped in black cloth to honor two deceased Senators, Henry Clay and Daniel Webster, and he asked, is that "a fearful omen of future calamities which await our [Federation] in event this Bill should become law? . . . I adjure you, harmonize and preserve this [Federation of States]. . . . Stir not up agitation! Give us peace!"

At 4:55 am, on March 4, after an exhausting 17-hour closing debate, the Senate voted and passed Stephen Douglas' Kansas-Nebraska Bill. The vote was an overwhelming 37 for and 14 against. [116]

The House Debates the Kansas-Nebraska Bill while Senator Douglas Coaches

The Kansas-Nebraska Bill then moved to the House for consideration there, but debate in the Senate continued.

During Senate debate on the Kansas-Nebraska Bill, Exclusion and Abolition Activists had succeeded in building a firestorm of agitation among the people living in Massachusetts and neighboring States, and westward along the Great Lakes. And Massachusetts ministers had joined together in a massive drive to collect protest signatures. Many people in Massachusetts supported the Exclusionist campaign, including Harriet Beecher Stowe, who had helped by donating some of the lucrative royalties from her novel, *Uncle Tom's Cabin*. The resulting Petition denounced Douglas' Kansas-Nebraska Bill, "in the name of Almighty God, and in His presence," damning the Bill as "a great moral wrong, . . . a breach of faith," and "a measure full of danger to the [Federation]." Sponsors selected Senator Edward Everett to present the Petition to the Senate.

On March 14, Edward Everett presented the Massachusetts Petition protesting "in the name of Almighty God" the Senate's approval of the Kansas-Nebraska Bill. The petition was 250 feet long. It bore the signatures of 3,000 ministers from Massachusetts and neighboring States. Many were Christian ministers, but many were Unitarians or Transcendentalists.

The immense petition revealed that these ministers were clearly distraught over the Kansas-Nebraska Bill. It even appeared that political activists had scared some of them into believing that passage of the Bill would likely cause thousands of families from the Southern States to migrate into the Northern States with their bonded African Americans and eventually also force poor European Americans into bondage. Of course, Southern States people had never seriously contemplated such a movement. Yet, political agitators alleged that the Kansas-Nebraska Bill just might be the start of such an offensive South-to-North migration. It is hard to believe that something so far-fetched could scare intelligent people, but it did scare some.

---

[116] *Stephen A. Douglas,* by Robert W. Johannsen, pages 410-432; *Charles Sumner and the Coming of the Civil War*, by David Herbert Donald, pages 252-254 and 259-260; *The Ravin, A Biography of Sam Houston*, by Marquis James, page 384.

In the Federal House, on March 21, 1854, William Richardson of Illinois moved to refer the Senate's Kansas-Nebraska Bill to the House Committee on Territories, of which he chaired. That was logical, but an opponent of passage, Francis Cutting of New York, succeeded by a 110 to 95 vote to direct the measure instead to a Committee of the Whole – a move that purposely buried the measure 50 bills deep in the House calendar. Proponents of the Bill would have to maneuver mightily to work the measure up through the legislative logjam. For the next 6 weeks Senator Stephen Douglas, President Franklin Pierce and his Cabinet would put intense pressure on Representatives to help advance the bill up the House calendar.

The House Votes to Pass the Kansas-Nebraska Bill

Finally, on May 8, 1854, Chairman William Richardson, acting in the House Committee of the Whole, succeeded in laying aside 18 bills to surface an earlier House version of a Kansas-Nebraska bill that had preceded the version that had been passed by the Federal Senate. He immediately proposed substituting the new Senate Bill (without Senator John Clayton's Amendment requiring Territory voters to be United States citizens) for the obsolete House bill. Apparently, Richardson, who represented Stephen Douglas' old northwest Illinois House District, favored letting every man in Kansas Territory and Nebraska Territory vote if he was simply old enough. Northern States politicians favored letting recent immigrants (non-citizens) vote to increase the likelihood that the Territory Legislatures and Constitutional Conventions would exclude bonded African Americans. Richardson's move to open debate on the Bill unleashed intense opposition from Exclusion and Abolition politicians — particularly politicians active in building the budding Northern States Republican Party. For the next 3 weeks, debate raged in the House as it had in the Senate during February and early March. More than once physical violence was threatened.

Many Northern States Democrats were so worked up over the Bill that they became known as "Anti-Nebraska" Democrats.

Stephen Douglas spent much time away from the Senate lobbying at the House. He was constantly at Chairman William Richardson's side, working to garner votes and control debate. When the House appeared to deteriorate into hopeless confusion, Representative Alexander Stephens of Georgia directed a series of shrewd parliamentary moves that steered the measure to a vote. On May 22, 1854, the supporters of Douglas' Bill succeeded in substituting the Senate bill for the outdated House bill, which had earlier been the vehicle for circumventing the calendar logjam. Supporters then succeeded in striking out Senator Clayton's Amendment, which had required Territory voters to be United States citizens. The final vote was taken. The Kansas-Nebraska Bill passed the House. The vote was very close, 113 for, versus 100 against. [117]

The Kansas-Nebraska Act Becomes Law

The Kansas-Nebraska Bill, as passed by the House, was quickly taken to the Senate to negotiate an adjustment for the difference in voter citizenship requirement. The Senate quickly approved a motion to delete Senator Clayton's Amendment, which required Kansas and Nebraska voters to be United States citizens. Finally, after mid-night on May 25, the Senate voted on the Kansas-Nebraska Bill in the form that matched the House Bill. The updated Bill passed. Proponents celebrated again. Only President Franklin Pierce's signature was required to make it law.

On May 29, 1854, Franklin Pierce signed the measure, making it Federal law.

President Franklin Pierce, Democrat of New Hampshire.

James Gadsden's Treaty to Purchase Mexican Land

While the Senate had struggled with sectional debate over Stephen Douglas' Kansas-Nebraska Act, President Franklin Pierce submitted to that body James Gadsden's Treaty to purchase a narrow strip of Mexican land that would make a transcontinental railroad out to California exceptionally inexpensive and quick to construct. Over the previous 6 months, James Gadsden had successfully negotiated with Mexican leaders his Treaty to purchase 45,535 square miles of Mexican land bordering on the southwest boundary of the United States. During the early days of President James Pierce's Administration, Jefferson Davis, Secretary of Defense, had recommended that James Gadsden of Charleston, South Carolina be America's Minister to Mexico and both men were delighted when, on December 30, 1853, Gadsden's Purchase Treaty was signed by Mexican leaders. The Treaty specified that 45,535 square miles of Mexican land would be sold to the United States for $15,000,000 — only 51 cents per acre. Yes, this land would allow Americans to build a fairly level railroad that bypassed the Rocky Mountains and the Sierra Nevada Mountains, enabling the building of a transcontinental railroad to California

---

[117] *Stephen A. Douglas*, by Robert W. Johannsen, pages 443-446; *Charles Sumner and the Coming of the Civil War*, by David Herbert Donald, pages 259-260.

in two or three years. President Pierce had proudly submitted the Treaty to the Senate on February 10, 1854.

Taking brief time-outs from the Kansas-Nebraska debate, the Senate had worked at resolving issues connected with purchasing the 45,535 square miles of Mexican land. Unfortunately, the Senate had first voted to reduce the purchase to 30,000 square miles for $10,000,000. Mexico agreed to the smaller land sale. At the end of June, 1854 the Senate ratified the Treaty and possession of the land changed hands. A fast-track railroad route to the Pacific was now available to Americans.

But this would be the beginning of a sad story in American history:

Politics would trump common sense and logical engineering. The first transcontinental railroad, via a central United States route would finally be completed on May 10, 1869, a long 15 years after the Gadsden Treaty approval, 12 years after the southern route would have been completed if the North had cooperated. The southern transcontinental railroad would not be completed until 1881, 27 years after the land for it had been purchased from Mexico. This nonsense was the North's way of punishing the South. Oh, yes, by the way, revenue coming into the Federal Government in those years was based on tariffs on imports, 80 percent of it collected at southern seaports. The South wanted to pay for the Southern Transcontinental Railroad. The North refused to allow it. [118]

---

[118] *Jefferson Davis, American Patriot, 1808-1861*, by Hudson Strode, pages 262-263.

Chapter 22: Bleeding Kansas and the Rise of the Northern States Republican Party

As Senator Sam Houston had Predicted, The Enacted Kansas-Nebraska Act Intensifies Northern Hatred of Southern People

Abraham Lincoln was drawn back into political activism by the uproar that Illinois Exclusionist and Abolitionist agitators had created over Stephen Douglas' Kansas-Nebraska Act. And his law partner, Billy Herndon, was even more intensely motivated. Although Billy's political energy erupted into a firestorm of activism of amazing intensity and diversity, Lincoln refrained from immediately jumping into the political fray.

During the first 7 months of 1854, Lincoln only read newspaper accounts and listened to debate around his Circuit Court District. But Billy Herndon was an ardent Abolitionist and kept in touch through many newspapers, which were being delivered to the law office, and through the correspondence he maintained with like-minded Abolitionists. In his biography of Lincoln, Herndon would write:

> "I was in correspondence with Sumner, Greeley, Phillips, and Garrison, and was thus thoroughly imbued with all the rancor drawn from such strong [Abolitionist] sources. . . . Every time a good speech on the great issue was made I sent for it. Hence you could find on my table the latest utterances of Giddings, Phillips, Sumner, Seward, and one whom I considered grander than all the others – Theodore Parker. Lincoln and I took such papers as the Chicago *Tribune*, New York *Tribune*, the *Anti-Slavery Standard*, the *Emancipator,* and the *National Era*. On the other side of the question we took the Charleston *Mercury* and the Richmond *Enquirer*. . . . I purchased all the leading histories of the [Abolitionist] Movement, and other works which treated on the subject." [119]

Lincoln usually read the newspaper articles that Billy recommended, thereby gaining a firm understanding of the anti-Nebraska anger.

Northern States Republican Parties begin to Rise in the Northern States.

On July 6, 1854, Exclusionist politicians held a mass meeting at Jackson, Michigan, to form a new political party, which would be based on the sole issue of exclusion of bonded African Americans from the National Territories. The men at

---

[119] Herndon's *Life of Lincoln*, by William Herndon, page 293; and *Lincoln*, by David Herbert Donald, page 167.

this meeting named their new political organization the "Republican Party." This was the first meeting in any State that was designed to create a State Republican Party. The movement would replicate across the northern States to become the Northern States Republican Party. [120]

During the same month a convention was held to organize a Massachusetts Republican Party, which included all members of the former Massachusetts Free Soil Party, many former members of the Massachusetts Whig Party and many Massachusetts Democrats who wanted to embrace Exclusionism. Furthermore, many political leaders in other northern States were holding similar statewide organizational efforts.

So, during the summer of 1854, Republican Parties were born in several of the Northern States. The Northern States Republican Parties had one plank in their platforms – Exclusionism. Most importantly, Republican Party organizers insisted that their Party only be organized in the Northern States, because a Southern States Republican Party would taint the Republican crusade. Of course almost all members were simply Exclusionists and Deportationists who insisted that independent African Americans not be allowed to migrate into their respective States (they did not want Blacks as neighbors). Republican propaganda would be directed against voters in the Southern States because the Northern States Republican Party needed an enemy around which to build support, and that enemy was to be the people of the Southern States. Its goal was to gain total control of the Federal Government without any Southern States votes. They recognized that, since the 1850 census, the Northern States could hold majorities in the Federal House and in the Electoral College. So they knew that it was possible to win control of the Federal House and the President's office without even one vote from the Southern States.

Exclusionists Political Activists Begin a Kansas Territory Settlement Crusade.

Kansas Territory was a vast land that spread westward from the Missouri State border. It was 200 miles, south-to-north, and nearly 700 miles, east to west. About three fourths of the eastern boundary was a straight line that ran southward from the confluence of the Missouri River and the Kansas River, allowing people of Missouri to simply walk cross the boundary into Kansas Territory. The remaining eastern border was the Missouri River, so a boat ride was necessary to enter from there. The northern border was 40 degrees latitude. People who had first migrated

---

[120] I will call this political party the "Northern States Republican Party" because it was only significant in the Northern States and that limited geographical extent was the intent of Party leaders. Within each Northern State, the party's official name was the "Republican Party." Collectively, I will be calling it the "Northern States Republican Party."

into Nebraska Territory could simply turn southward and walk across the southern Nebraska border into Kansas Territory. The southern border, which was at 37 degrees latitude, corresponded to the northern boundary of present-day Oklahoma, then designated as land given permanently to the Cherokee Nation, the homeland of Cherokees who had agreed to migrate west, cross the Mississippi and live in that Indian Territory which had been given to them forevermore. The western border

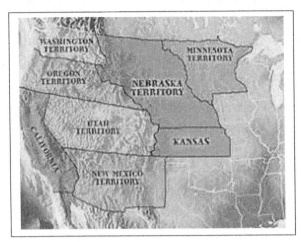

was the eastern crest of the Rocky Mountains, way out in present day Colorado. Less than 800 European Americans lived in Kansas Territory when it became an official Territory in May 1854. At that time, most of the land in Kansas Territory belonged to Native American nations.

Yes, Kansas Territory was home to several Native American nations. Eastern Kansas Territory contained land belonging to (from north to south) Ioways, Kickapoos, Pottawattamies, Delawares, Shawnees, Piankshaws, Sacs and Foxes, Kansas, Miamies, Cherokees, and Osages. The western dry plains belonged to Arapahoes, Cheyennes, Kioways and Comanches, tribes engaged in a more nomadic way of life, following buffalo herds for their food source.

Alice Nichols, in her must-read history, *Bleeding Kansas*, would write:

"It was announced, with no mention of method, that these [Native American nations] had ceded such and such lands. Millions of deep-loamed acres were thrown open for settlement. The land was there for the claiming. Shake together a cabin or pitch a tent, break half an acre of sod and fence it, file a notice of intention to preempt your chosen 160 acres at the nearest sutler's office. The price, $1.25 per acre, but you will have months or years of free use of the land to help you raise the money, since the land cannot be sold until government surveys are completed. Then, for $200, that quarter-section piece of God's earth will be assigned to you and your heirs forever." [121]

Settlement of Kansas Territory picked up substantially in the summer of 1854. By summer's end settlers, mostly from Missouri, had established 3 towns along the west bank of the Missouri River, named Leavenworth, Kickapoo and Atchison. However, with no Southern, organized migration campaign, that first summer

---

[121] *Bleeding Kansas*, by Alice Nichols, pages 19-22.

produced only modest settlement from the Southern culture prior to enactment of the Kansas-Nebraska Act.

The Massachusetts Emigrant Aid Company.

During the summer of 1854, after the Kansas-Nebraska Act was signed, an organized effort to fund settlement from Massachusetts was launched when a Massachusetts Representative from Worcester, Eli Thayer, convinced the State Legislature to grant him a Charter to establish the "Massachusetts Emigrant Aid Company." Thayer's Charter permitted him to raise up to $5,000,000 to finance the venture. He reasoned that Massachusetts settlers would need organized political, financial and military support to win Kansas Territory for the Exclusionist cause. He also hoped to make a lot of money on Kansas land and on whatever other opportunities arose. Thayer told potential investors the money would be spent to build temporary housing for settlers just arriving in Kansas, to construct grist mills and steam-driven saw mills, and to establish newspapers. The company would purchase 640 acres of land around the locations selected for these facilities and sell off lots as each section grew into a town. When Kansas became a State, the company would sell off its assets and pay a dividend to stockholders. Thayer printed his prospectus and started selling stock. On July 17, 1854, a group of 29 men, aiming to be Kansas settlers, was sent off from Boston with much the same fanfare with which heroes are sent off to war.

When the group of 29 Massachusetts men arrived at St. Louis, this first band of Emigrant Aid Company settlers was directed to the Kansas site where Charles Robinson wanted to build the first Emigrant Aid town, located on the Kansas River, about 40 miles upriver from its juncture with the Missouri River. The town was named Lawrence in honor of Amos Lawrence, the treasurer of the Emigrant Aid Society. [122]

The Federal House and Senate adjourned on August 7, 1854. Two weeks later Stephen Douglas arrived in combative Chicago. Abolition and Exclusion Agitators had been busy all summer inciting political discord among Democrats and wooing Whigs and Exclusionist Democrats toward a new Northern States party. Ohioans Salmon Chase and Joshua Giddings, and Kentuckian Cassius Clay, had been stumping the State denouncing the Kansas-Nebraska Act. Illinois Exclusionists, such as Ichabod Codding of Chicago, were spreading fear of a mass movement of African Americans into the Northern States and the National Territories, and they were also promoting a new perceived Illinois Republican Party. Northern Illinois was especially fearful of the alleged Southern threat.

---

[122] *Bleeding Kansas*, by Alice Nichols, pages 13-16.

An Illinois State Convention of all opponents to the Kansas-Nebraska Act was announced. Many opponents feared people of full or partial African ancestry becoming their neighbors in Illinois, where those opponents presently resided, or in Kansas to which they or their children might relocate at some future time. Other Illinois political activists were opposed to recent immigrants from Europe moving into Illinois and Catholic influence in their schools and government. Others were promoting statewide prohibition of beer, wine and liquor. Also, Lieutenant Governor Gustave Koerner, himself a German immigrant, was leading a protest against the Kansas-Nebraska Act. It appeared that all political organizations in Illinois were arrayed against Senator Douglas and his Kansas-Nebraska Act. Opposition to Douglas was extreme in Chicago and far-north Illinois. Douglas resolved to win the election for the Democratic Party by campaigning elsewhere in the State

Against this massive array of political opposition, Stephen Douglas fought back with his newspaper, the Chicago *Times*, and with his political influence. He felt forced to demand that support of the Kansas-Nebraska Act be a test of Illinois Democratic Party loyalty. [123]

During June, leaders of the Massachusetts Free Soil Party disbanded and prepared to take the lead in forming a new Massachusetts Republican Party. This new proposed Massachusetts Republican Party opened its first Convention in Worcester on September 6, 1854, but many of the state's political leaders who were opposed to the Kansas-Nebraska Act decided to stay clear of what they considered the Massachusetts Free Soil Party by another name. Attendance at the Massachusetts Republican Convention was small, primarily because of the meteoric rise of the Massachusetts Know Nothing Party. But the core organizations in the Massachusetts Whig and Democratic parties avoided involvement with Know Nothing politicians. [124]

The first Governor of Kansas Territory arrived during October to begin his duties. Franklin Pierce had appointed Andrew Reeder to this difficult and thankless job. Reeder set up living quarters at Fort Leavenworth, which the Army had constructed in 1827. Two miles away, Leavenworth City, just getting off the ground, would be growing rapidly. The February 1855 issue of the Leavenworth *Herald* would say:

"Five months ago there was not a building in the place. The town had just been laid off and the brush cut down. Leavenworth now has a hotel, a saw mill, a

---

[123] *Stephen A. Douglas*, by Robert W. Johannsen, pages 451-459.
[124] *Charles Sumner and the Coming of the Civil War*, by David Herbert Donald, page 267; *Nativism and Slavery, the Northern Know Nothings and the Politics of the 1850s*, by Tyler Anbinder, pages 87-96, and *The Origins of the Republican Party, 1852-1856*, by William E. Gienapp, pages 133-138.

tailor's shop, a shoemaker, a barber, 2 blacksmiths, 3 carpenter shops, several law and 2 doctor's offices." [125]

Billy Herndon is Springfield Mayor and Abe Lincoln, now Politically Active, Advocates Exclusionism.

Meanwhile, during this historically important year of 1854, Billy Herndon had been elected Mayor of Springfield, then a town of 6,218 people. Herndon "was not going to be just another Mayor. There was a new spirit in the air. Citizens were tired of letting things jog along in the old way. The *State Journal* came out bluntly for changes: 'a school house, a city hall, gas lights, plank streets, water works, fire engines'." [126]

During the first 8 months of 1854, Abraham Lincoln had been listening and reading, but declining to speak out on political matters. But, near the end of August, he thought it time to speak out at the Scott County Whig Convention. There, he attacked "the great wrong and injustice" of allowing bonded African Americans to move into National Territory north of 36 degrees and 30 minutes. On September 3, Lincoln allowed a mix of local politicians (Whig Party men, Know Nothing Party men and men of the Faction of Democrats that opposed Stephen Douglas) to nominate him for the State Legislature. It seemed to Lincoln to be a politically regressive move, for his real goal was to win election to the Federal Senate seat held by James Shields, which was up for reelection. [127]

---

[125] *Bleeding Kansas*, by Alice Nichols, pages 23-25.
[126] *Lincoln's Herndon, a Biography*, by David Herbert Donald, page 60.
[127] *Lincoln*, by David Herbert Donald, pages 171-172.

Chapter 23: Abe's and Mary's Renewed Political Ambitions

Douglas and Lincoln Speak at the 1854 Illinois State Fair in Springfield

The political debates during the Illinois State Fair in Springfield were the climax of the state's 1854 mid-term election campaign, midway between Presidential election years. On October 3, Abe Lincoln stood outside the Hall of Representatives in Springfield, listening to Senator Douglas speaking inside. Then, at the very end of the speech, he burst inside and announced to the audience that tomorrow he or Lyman Trumbull would deliver a speech in answer to Douglas.

As promised, the next day, Lincoln delivered his speech in the Hall of the House of Representatives in opposition to Senator Douglas. It was a hard-hitting denunciation of the Kansas-Nebraska Act, full of Abolitionist feeling and moral outrage. Lincoln denounced "the monstrous injustice of slavery." He charged that "there can be no moral right in connection with one man's making a slave of another." Permitting bonded African Americans to live in a National Territory or "to every other part of the wide world, where men can be found inclined to take slaves" was equally wrong, he shouted. He accused Stephen Douglas of secretly harboring "real zeal" for allowing bonded African Americans to live in the National Territories. Misquoting the meaning of the Declaration of Independence, as

Springfield Lawyer Abraham Lincoln in 1954.

Exclusionists and Abolitionists loved to do, Lincoln asserted, "All men are created free and equal." He alleged that "our revolutionary fathers" had understood that slavery was wrong, but, being unable to abolish it, they had "hedged and hemmed where slavery was allowed to exist to the narrowest limits of necessity." On and on, Lincoln persisted, consuming a full three hours of the time of listeners, many of them in town attending the State Fair. We should remember that, when American leaders wrote the Declaration of Independence, New England states were the home base of those sailboats that were involved in transporting slaves from West Africa to the Caribbean islands, South America and the American colonies. Furthermore, slavery was widespread in most Northern colonies. During that time, at the birth of our nation, no one conceived of "all men" including African slaves.

That evening, following Lincoln's speech in answer to Douglas, Billy Herndon wrote up his law partner's speech for the next day's editorial page of the Springfield *Journal*. Herndon was a zealous Abolitionist, so it is understandable that he might overly glorify Lincoln's Exclusionist rhetoric, but his Springfield *Journal* editorial is worthy of quoting to help readers understand the high level of passion and holier than thou zeal that characterized the period:

"The [Exclusionist] speech of Mr. Lincoln was the profoundest in our opinion that he has made in his whole life. He felt upon his soul the truth's burn, which he uttered, and all present felt, that he was true to his own soul. His feelings once or twice swelled within and came near stifling utterance. He quivered with emotion. The whole house was as still as death. He attacked the [Kansas-Nebraska Act] with unusual warmth and energy; and all felt that a man of strength was its enemy, and that he intended to blast it, if he could, by strong and manly efforts. He was most successful, and the house approved the glorious triumph of truth by loud and continued huzzahs. . . . At the conclusion of this speech, every man and child felt that it was unanswerable. He took the heart captive and broke like a sun over the understanding."

Immediately after Lincoln concluded his 3-hour address, Stephen Douglas took the floor and delivered a 2-hour rebuttal. [128]

The First Attempt to Found the Illinois Republican Party

Immediately after Lincoln concluded his speech, two Abolitionist Activists, Ichabod Codding and Owen Lovejoy, stood up and gave notice of a meeting that evening to organize an Illinois political party that would be focused on forbidding bonded African Americans from moving into any part of the National Territory. It was understood they intended to organize an Illinois Republican Party. Twenty-six men, including Billy Herndon, attended that night's meeting. But Lincoln did not attend! Many years later, in his biography of the late President, Herndon would explain how he had encouraged his law partner to immediately leave Springfield:

". . . I hunted up Lincoln and urged him to avoid meeting the enthusiastic champion[s] of Abolitionism. "Go home at once," I said. "Take Bob with you and drive somewhere into the country and stay till this thing is over." . . . [Lincoln], who was aspiring to succeed his old rival, James Shields, in the

---

[128] *Stephen A. Douglas*, by Robert W. Johannsen, pages 455-459; *Lincoln*, by David Herbert Donald, pages 175-176, and *Herndon's Life of Lincoln*, by William Herndon, page 296.

[Federal] Senate, was forced to avoid the issue by driving hastily in his one horse buggy to the Court in Tazewell County."

Codding and Lovejoy's meeting to organize an Illinois Republican Party adjourned to be reconvened the next day. More attended the second meeting and the attendees, mostly from northern Illinois, adopted a Party Platform. Although, Abe Lincoln was not present, his involvement in the Party was eagerly sought, so the Delegates voted him to membership on the State Central Committee. The new Party adopted the name "Republican." [129]

The 1854 Election in Illinois Results in Large Loses for Stephen Douglas and Democrats.

The Illinois November, 1854 elections destroyed the Democratic Party's hold on the State. In the 9 Illinois Federal House Districts, only 4 Democrats were elected. Exclusionists, who would align with Republicans, took the 3 northern Districts. But Stephen Douglas was pleased that loyal Democrat Thomas Harris had defeated the incumbent Whig Representative in the House District that included Springfield.

Politicians opposed to the regular Democratic Party won a majority of the seats in the State House and the State Senate. Being "fused" into a political alliance on State issues by their opposition to the Kansas-Nebraska Act, Legislators opposed to the regular Democratic Party were expected to act in unison to have their way with State legislation and to control the election of the next Federal Senator.

The 1854 election campaigns all over the northern States had focused on controversy over the Kansas-Nebraska Act, agitation against Catholics, and often over prohibition of alcohol beverages as well. The political results proved to be a resounding victory for candidates opposed to permitting settlers in Kansas Territory to vote to exclude or include bonded African Americans. Among elections for the U. S. House of Representatives, candidates favoring Exclusion of bonded African Americans from all National Territories won 29 of 31 seats in New York, 21 of 25 seats in Pennsylvania, all seats in Ohio, all but 2 in Indiana, and 5 of 9 in Illinois. The Know-Nothing Party swept Massachusetts. Most of the States bordering Massachusetts were also lost to the Democrats. In fact the Democratic Party was to be the minority party in the Federal House for the first time in many years. Only two northern, non-Southern States would send mostly Democrats to the Federal House: sparsely settled California and little New Hampshire. The destruction of the Democratic Party in the northern States by the Know Nothing Party and Exclusion Activists was a watershed event in the politics of the United States.

---

[129] *Lincoln*, by David Herbert Donald, page 177; *Herndon's Life of Lincoln*, by William Herndon, page 299, and *Bloodstains*, Volume 2, by Howard Ray White, page 166-168.

Yet, the idea and the passion for an Exclusionist party remained in the hearts of many Illinoisans, especially those living in the northern part of the State. They were advocating a reconstituted Illinois Republican Party, a party with the same name as the 1854 effort, but a party reconstituted at a new, seemingly disconnected political convention. They believed Illinoisans would better follow political leaders, bent on the same crusade, if those leaders applied their craft with more subtlety. Time was short because a new Federal President would be elected in the fall of 1856, and politicians in most other northern States were much further along toward building their state Republican parties than were the politicians in Illinois. Abraham Lincoln understood that a Republican Northern States Convention would take place, probably in June, 1856. And he was wondering how he might become involved. [130]

The Climax of the North-South Struggle in Kansas Territory: December, 1855

By the close of 1855, political agitation over Bleeding Kansas had risen to a fever-pitch. Let us take a look at the North-South political and military struggle in Kansas Territory as 1855 came to a close and 1856 began.

On December 7, 1855, the local Lawrence, Kansas newspaper, the *Herald of Freedom*, reported the arrival of terrorist John Brown and his four sons:

Murders by John Brown's gang at Pottawatomie in Kansas Territory were especially horrible. It was another attempt to force Southern families to abandon their claims and flee.

"As they drove up in front of [Lawrence Kansas Territory's] Free State Hotel, they were all standing in a small lumber wagon To each of their persons was strapped a short heavy broad sword, Each was supplied with a goodly number of firearms and navy revolvers, and poles were standing endwise around the wagon box with fixed bayonets pointing upwards. They looked really formidable and were received with [manifest brilliance]. A small military company was organized at once, and the command was given to Old [John] Brown. From that hour he

---

[130] *Stephen A. Douglas*, by Robert W. Johannsen, pages 460-461 and 468; *Lincoln*, by David Herbert Donald, pages 178-179 and 187-189, *Jefferson Davis, American Patriot, 1808-1861*, by Hudson Strode, page 269 and *Bloodstains*, Volume 2, pages 171-173.

commenced fomenting difficulties in [the Exclusionist Lawrence military] camp, disregarding the commands of superior officers, and trying to induce the men to go down to Franklin and make an attack on [Kansas Territory Governor Wilson Shannon's 1,500-man peace-keeping force, under the command of Sheriff Jones, which was] encamped there."

The day following the newspaper report, Governor Shannon ventured personally into Lawrence to negotiate with Exclusionist leaders, including the primary leader, Charles Robinson, the man from Massachusetts who had led the first wave of 29 men from that state to Kansas Territory and settled them at a new town he had named "Lawrence."

Governor Wilson Shannon had no stomach for a territory war in which settlers from the North, such as John Brown-inspired terrorists and the militant faction within the Massachusetts Immigrant Aid Society, attacked and killed settlers from the South. The majority of Territory voting men were from the South and the Lawrence Exclusionists were becoming desperate to gain control over the Kansas Territory Legislature. Many seemed to be planning to kill Southern settlers and burn houses, in hopes many would flee back to their previous homes in search of safety, thereby reducing the Southern vote total for the Territory Legislature.

So, the day following John Brown's terrorist-inspired arrival in Lawrence, December 8, 1855, Territory Governor Wilson Shannon signed a weak treaty between the militant Lawrence settlers (Charles Robinson being their leader) and his Kansas Territory Government. Basically, Robinson agreed "to aide in the execution of any legal process" against offending citizens. In other words, if a party of Lawrence Exclusionists went on a rampage, burning Southern settler homesteads and driving them out of the Territory, the leaders of the settlers of Lawrence pledged to help find those responsible and assist with prosecution.

After signing this treaty promising aide in prosecution of Exclusion terrorists, Governor Shannon explained to the Lawrence crowd their relevant obligations. Immediately, John Brown jumped up on a dry-goods box and shouted:

"Those laws we denounce and spit upon and will never obey! No, no! Down with the [laws passed by] the Kansas Territory Legislature! Lead us down to fight first."

Ignoring John Brown's gang, Governor Shannon and Lawrence Exclusionist leaders, Charles Robinson and Jim Lane, went to Franklin, met with the leaders of the 1,500-man law enforcement posse and arranged for it to disband.

Exclusionists would not obey the treaty signed in Lawrence. Many Exclusionists would remain armed with Sharps repeating rifles.

John Brown's gang would move on — taking captured slaves to Canada, releasing them there, moving east to Virginia and staging what he hoped to be the start of a slave uprising.

Using the weaponry at the Federal armory at Harpers Ferry Brown's gang would hope to arm thousands of newly recruited Colored terrorists and lead them against the White people of Virginia. It would prove to be a stupid idea — Virginia slaves would not take the gangs stockpile of spears, would not take the armory's weapons, would ignore the gang's call to rebel against their owners. The gang would only kill a few Harper's Ferry people. The gang members would die, including John Brown. The North would praise the late John Brown. America's patriotic Yankee song, "The Battle Hymn of the Republic," would be based on praise for the late John Brown. [131]

Abolition Terrorist Leader John Brown, known for leading his terrorist gang in Kansas Territory and at Harpers Ferry, Virginia.

I have just given you a detailed look at one of the scores of major political and terrorist efforts of the minority population in Kansas Territory — settlers from the Emigrant Aide Societies — during the administrations of Democrat President Franklin Pierce of New Hampshire and Democrat President James Buchanan of Pennsylvania. During these years, reporters from Northern newspapers were reporting and would be reporting all North-South incidents, slanting stories to make Northern settlers appear saintly and Southern settlers appear as rouges and detestable "ruffians." It would be a long propaganda war of words. It was in the early days of this North-South struggle in Kansas Territory that Abe Lincoln decided to become a fervent Exclusionist, somewhat of an Abolitionist and play a major role in launching the Illinois Republican Party.

---

[131] *Bleeding Kansas*, by Alice Nichols, pages 13-15; and *Bloodstains*, Volume 2, by Howard Ray White, pages 158 and 202-204.

Lincoln attends February 22, 1856 Conference of Anti-Slavery Newspaper Men

In January 1856, Paul Selby of the Jacksonville, Illinois *Morgan Journal* proposed a conference of all editors who were opposed to slavery in Kansas Territory. They were invited to gather and plan for the next presidential election. Abe Lincoln was now ready to take a leading role in Exclusionist-Republican political efforts, so he endorsed the idea of a meeting of non-Democrat newspaper editors. [132] Selby's meeting took place at Decatur on February 22, 1856 with many non-Democrat editors in attendance. Abe Lincoln was also at the meeting, the only person present who was not a newspaperman. The attending newspaper editors discussed political platform planks and called for all non-Democrat leaders in Illinois to gather at a fusion convention at Bloomington, Illinois on May 29 to unite all non-Democrats under one political party banner.

A banquet was held that evening. At the banquet, one editor suggested that Abe Lincoln become the new fusion party's candidate for state governor. Lincoln declined, but, after a toast praising him "as the warm and consistent friend of Illinois, and our next candidate for the U. S. Senate," Lincoln agreed, replying, "The latter part of that sentiment I am in favor of." Lincoln then expressed "his willingness to buckle on his armor" and engage in the upcoming struggle against Senator Stephen Douglas and the Illinois Democratic Party. [133]

---

[132] In those days almost all newspapers were published to support a specific political party.

[133] *Lincoln*, by David Herbert Donald, pages 189-190; *The Origins of the Republican Party, 1852-1856*, by William E. Gienapp, pages 288-289; *Bloodstains*, Volume 2, by Howard Ray White, page 209.

Chapter 24: The Birth of the Illinois Republican Party and the John Fremont Campaign

Formation of the Illinois Republican Party — May 29, 1956

On May 10, Billy Herndon called for a meeting of Sangamon County citizens who were opposed to allowing African Americans to live in Kansas Territory, the purpose being to elect delegates to the upcoming Illinois non-Democrat fusion convention scheduled for May 29, 1856 at Bloomington. Those gathered voted to include Herndon and Abe Lincoln among the convention delegates from the Springfield area.

It was amid excited newspaper stories about Bleeding Kansas that Illinois politicians gathered on May 29 to re-ignite the Illinois Republican Party. The new Illinois Party, which would soon adopt the name "Republican" opened its State Convention at Bloomington, attended by 270 Delegates. Five prominent political leaders had joined in encouraging unification of all politicians opposed to the Democratic Party. Lyman Trumbull and James Woodworth had been encouraging dissatisfied Democrats — Jesse Norton and Thomas Knox had been encouraging Know Nothing Party political leaders — and Elihu Washburne had been encouraging Whigs, as had former Whig Abe Lincoln. Clearly recognizing the impossibility of sustaining an independent Whig Party, Washburne had written fellow Whig leader Richard Yates in April, "If we do not take hold of this Bloomington Convention, what shall we do? We all think it is the only way. If we cannot come together as opponents of the [Kansas-Nebraska Act] infamy, how can we?"

Billy Herndon and Abe Lincoln were joined in Bloomington by other prominent past Whigs, including Richard Yates, David Davis, Orville Browning and Edward Baker. Past Democrats included Elihu Washburne, John Wentworth, Norman Judd and John Palmer, who would preside over the Convention. Leaders among German-speaking voters included George Schneider and Adolph Mayer. Past Know Nothing Party men included Joseph Gillespie, William Jayne and Jesse Dubois. Longtime Free Soil Party Abolitionists included Owen Lovejoy, Ichabod Codding and John Bryant, brother of the prominent literary Abolitionist, William Bryant.

However, and this is important, future Republicans had not organized and elected Delegates from more than 30 counties in the State, almost all of them in southern Illinois. The southern part of the state, where Democrats were popular, was unrepresented at Bloomington. So the Bloomington gathering did not represent a statewide political organization, instead it represented an Illinois central-and-northern-counties organization. [134]

The reason for the lack of support for a new Exclusionist Republican Party in the southern Illinois counties is simple: Southern Illinois had been primarily settled by Southern families. Many had relatives in the South.

Abe Lincoln Delivers a Politically-Advancing Speech at Bloomington

In recognition of Abraham Lincoln's role in creating the new fusion party, soon to be called the Illinois Republican Party, he was invited to make the closing address at the Bloomington Convention. Speaking without notes, Lincoln delivered what Billy Herndon believed to be the greatest speech of his law partner's life.

The only record of this speech was published on June 5, 1856 by the Alton *Weekly Courier*. Being an important Lincoln speech, I simply quote the summation by the Alton reporter:

Lincoln at the Bloomington Convention. (permission to use this art was granted by Neil Gale of Living History of Illinois).

"Abraham Lincoln of Sangamon, came upon the platform amid deafening applause. He enumerated the pressing reasons of the present movement. He was here ready to fuse with anyone who would unite with him to oppose slave power; spoke of the bugbear disunion which was so vaguely threatened. It was to be remembered that the Union must be preserved in the purity of its principles as well as in the integrity of its territorial parts. It must be 'Liberty and Union, now and forever, one and inseparable.' The sentiment in favor of White slavery now prevailed in all the slave state papers, except those of Kentucky, Tennessee, Missouri and Maryland. Such was the progress of the National Democracy. Douglas once claimed against

---

[134] *Herndon's Life of Lincoln*, by William Herndon, page 312; *Lincoln*, by David Herbert Donald, pages 191-192; *The Origins of the Republican Party, 1852-1856*, by William E. Gienapp, page 294.

him that Democracy favored more than his principles, the individual rights of man. Was it not strange that he must stand there now to defend those rights against their former eulogist? The Black Democracy were endeavoring to cite Henry Clay to reconcile old Whigs to their doctrine, and repaid them with the very cheap compliment of National Whigs." [135]

This speech by Springfield lawyer, Abraham Lincoln, must have been a major boost to his political advancement because, only one month later, he would be nominated for Vice-President of the United States.

I need to repeat this observation to ensure you understand:

This speech by Springfield lawyer, Abraham Lincoln, must have been a major boost to his political advancement because, only one month later, he would be nominated for Vice-President of the United States.

Let us try to figure out what Lincoln said in that important May 29, 1856 speech:

- "He enumerated the pressing reasons of the present movement." He had organized his speech as a list of the pressing reasons that had given rise to the Illinois Republican Party.

- ". . . unite with him to oppose slave power . . ." "The slave power" was a term often used to mischaracterize Southern Democrats and, by association, denounce Illinois Democrats.

- ". . . spoke of the bugbear disunion which was so vaguely threatened. It was to be remembered that the Union must be preserved in the purity of its principles as well as in the integrity of its territorial parts. It must be 'Liberty and Union, now and forever, one and inseparable'." He called "State Secession," which we realize was not prohibited by the Federal Constitution, "the bugbear disunion." We can assume he pledged to conquer any seceded state by military force.

- "The sentiment in favor of White slavery now prevailed in all the slave state papers, except those of Kentucky, Tennessee, Missouri and Maryland. Such was the progress of the National Democracy." Totally fallacious and unfounded was Lincoln's alleged threat of the existence of a white people enslavement movement in Virginia, Tennessee and Arkansas, and all states further south and out to Texas. He had omitted the border states of Maryland, Kentucky and Missouri because, if he had included them in his fallacious threat, it would have been too easy for people in Illinois to discover that the whole idea was a lie. The only

---

[135] *Lincoln*, by David Herbert Donald, page 191.

possible evidence to support Lincoln's claim would have been a very few cases where a person who exhibited very slight physical evidence of African ancestry was being held as a slave. In the South, it was legal to hold as a bonded slave a person with <u>more than one-eighth</u> African ancestry. A person of one-eighth African ancestry, or less could, not be held as a slave. Anyway, Lincoln's presentation of this threat to White people in Illinois was ridiculous. [136]

The 1856 Republican Party's Northern States Convention in Philadelphia on June 17-19, 1856

The 1856 Republican Party Northern States Convention was held on June 17 to 19 in Philadelphia, Pennsylvania. Neither Abraham Lincoln nor Billy Herndon was among the Illinois Republican Party delegation that attended the convention.

Three men were considered in the running for the Party's nomination for Federal President. Salmon Chase of Ohio, a Republican Governor, past Free Soil Democrat and Republican pioneer, was a favorite of fervent Exclusionists. William Seward of New York, a past Whig, a Federal Senator and a clever pragmatist, although a late joiner of the Party, was generally considered the strongest candidate. Finally, there was a man who was clearly not qualified to be President, but many of the more clever Republican image-makers figured they could successfully package that man and sell him to gullible voters. That man's name was "John C. Fremont."

John Fremont was, by all rational measures, totally incompetent to be Federal President. His most useful asset was his wife, the former Jessie Benton, the vivacious and politically astute daughter of Thomas Benton of Missouri. Thomas Benton had been elected U. S. Senator five consecutive times, representing Missouri from 1821 to 1851. Benton had vast experience in the Federal Government, and must have rather shuttered at the prospect of his son-in-law becoming responsible for the office of Federal President. And Benton would never publicly support his son-in-law's candidacy.

But his daughter Jessie longed to become First Lady and was working hard and capably to make that happen. John Fremont, age 43, had been born in Georgia. His father had been a French immigrant. Upon coming of age, he had joined the Federal Army, moved into the Topographical Engineers group, and worked on Army expeditions to explore and map the upper Mississippi and Missouri rivers. In the 1840's he had led 3 major Army expeditions to the far west, mapping the Oregon Trail, and trails into Mexican Alto Californio.

---

[136] *Bloodstains*, Volume 2, by Howard Ray White, pages 231-233; and *Lincoln*, by David Herbert Donald, page 191.

He had been stationed there during the War with Mexico. After California statehood, Fremont had been elected U. S. Senator as a Democrat, but had only been able to work in the Senate in Washington City for 17 days before his short term had expired. He had failed at his bid for reelection. Partly due to the efforts of his

wife and father-in-law, Fremont's exploits had received considerable publicity; he had gained the nickname "Pathfinder" and a reputation for toughness and independent action. It was that reputation that Republican Delegates wanted to exploit in the campaign for President. They figured he could be packaged and sold to the voters. Meanwhile, John and Jessie Fremont stayed in New York City, readily available to politicians, newspapermen and financial interests. [137]

The first day of the Convention was devoted to writing the Northern States Republican Party Platform. It proclaimed that State Secession would be considered treason. It stipulated that the Federal House and Senate had "sovereign power over the [National] Territories." It advocated that Kansas Territory be granted immediate statehood under the Revolutionary Kansas Constitution written in Lawrence, Kansas Territory. To retard economic development of the southern States, it excluded consideration of the southern railroad route through Texas and the Gadsen Purchase to the Pacific, which would be far cheaper and far more quickly built than a railroad across the Rocky Mountains and the California mountains.

John and Jessie Fremont

The second day of the convention, June 18, was devoted to choosing the Party's nominee for President. Fremont had the nomination sewed up before balloting

[137] *The Origins of the Republican Party, 1852-1856*, by William E. Gienapp, pages 316-329 and 334-335; *An Historian and the Civil War*, by Avery Craven, page 192;

began. On the second ballot, the nomination was decided for Fremont by a vote of 520 to 37.

Republican Delegates Nominate Abraham Lincoln for Vice President of the United States

The third day of the convention, June 19, was devoted to choosing the party's nominee for Vice president. It seemed agreed that the nominee be a former Whig. In the evening of the 18th, William L. Dayton, a former Whig U. S. Senator from New Jersey seemed the overall favorite. But the Midwestern states were eager to put forward their choice. That evening, the Illinois delegation caucused to discuss choices. Delegate Nathaniel G. Wilcox, perhaps favorably remembering Lincoln's May 29 speech at Bloomington, proposed that the Illinois delegation push Abraham Lincoln for Vice President. So, Illinois delegates campaigned for support for Lincoln among other delegations. Although not a delegate, U. S. Senator Lyman Trumbull of Illinois was attending the Convention and the caucus as an observer. Having been thrown out of the Democratic Party at its National Convention in early June, Trumbull was maneuvering to become a powerful Republican leader. He offered to help encourage Delegates in neighboring States to join Illinois in support of

Lawyer Abraham Lincoln, the second place 1856 Vice Presidential Nominee for the Northern States Republican Party.

Lincoln for Vice President. The results were impressive. Delegate John Allison of Pennsylvania agreed to nominate Abraham Lincoln the next day.

On June 19, a delegate nominated William Dayton, a former Whig and Federal Senator from New Jersey, for Vice President. Then Delegate John Allison of Pennsylvania nominated Abe Lincoln of Illinois for Vice President, proudly praising him as "the prince of good fellows and an Old-Line Whig." Then Illinois Delegate William Archer seconded, saying he had known Lincoln for 30 years and had always found him "as pure a patriot as ever lived."

The vote was 253 votes for Dayton, 110 votes for Lincoln and 202 for others.

James Buchanan and Fremont's Political Opponents

The Fremont-Dayton ticket would oppose the National Democratic Party's Buchanan-Breckinridge ticket. Incumbent President Democrat Franklin Pierce of New Hampshire was willing to serve a second term, but the Democratic Party delegates felt that James Buchanan would make a stronger candidate, free of having to defend a 1852-1856 record against a strong Northern States Republican Party. Also, Buchanan was from the large battleground state of Pennsylvania whereas Pierce was from little New Hampshire. And, for 25 years, Buchanan had been a proven government leader: Minister to the United Kingdom, 1853-1856; Secretary of State, 1845-1849; U. S. Senator, 1834-1845; Minister to Russia, 1832-1833; and Representative in the U. S. House, 1821-1831. Vice President Candidate James Breckinridge had been recently elected U. S. Senator for Kentucky, having served in the House from 1851 to 1855. A third party, the American Party (formerly the Know Nothings), nominated Millard Filmore of New York State. [138]

Billy Herndon and Abe Lincoln Campaign for the Fremont-Dayton Presidential Ticket, Hoping to Defeat Democrat James Buchanan

Meanwhile, in Illinois, during the 1856 political campaign season, Billy Herndon was working hard advocating for Republican Presidential candidate John Fremont and other Republican candidates. As a member of the Illinois Republican Party State Central Committee, Billy was often called on to help organize campaign groups and help train political leaders. The Lincoln & Herndon law office was the meeting place for central Illinois Republican politicians. Also Billy was called on to address Republican rallies all over the State. Billy's speeches focused on Exclusionism and an alleged fanciful Southern Democrat conspiracy to introduce bonded African America slaves into the northern States.

Now, you should realize that American history proves that there had never been any effort by any faction of Southern slave owners to change laws in any Northern State to enable the existence of slavery within its borders. Nevertheless, that fear tactic was a widely used campaign tool in the Republican political weaponry.

Before Herndon's audiences he alleged that, if bonded African Americans were permitted to move into Kansas Territory, they would inevitably be eventually permitted to move into northern States, even into Illinois, which, since 1853, had been legally prohibiting anyone of African descent from moving into the State.

---

[138] *The Origins of the Republican Party, 1852-1856*, by William E. Gienapp, pages 335-346; *A Review of the Political Conflict in America*, by Alexander Harris, page 173; *Lincoln*, by David Herbert Donald, pages 192-193; *Stephen A. Douglas*, by Robert W. Johannsen, page 534.

That's right. Since the enactment of the Illinois Black Code of 1853, state law had prohibited any person to take residence in that state if he or she showed evidence of noticeable African ancestry.

President James Buchanan, Democrat of Pennsylvania.

Abe Lincoln worked hard campaigning for Republican John Fremont. Lincoln argued that everyone opposed to the Democrats, and everyone opposed to settlers from the southern States moving to the National Territories with bonded African Americans, must unite behind Republican John Fremont because American Party candidate Millard Fillmore of New York State was not electable in Illinois.

It seems Lincoln convinced many people not to waste a vote on Fillmore. But his wife Mary Todd Lincoln favored the American Party candidate. She had written that her "weak woman's heart" attracted her to Millard Fillmore of New York State of the party that had formerly called itself the "Know Nothing Party," but had renamed itself the "American Party." Why? She said she favored Fillmore because of "the necessity of keeping foreigners within bounds."

Republican Fremont was defeated in the race for President.

Billy Herndon had campaigned hard for Northern States Republican candidates. In a letter to Theodore Parker, Billy would estimate that he had delivered over 100 speeches during the campaign. Yes, even in defeat, Billy would be proud of his political accomplishments. A few months after the elections he would emote in a letter to Charles Sumner, "I shall ever hold the year 1856 the crown of my life." [139]

Mary's Huge Birthday Party for Husband Abe in February, 1857

The previous year, in the spring of 1856, Mary had contracted for a major expansion of their modest Springfield house. The Lincoln income was good and Abe expected to eventually receive a big legal fee from the Illinois Central Railroad case

---

[139] *Lincoln*, by David Herbert Donald, pages192-195; *Lincoln's Herndon, a Biography*, by David Herbert Donald, pages 93-97; *Bloodstains*, Volume 2, by Howard Ray White, pages240-245.

that Lincoln & Herndon had litigated. Also, Mary had received money from the sale of some inherited Todd land in Kentucky. Contractors had raised the roof and built a second story onto the house that she and Abe had purchased 12 years earlier. The resulting Greek revival two-story house had separate bedrooms for Mary and husband Abe (they did not normally share a bed). Robert had his own room.

Another bedroom was shared by Willie and Tad. There was also a guest bedroom, a maid's quarters, parlors, a sitting room, and of course a kitchen and dining room. It by no means rivaled the much grander Springfield mansion where her sister Elizabeth Todd Edwards lived, but the expanded Lincoln home was now one of the best in Springfield. Yes, the house was quite nice, and Mary had money to properly decorate the place.

In February, 1857, Mary Todd Lincoln proudly showed off the expanded home during a grand 48th birthday party she gave for her husband Abe. About 300 guests attended the party. The guest list was

Mary Todd Lincoln a few years before the big birthday party.

designed to maintain her husband's network of political friends and acquaintances. Mary was always ambitious for her husband to reach great heights in politics and artfully applied lessons learned while growing up among powerful politicians in Lexington, Kentucky. Her father, Robert Todd, had often been involved in politics, and had run unsuccessfully for the Federal Senate. The Todd's had been family friends of Lexington's most famous resident, Henry Clay, one of the primary founders of the Whig Party. So, with Abe's prominence in the Illinois Republican Party, with his national recognition growing, and with Tad and Willie becoming old enough to allow Mary substantial free time, she had become much more involved in supporting her husband's ambitions.

But was Abe Lincoln's birthday party free of ulterior motives? Of course not! He was really about fifty-two years old, not forty-eight. He had come into this world in Western North Carolina, not Kentucky, and two years before his parents had married. When his mother, Nancy Hanks, had married Thomas Lincoln, little Abe had been running around the room, seemingly a year and a half years old. That little boy's father was Abraham Enloe. Furthermore, Thomas Lincoln's horrible bout with the mumps had rendered him sexually sterile.

Now that Lincoln was rising to prominence, it was essential that his true parentage be hidden from all political opponents. We can assume that Abe and Mary threw the February birthday party to help fix Abe's age at 48 years. Abe had claimed a birth date of February 10, 1809, the date that corresponded to the birth of his mother's third child that she had named Thomas, the child that had died in infancy. That was the date Abe had written as his birth date in the new Bible in which he had recorded family births, marriages and deaths while sitting beside Sarah Bush Johnston Lincoln about one or two years after her second husband's death. This birthday party was Mary's defense against future questions about her husband's paternity.

You will recall that, about four years previously, in 1853, after Thomas Lincoln's death in 1851, Abe had visited his stepmother Sarah Bush Johnston Lincoln and had written a series of family birth, marriage and death dates in a new Bible he had purchased for the occasion. That was the first written record of Abe's birth as February 10, 1809 and it is without merit because it is unverified. Billy Herndon had discovered the tattered family record page torn from that Bible on a visit to Col. Chapman. On that page, Lincoln had written, all in one day, the family record, mostly of the Johnston family. [140]

---

[140] *Bloodstains*, Volume 2, by Howard Ray White, page 272.

Chapter 25: With Billy Herndon's Help, Abraham Lincoln's Prominence Rises Rapidly

In Early 1858, Billy Herndon Promotes Lincoln's Political Image among Northeastern Abolitionists and Republican Leaders

In late February or early March, 1858, Billy Herndon, made a pilgrimage to the northeastern States. The purpose of the trip seemed to have been advancing Lincoln's political image in the Northeast. This was Herndon's first-ever trip beyond his home region about Illinois. Most anxious that Billy call on Horace Greeley, Lincoln instructed his partner with these words: "I fear Greeley's attitude will damage me with Sumner, Seward, Wilson, Phillips, and other friends in the [Northeastern States]." In addition to Greeley, Herndon wanted to meet many other Exclusion and Abolition Activists and politicians in Washington City, New York State and Massachusetts.

Horace Greeley, publisher and editor of America's most widely read newspaper.

Herndon arrived in Washington City in mid-March. Of this trip, he would later write in his biography of Abraham Lincoln:

> "I had been in correspondence on my own account with [Horace] Greeley, [William] Seward, [Charles] Sumner, [Wendell] Phillips, and others for several years, had kept them informed of the feelings of our people and the political campaigns in their various stages, but had never met any of them, save Greeley."

> "I enjoyed heartily the journey and the varied sights and scenes that attended it. Aside from my mission, the trip was a great success. The magnificent buildings, the display of wealth in the large cities and prosperous manufacturing towns, broadened the views of one whose vision had never extended beyond the limits of the Illinois prairies."

In Washington City, Herndon stopped by the Washington home of Democrat Stephen Douglas, briefly speaking with the Senator from Illinois as he lay in his sick bed. At this time in American political history, many influential Republicans and former-Democrats-turned-Republicans across the Northern States were encouraging Senator Douglas, the leading Democrat in the North, to switch parties.

If Douglas switched, Lincoln's future would be severely weakened. So, while Herndon sat beside Senator Douglas' sick bed, it seems that the Illinois Democrat was surprisingly agreeable with Exclusionism in spite of past political differences. In his biography of Lincoln, Herndon would record the following account of the sick bed encounter:

"Douglas was confined to his house by illness, but, on receiving my card, he directed me to be shown up to his room. We had a pleasant and interesting interview. Of course, the conversation soon turned on Lincoln. In answer to an inquiry regarding the latter, I remarked that Lincoln was pursuing the even tenor of his way. 'He is not in anybody's way,' I contended, 'not even in yours, Judge Douglas.' [141] He was sitting up in a chair smoking a cigar. Between puffs, he responded that neither was he in the way of Lincoln or anyone else and did not intend to invite conflict. He conceived that he achieved what he had set out to do, and hence did not feel that his course need put him in opposition to Mr. Lincoln or his party. 'Give Mr. Lincoln my regards,' he said rather warmly, 'when you return, and tell him I have crossed the river and burned my boat.'

Before leaving Washington City, Herndon also "saw and dined with [Lyman] Trumbull, who went over the situation with me." He also "saw [William] Seward, [Henry] Wilson, and others of equal prominence." Then, he headed to New York City, eager to meet with Horace Greeley.

Horace Greeley, raised in New Hampshire and a longtime resident of New York City, had, by 1858, built his newspaper, the New York *Tribune*, into the foremost American newspaper, with 600,000 subscribers to its weekly edition. His editorials and news selectivity made the *Tribune* the North's most powerful advocate for Exclusionism, Abolitionism, and, since 1854, the Republican Party of the Northern States. Herndon was eager to convince Greeley to be supportive of his law partner's political future:

"Leaving Washington [City], my next point was New York [City], where I met the editor of the Anti-Slavery Standard, Horace Greeley [as well as] Henry Ward Beecher, and others. I had a long talk with Greeley, whom, I noticed, leaned toward Douglas," if he chose to switch parties.

"I found, however, he was not at all hostile to Lincoln. I presented the latter's case in the best phase I know how, but while I drew but little from him, I left feeling that he hadn't been entirely won over. He introduced me to Beecher, who, as everybody else did, inquired after Lincoln and through me sent him words of encouragement and praise."

---

[141] Stephen Douglas was addressed as "Judge Douglas" ever since serving as a judge in Illinois, long before entering the U. S. Senate.

Herndon's letter to Lincoln, written from the Revere House in Boston on March 24, tells of his political discussions in New York and Boston with Exclusionists, Abolitionists and politicians.

"Since I have landed in Boston I have seen much that was entertaining and interesting. This morning I was introduced to Governor [Nathaniel] Banks. He and I had a conversation about Republicanism and especially about Douglas. He asked me this question, 'You will sustain Douglas in Illinois, won't you?' and to which I said, 'No, never!' He affected to be much surprised, and so the matter dropped and turned on Republicanism, or in general, Lincoln. Greeley's and other [newspapers] that laud Douglas, Harris et al., want them sustained, and will try to do it. Several persons have asked me the same question that Banks asked, and evidently they get their cue, ideas, or what, not from Greeley, Seward, et al. By the bye, Greeley remarked to me this: 'The Republican standard is too high; we want something practical'."

We must realize that wise Northeastern political leaders did not want to drive the Southern States to Secession. The import taxes raised in Southern seaports (about 80 percent of Federal Tariff revenue was collected in Southern seaports), the banker's cotton factoring businesses and the sales of Northern-made goods to the South needed to be sustained. These were important economic realities. [142]

---

[142] Herndon's *Life of Lincoln*, pages 321-323; *Bloodstains*, Volume 2, by Howard Ray White, pages 413-315.

Chapter 26: "A House Divided," the Lincoln-Douglas Debates and Senator Jefferson Davis of Mississippi

Abe Lincoln, the 1858 Illinois Republican State Convention in Springfield and "A House Divided"

On June 16, 1858, the Illinois Republican State Convention assembled in Springfield. To the normal agenda, leaders added the task of formally endorsing a candidate to compete for Stephen Douglas' Senate seat, which was up for reelection at the next session of the Illinois Legislature. By the way, back then, state legislatures — not the voting citizens — elected each state's two senators. Abe Lincoln and his supporters wanted to squelch the nagging newspaper stories about various potential candidates, such as John Wentworth of Chicago, or even Douglas if he would switch parties. So Lincoln's supporters arranged for Republican Delegates at the State Convention to vote to endorse a preference for the Federal Senate job, which was not normal procedure in those days. The plan worked beautifully. Delegates recognized Lincoln as the

Democrat Senator Stephen A. Douglas of Illinois, considered the leader of the Democratic Party in the Northern States.

founder of the Illinois Republican Party in 1856 and they showed their appreciation. They voted to endorse Lincoln as the Republican recommended for the Federal Senate seat held by Stephen Douglas. The Party endorsement of Lincoln was not a binding arrangement, and Illinoisans would not go to the polls, as they do today, to vote for Lincoln or Douglas, they would just vote for their local Representative and Senator to the State Legislature. If the Republican Party held the most seats in the State Legislature, it would elect the man to take the U. S. Senate seat long held by Stephen Douglas.

On the evening of June 17, 1858, having received the Party's endorsement as its choice to replace Douglas, Abe Lincoln gave his acceptance speech before a crowd of enthusiastic Republican Delegates and politicians. Lincoln began his speech with the following introductory demagoguery — remarkable nonsense designed to scare the large population of gullible and inexperienced northern States voters:

"If we could first know where we are, and whither we are tending, we could then better judge what to do, and how to do it.

"We are now far into the fifth year, since a policy was initiated, with the avowed object, and confident promise, of putting an end to [agitation over what to do about bonded African Americans]. [143]

"Under the operation of that policy, that agitation has not only, not ceased, but has constantly augmented.

"In my opinion, it will not cease, until a crisis shall have been reached, and passed.

"'A house divided against itself cannot stand.'

"I believe this government cannot endure, permanently half [with bonded African Americans] and half [without bonded African Americans].

"I do not expect the [Federation of States] to be dissolved – I do not expect the house to fall – but I do expect it will cease to be divided.

Springfield lawyer and Illinois Republican Party leader, Abraham Lincoln.

"It will become all one thing, or all the other.

"Either the opponents of [African American bonding], will arrest the further spread of it, and place it where the public mind shall rest in the belief that it is in the course of ultimate extinction; or its advocates will put it forward, till it shall become alike lawful in all the States, old as well as new – [in the northern States] as well as in [the southern States]." [144]

Lincoln said, "We are far into the fifth year." This he spoke of in 1858. Five years previously was 1853. What happened in 1853? Illinois politicians passed the "Illinois Black Code of 1853," which prohibited people of noticeable African ancestry from coming into Illinois to live.

---

[143] Concerning racial and slavery issues, I am changing words, as you can see, and putting the revisions in square brackets. The meaning is the same, but the replacements help the reader comprehend the meaning of what was said or written.

[144] *Lincoln*, by David Herbert Donald, pages 205-206; *Abraham Lincoln — His Speeches and Writings*, edited by Ray P. Basler, pages 372-373; *Bloodstains*, Volume 2, by Howard Ray White, page 329.

This speech would become the most important ever delivered by Abe Lincoln. Although not a Christian, it was not uncommon for him to use phraseology from the *Bible*. In this case he encouraged the North's Exclusionist political crusade by invoking the words of Jesus Christ. "A house divided against itself cannot stand" would become, for political historians, Lincoln's most important warmongering sound bite – his allegation of the unavoidability of eventual war between the northern States and the southern States. About 2,000 years ago, Jesus Christ had been confronted by pious religious men, called "scribes," who blasphemously accused Him (He had been seen performing healing miracles) of employing (instead of God's power) allegedly Satan's supernatural power to cast demons from afflicted people – much like witchcraft. Jesus responded to his accusers with a parable. John Mark, a close associate of the apostle Peter, recorded the event in the *Bible* as follows (Mark, Chapter 3, verses 22 through 30). The King James translation, which was used during Lincoln's day, is presented:

"And the scribes which came down from Jerusalem said, He hath Beelzebub, and by the Prince of the devils casteth he out devils. And He called them unto him, and said unto them in parables.

"How can Satan cast out Satan? And if a kingdom be divided against itself, that kingdom cannot stand. And if a house be divided against itself, that house cannot stand. And if Satan rise up against himself, and be divided, he cannot stand, but hath an end. No man can enter into a strong man's house, and spoil his goods, except he will first bind the strong man; and then he will spoil his house. Verily I say unto you, All sins shall be forgiven unto the sons of men, and blasphemies wherewith so-ever they shall blaspheme: But he that shall blaspheme against the Holy Ghost hath never forgiveness, but is in danger of eternal damnation: Because they said, He hath an unclean spirit."

Luke recorded the same event in the *Bible* (Luke, Chapter 11, verses 17 through 20). I use the New International Version translation of the Greek here:

"Any kingdom divided against itself will be ruined, and a house divided against itself will fall. If Satan is divided against himself, how can his kingdom stand? I say this because you claim that I drive out demons by Beelzebub. Now if I drive out demons by Beelzebub, by whom do your followers drive them out? So then, they will be your judges. But if I drive out demons by the finger of God, then the kingdom of God has come to you."

The "house-divided-against-itself-cannot-stand" quotation from Jesus Christ had been previously applied in agitation against the southern States. It was basically a scare tactic, designed to produce fear that northern States European Americans (White people) might someday become bonded or, at least, be made to live alongside bonded African Americans. Massachusetts Abolitionist Edmund Quincy had applied the quotation in an 1852 speech. Lincoln had considered using it in a speech in 1856. It seemed to graphically picture the Abolitionist argument that, 1) the Federation of States was cursed by the demon-sin of African American bonding, 2) agitation over bonded African Americans produced a sinful "house divided against itself" because many favored bonding most African Americans and many opposed the relationship, 3) the sin of African American bonding tainted even those opposed to it, because their forefathers had permitted it to flourish, 4) yet, we know from the teachings of Jesus that [African American bonding] will, someday, eventually become extinct because a sinful house divided against itself will fall, 5) to hasten the extinction of African American bonding, the righteous must cleanse their souls of the sins of African American bonding and strike against the southern States sinners, to "drive out demons by the finger of God", 6) "then the kingdom of God has come" to a purified Federation of States. What happens to African Americans at that point is purposely not discussed.

Using the teachings of Jesus Christ to justify a war against southern States to ensure exclusion of bonded African Americans from western territory required that Abe Lincoln engage in very selective reading, because, Jesus also taught:

On charity: "When you give a luncheon or dinner, do not invite your friends, your brothers or relatives, or your rich neighbors; if you do, they may invite you back and so you will be repaid. But when you give a banquet, invite the poor, the crippled, the lame, the blind, and you will be blessed. Although they cannot repay you, you will be repaid at the resurrection of the righteous." [145]

On judging others: "Do not judge, and you will not be judged. Do not condemn, and you will not be condemned. Forgive, and you will be forgiven. [146]

Again on judging others: "Why do you look at the speck of sawdust in your brother's eye and pay no attention to the plank in your own eye? How can you say to your brother, 'Brother, let me take the speck out of your eye,' when you yourself fail to see the plank in your own eye? You hypocrite, first take the plank out of your eye, and then you will see clearly to remove the speck from your brother's eye." [147]

On enemies: "Love your enemies, do good to those who hate you, bless those who curse you, pray for those who mistreat you. If someone strikes you on one cheek, turn to him the other also." [148]

---

[145] (Luke, 14:12, NIV)
[146] (Luke, 6:37, NIV)
[147] (Luke, 6:41, NIV)
[148] (Luke, 6:27, NIV)

On Giving: "Give, and it will be given to you. A good measure, pressed down, shaken together and running over, will be poured into your lap. For with the measure you use, it will be measured to you." [149]

On forgiveness: "Father, forgive them, for they do not know what they are doing". [150]

On lawyers: "Woe to you experts in the law, because you have taken away the key to knowledge. You yourselves have not entered, and you have hindered those who were entering." [151]

The Republican Party was not proposing to go into the South and purchase bonded African Americans and make them independent, or in any other way give charity to bonded African Americans; it was not hesitant to judge others; it was not tolerant toward enemies; it was not seeking personal salvation; and its politics were not about personal forgiveness of sins. The Republican Party was about self-righteousness; about inciting conflict with enemies over matters about which they knew too little; about matters sanctified in tangled issues of law; about too many lawyers manipulating for political power; about political deception; about inventing threatening demons that did not exist; about deceitfully manipulating a naive population into a state of angry emotion to further political ambitions.

Lincoln Had Wanted to Proclaim that "A House Divided Cannot Stand" Two Years Earlier, in 1856

Two years earlier, in 1856, Lincoln's Illinois Republican supporters had strongly advised him against making such an aggressive and warmongering statement as "a house divided against itself cannot stand." Many years later Lyle Dickey would write a letter about his view on Lincoln's "a house divided itself cannot stand" speech. Dickey's letter would be written to Billy Herndon and dated December 8, 1866. In the letter Lyle Dickey would tell of his reaction to Lincoln's disclosure that he, [Lincoln,] wanted to include the "a-house-divided-against-itself-cannot-stand" argument in the speech he was about to give at the 1856 Republican State Convention at Bloomington. Lyle Dickey would write::

"After the meeting was over Mr. Lincoln and I returned to the Pike House, where we occupied the same room. Immediately on reaching the room I said to him, 'What in God's name could induce you to promulgate such an opinion?' He replied familiarly, 'Upon my soul, Dickey, I think it is true.' I reasoned to show it was not a correct opinion. He argued strenuously that the opinion was a sound

---

[149] (Luke, 6:38, NIV)
[150] (Luke, 23:34, NIV)
[151] (Luke, 11:52, NIV)

one. At length I said, 'Suppose you are right, that our [Federal] Government cannot last part [with bonded African Americans] and part [without], what good is to be accomplished by inculcating that opinion (or truth, if you please) in the minds of the people?' After some minutes reflection he rose and approached me, extended his right hand to take mine, and said, 'From respect for your judgment, Dickey, I'll promise you I won't teach the doctrine again during this campaign.'"

Two years later, in 1858, Lincoln had again solicited reactions from fellow Illinois Republican leaders the day before delivering his "house-divided-against-itself-cannot-stand" acceptance speech to the 1858 Republican State Convention. He had read a draft of his speech to Billy Herndon in their law office a few days earlier so they could jointly consider if the timing was politically wise. In his biography of Lincoln, Billy Herndon tells of the meeting the day before Lincoln was to deliver the 1858 address:

"Before delivering his speech he invited a dozen or so of his friends over to the library of the State House, where he read and submitted it to them. After the reading he asked each man for his opinion. Some condemned and not one endorsed it. One man, more forcible than elegant, characterized it as a 'damned fool utterance;' another said the doctrine was 'ahead of its time;' and still another contended that it would drive away a good many voters fresh from the Democrats ranks. Each man attacked it in his criticism. I was the last to respond. Although the doctrine announced was rather rank, yet it suited my views, and I said, 'Lincoln, deliver that speech as read and it will make you [Federal] President.' At the time I hardly realized the force of my prophecy. Having patiently listened to these various criticisms from his friends – all of which with a single exception were adverse – he rose from his chair, and after alluding to the careful study and intense thought he had given the question, he answered all their objections substantially as follows: 'Friends, this thing has been retarded long enough. The time has come when these sentiments should be uttered; and if it is decreed that I should go down because of this speech, then let me go down linked to the truth [as I allege it to be] – let me die in the advocacy of what [I allege to be] just and right.'

"The next day, the 17th, the speech was delivered just as we had heard it read. Up to this time Seward had held sway over [northern States Republicans] by his 'higher-law' sentiments, but the 'house-divided-against-itself' speech by Lincoln in my opinion drove the nail into Seward's political coffin." [152]

---

[152] Herndon's *Life of Lincoln*, page 325-326; *Lincoln's Herndon, a Biography*, by David Herbert Donald, page 118.

August 21, 1858, Ottawa — the First Douglas-Lincoln Debate

Our history now advances two months to August, 1858. Senator Stephen Douglas launched the first of seven debates with Abe Lincoln on August 21, 1858, in the mid-northern Illinois town of Ottawa. Between 10,000 and 20,000 attended. Opening the debate, Douglas continued with his attacking theme, alleging that, since 1854, Republican candidate Abe Lincoln and Democrat-turned-Republican Senator Lyman Trumbull had been conspiring to subvert both the Democratic Party and the remnant of the Whig Party in order to create "an Abolition Party, under the name and guise of a Republican Party." He threw many loaded questions at Lincoln, each aimed at proving this charge.

The most significant segment of Lincoln's speech at Ottawa concerned his attitudes toward the African race:

Lincoln and Douglas during their seven 1858 Debates.

". . . I have no purpose, directly or indirectly, to interfere with [African American bonding] in the States where it exists. I believe I have no lawful right to do so, and I have no inclination to do so. I have no purpose to introduce political and social equality between the [European] and [African][153] races. There is a physical difference between the two, which, in my judgment, will probably forever forbid their living together upon the footing of perfect equality; and inasmuch as it becomes a necessity that there must be a difference, I, as well as [Stephen] Douglas, am in favor of the race to which I belong having the superior position. I have never said anything to the contrary, but I hold that, notwithstanding all this, there is no reason in the world why the [African American] is not entitled to all the natural rights enumerated in the Declaration of Independence – the right to life, liberty, and the pursuit of happiness. I hold that he is as much entitled to these as the [European American]. I agree with

---

[153] Lincoln said "White" and "Black" races. In reality, African Americans were then a mixed-race people, ranging from one-eighth White to 100 percent Black, the average racial ancestry being about 25 percent White.

Douglas [that the African American] is not my equal in many respects – certainly not in color, perhaps not in moral or intellectual endowment. But in the right to eat the bread, without the leave of anybody else, which his own hand earns, he is my equal, and the equal of Douglas, and the equal of every living man."

Lincoln further said:

"Now I believe if we could [exclude bonded African Americans from all National Territories, African American bonding] would be in the course of ultimate extinction . . . The crisis would be past, and [African American bonding] might be let alone for a hundred years, if it should [be in effect] so long, in the States where it exists; yet it would be going out of existence in the way best for both the [African] and the [European] races."

One hundred years is a long time. That would preserve slavery until it would be finally terminated in 1958, twenty years after I was born!

I suspect Lincoln was alluding to gradual deportation, or at least, that he expected his audience to think that he was. He definitely did not want to scare his listeners into fearing Colored people with evidence of African ancestry might move into Illinois and become their neighbors.

Of his allegation that "a house divided against itself cannot stand," Lincoln submitted:

"I really was not thinking . . . that I was doing anything to bring about a war between the [Northern States] and the [Southern States]. I had no thought in the world that I was doing anything to bring about a political and social equality of the [African] and the [European] races."

This was a dodge. State Secession was the fear that would likely precipitate war. There would be no war to force emancipation of Southern slaves.

A bit later Lincoln complained:

Douglas "goes on and deduces, or draws out, from my speech this tendency of mine to set the States at war with one another, to make all the institutions uniform, and set the niggers and white people to marrying together."

Yet, Lincoln alleged:

". . . the course that Douglas is pursuing every day has bearing upon this question of making [the bonding of workers] national. . . . There is no danger that the people of Kentucky will shoulder their muskets, and, with a young nigger stuck to every bayonet, march into Illinois and force them upon us. **There is no danger of our going over there and making war upon them.** Then what is necessary for the nationalization of [the bonding of

179

workers]? It is simply the next Dred Scott decision. It is merely for the Supreme Court to decide that no State under the [Federal] Constitution can exclude [bonded African Americans]. . . . This being true, and this being the way, as I think, that [the bonding of workers] is to be made national, let us consider what Douglas is doing every day to that end."

Lincoln said, **"There is no danger of our going over there and making war on them."** To historians, that was a very important statement. As we sadly know — two and a half years later Republican President Lincoln would lead a military effort to "make war upon the South," which would last four years and result in one million unnecessary deaths.

Lincoln then alleged that Douglas was encouraging policies that would eventually lead to bonded African Americans living and working in the northern States.

But, overall, Douglas was effective with this line of heavy attack. Lincoln seemed overwhelmed by Douglas' incessant accusative tactic, and most observers believed Lincoln did not effectively counter. [154]

August 27, 1858, Freeport — the Second Douglas-Lincoln Debate

The second debate took place on August 27, 1858 in the far-north town of Freeport, before an audience of 15,000, which was heavily sympathetic toward preventing people of full or partial African descent from living in a new Territory or State. Opening the debate this time, Lincoln hurled four questions at Douglas that had been suggested by campaign advisers from Chicago. Douglas' answer to the second question received important newspaper coverage. Lincoln's second question:

"Can the people of a [National] Territory, in any lawful way, against the wish of any citizen of the United States, exclude [bonded African Americans] from its limits prior to the formation of a State Constitution?"

Overall, the Freeport debate would receive much heated newspaper coverage for many months. Douglas' answer to Lincoln's second question would be termed the "Freeport Doctrine." Douglas' answer:

"It matters not what way the [Federal] Supreme Court may hereafter decide as to the abstract question whether [bonded African Americans] may or may not go into a [National] Territory; under the [Federal] Constitution, the people have the lawful means to introduce [them] or exclude [them] as [the people] please,

---

[154] Text of debate at www.bartleby.com; *Lincoln*, by David Herbert Donald, pages 215-218; *Abraham Lincoln — His Speeches and Writings*, edited by Ray P. Basler, page 441-461; *The American Conscience, The Drama of the Lincoln-Douglas Debates*, by Saul Sigelschiffer, pages 173-202.

for the [alleged] reason that [African American bonding] cannot exist a day or an hour anywhere unless it is supported by local police regulations. Those police regulations can only be established by the local [Territory] Legislature, and if the people are opposed to [African American bonding] they will elect Representatives to that body who will, by unfriendly legislation, effectually prevent the introduction of it into their midst. If, on the contrary, they are for it, their legislation will favor [inclusion of bonded African Americans]."

September 15, 1858, Jonesboro — the Third Douglas-Lincoln Debate

The third debate between Douglas and Lincoln took place on September 15, 1858 in the small, rural, southern Illinois town of Jonesboro. It drew a small crowd of no more than 1,500, which was quite antagonistic toward Abolitionist rhetoric. Opening the debate, Stephen Douglas denounced Political Sectionalism and encouraged respect for State Rights. He ridiculed the practice of Illinois Republicans to present different policies in different sections of the State. A bit later in his speech, Douglas assured the audience that Lincoln's scare-tactic allegation, "a house divided against itself cannot stand," was nonsense so long as people respected State Rights:

"[Lincoln] says that [the States] must all [exclude bonded African Americans] or all [include bonded African Americans], that they must all be one thing or all be the other, or this [Federal] Government cannot last. Why can it not last, if we will execute the Government in the same spirit and upon the same principles upon which it was founded? Lincoln, by his proposition, says to the [southern States]: "If you desire to [continue to include bonded African Americans], you must not be satisfied with minding your own business, but you must invade Illinois and all the other northern States, establish [there laws permitting workers to be bonded], and make [such laws] universal;" and in the same language he says to the [northern States]: "You must not be content with regulating your own affairs, and minding your own business, but if you desire to maintain your [personal independence], you must invade the southern States [and make all the bonded African Americans independent]. [One of these events must happen] to have the States all one thing or all the other. I say that this is the inevitable and irresistible result of Lincoln's argument, inviting a warfare between the [northern States] and the [southern States], to be carried on with ruthless vengeance, until the one section or the other shall be driven to the wall, and become the victim of the rapacity of the other. What good would follow such a system of warfare? Suppose the [northern States] should succeed in conquering the [southern States], how much would [the northern States] be the gainer? Or suppose the [southern States] should conquer the [northern States], could the [Federation] be preserved in that way? Is this sectional warfare to be waged between the northern States and the southern States until they all shall become uniform in their local and domestic institutions merely because Lincoln says that "a house divided against itself cannot stand," and pretends that this scriptural quotation, this language of our Lord and Master, is applicable to the American [Federation] and the [Federal] Constitution? [George] Washington and his compeers, in the Convention that framed the [Federal] Constitution, made this [Federation of States, which at the time was] divided into [one state that prohibited African American bonding] and [twelve states that allowed it]. It was composed then of 13 sovereign and independent States, each having sovereign authority over its local and domestic institutions, and all bound together by the Federal Constitution. Lincoln likens that bond of the Federal Constitution . . . to a house divided against itself, and says that it is contrary to the law of God, and cannot stand. When did he learn, and by what authority does he proclaim, that this [fabric of State and Federal governments] is contrary to the law of God and cannot stand? It has stood thus divided into [States that include bonded African Americans and States that do not] from its organization up to this day. During that period we have increased from 4,000,000 to 30,000,000 people; we have extended our territory from the Mississippi to the Pacific Ocean; we have acquired the Florida's and Texas, and other territory sufficient to double our geographical extent; we have increased in population, in wealth, and in power beyond any example on earth; we have risen from a weak and feeble power to become the terror and admiration of the civilized world; and all this has been done under a [Federal] Constitution which Mr. Lincoln, in substance, says is in violation of the law of God, [all while divided, in that some States include bonded African Americans and some do not], which Mr. Lincoln thinks, because of such division, cannot stand."

September 18, 1858, Charleston — the Fourth Douglas-Lincoln Debate

The fourth debate took place on September 18 at Charleston, in Coles County, the county where Abe Lincoln's father had lived and where his stepmother, Sarah Bush Johnston Lincoln, and some Hanks cousins still lived. Here, Lincoln opened the debate before a crowd of 12,000, meeting the race issue head-on.

But, before viewing segments of the debate language, let us explore any attendance by Abe's stepmother, Sarah Bush Johnston Lincoln, and cousins Dennis Friend Hanks and others. One would think such close relatives would have arranged to be present at the debate grounds in nearby Charleston. But, I've found no record of attendance by his stepmother or any Hanks relatives. In fact, I suspect that, with many newly-arrived newspaper reporters present in the County, Abe was careful to sweep into Charleston, debate and sweep away. As his public prominence increased, more than ever, he wanted to avoid contact with relatives to minimize the chance that a reporter or Democrat activist might realize that, in Lincoln's parentage, there was an amazing story to be investigated.

Lincoln began (you will notice that I am substituting in square brackets substitute words for the white race, negro race and other terms that today seem inappropriate):

"I will say then that am not, nor ever have been, in favor of bringing about in any way the social and political equality of the [European] and [African] races, that I am not, nor ever have been, in favor of making voters or jurors of [African Americans], nor of qualifying them to hold office, nor to intermarry with [European Americans]; and I will say in addition to this that there is a physical difference between the [European] and [African] races which I believe will forever forbid the two races living together on terms of social and political equality. And

Lawyer and Illinois Republican Party leader Abraham Lincoln speaking at one of the seven debates while Democrat Senator Stephen Douglas awaits his turn to counter Lincoln's argument.

inasmuch as they cannot so live, while they do remain together there must be the position of superior and inferior, and I, as much as any other [European American] man, am in favor of having the superior position assigned to the [European] race.

"I say upon this occasion I do not perceive that because the [European race] is to have the superior position the [African race] should be denied everything. I do not understand that, because I do not want [an African American] woman for [my bonded worker], I must necessarily want her for a wife. My understanding is that I can just let her alone. . . .

"I will, to the very last, stand by the law of this State, which forbids the marrying of [European Americans] and [African Americans]. I will add one further word, which is this: that I do not understand that there is any place where an alteration of the social and political relations of the [African American] and the [European American] can be made, except in the State Legislature."

Senator Stephen Douglas closed his speech by accusing lawyer Lincoln of favoring equal political rights for African Americans:

"Lincoln maintains [in the northern counties of our State] that the Declaration of Independence asserts that the [African American] is equal to the [European American], and that under Divine law; and if he believes so, it [would be] rational for him to advocate [African American] citizenship, which, when allowed, puts the [African American] on an equality under the law.

"I will say to you in all frankness, gentlemen, that in my opinion [an African American] is not a citizen [of all the States], cannot be, and ought not to be, under the [Federal Constitution]. . . . I say that this government was established on the [European American] basis. It was made by [European American] men, for the benefit of [European American] men and their posterity forever, and never should be administered by any except [European American] men. I declare that [an African American man] ought not to be a citizen, whether his parents were imported into this country as [bonded workers] or not, or whether or not he was born here. It does not depend upon the place [his] parents were born, or whether they were [bonded] or not, but upon the fact that he is [of African descent], belonging to a race incapable of self-government, and for that reason ought not to be on an equality with [European American] men."

In his rebuttal, Lincoln presented his "a-house-divided-against-itself-cannot-stand" fear-tactic allegation:

"There is no way of putting an end to the [agitation concerning bonded African Americans] but to . . . keep it out of our new Territories – to restrict it forever to the old States where it now exists. Then the public mind will rest in the belief that it is in the course of ultimate extinction. That is one way of putting an end to the slavery agitation.

"The other way is for us to surrender, and let [Stephen] Douglas and his friends have their way and plant [bonded workers] over all the States; cease speaking of it as in any way a wrong; regard [African American bonding] as one of the common matters of property, and speak of [people of African descent] as we do our horses and cattle. But while [the Inclusion Movement] [155] drives on in its state of progress as it is now driving, and as it has driven for the last 5 years, I have ventured the opinion, and I say to-day, that we will have no end to the

---

[155] The "Inclusion Movement" is the opposite of the "Exclusion Movement," which strives to Exclude bonded African Americans from all Territories and State outside of the South.

[agitation concerning bonded African Americans] until it takes one turn or the other. I do not mean that when it takes a turn toward ultimate extinction it will be in a day, nor in a year, nor in two years. I do not suppose that in the most peaceful way ultimate extinction would occur in less than 100 years at least; but that it will occur in the best way for both races, in God's own good time, I have no doubt." [156]

You may share with me the suspicion that Lincoln's intent was that African Americans would become "extinct" — that they would become victims of the "ultimate extinction." You will remember that the Illinois State Legislature had enacted the Black Code of 1853, which only five years earlier, prohibited independent African Americans from moving into the State. The Black Hawk War had excluded the last band of Native Americans from growing corn at the Illinois border. With voters so recently endorsing as much racial purity as practical throughout Illinois, Lincoln's remarks were obviously calculated to reassure Illinois voters that, should bonded African Americans be made independent in the southern States, that did not mean that newly independent and newly mobile African Americans would be moving into Illinois. By implication, all of Lincoln's speeches were designed to assured his audience that racial purity in Illinois and making independent bonded African Americans in the southern States would not be conflicting political agendas. It must have sounded reassuring.

But in fact, examination of the history of Lincoln's limited inquiry into that question reveals that he had no earthly idea of what to do with 4,000,000 newly independent African Americans, should they become independent and strive to make their own living. Where would they go? Would they work cotton fields on southern States farms for wages or would they tend textile machines in northern States cotton mills? What would they do for a living? Would their competition for available jobs be a peaceful process? Lincoln was a supporter of much of the Abolition Movement, but like essentially all Abolition Activists, he had no plan for helping African Americans prosper as independent and responsible citizens. Unlike the most fervent Abolitionists, he did not want to help bonded African Americans become emancipated and, remaining in America, live successful lives for themselves and their families as independent people. Biographer David Donald would explain why: "[Lincoln] continued to think of [deportation to Africa or South America] as the best solution to the [Federation's] race problem."

---

[156] Numbers in this segment of Lincoln's argument are significant. Five years previously, Illinois passed the Black Code of 1853. Somehow, Lincoln perceived that people of African ancestry would become "extinct" in America in 100 years or later. We must assume he believed that, through deportation, those people would become extinct in the United States.

So, Lincoln told the audience at the Charleston debate that political agitation concerning bonded African Americans would only be resolved one of two ways: either by bonded African Americans becoming extinct, or by moving a large portion of the bonded African American population into the northern States where they would remain enslaved. Of course, we readers realize that both suggested outcomes were nonsense. Lincoln's was a typical trained-lawyer argument — to pretend that only two solutions to a problem existed, encouraging the jury to not consider a third or fourth solution. [157]

While Lincoln Debated Douglas, Herndon Wrote Letters Advocating Abolitionism

While Stephen Douglas debated Abe Lincoln, Billy Herndon wrote many letters, and he spoke in favor of Republican candidates and his law partner throughout central Illinois. Although a fervent Abolitionist within his heart, Herndon coyly assured these audiences — who were mostly made up of old Whigs — that, regarding bonded African Americans, Lincoln shared the attitudes espoused earlier by George Washington and Henry Clay (Washington had made his bonded African Americans independent and Clay had been a key founder of the American Colonization Society). Herndon argued that Douglas was the one in conflict with the teachings of Clay. By the way, Henry Clay was a prominent founder of the American Colonization Society, which advocated deportation of people of over one-eight African ancestry to Liberia, a country in West Africa, immediately after making them independent. At the same time, Billy assisted Lincoln much like a private secretary, collecting newspaper clippings, writing letters, responding to telegrams and the like.

When it came to manipulations designed to keep Isaac Cook's Illinois National Democrats (a third party movement) strong enough to hurt Douglas, Herndon was there in the political trenches doing Lincoln's bidding. Herndon's father, Archer, and brother, Elliott, were among the leaders of the National Democrats in Illinois, and, as Billy related to Theodore Parker in a June letter, "they make 'no bones' in telling me what they are going to do." [158]

---

[157] Text of debate at www.bartleby.com; *Lincoln*, by David Herbert Donald, pages 220-221; The American Conscience, *The Drama of the Lincoln-Douglas Debates*, edited by Saul Sigelschiffer pages 278-295.

[158] *Lincoln's Herndon*, by David Herbert Donald, page 123.

September 21, 1858, Galesburg — the Fifth Douglas-Lincoln Debate

The fifth debate was held on September 20, 1858 at Galesburg in the northwestern part of the State. Populated by 5,500 people, primarily of Swedish descent, Galesburg was the home of Knox College, founded in 1836 by George Gale of New York State, a fervent Abolitionist and a Presbyterian minister, and presided over during 1858 by college president Jonathan Blanchard, also a leading Abolition activist.

Stephen Douglas opened the debate. In part he said:

"Now, let me ask you whether the [Federation] has any interest in sustaining this organization, known as the Republican Party. . . . The leaders of that Party hope that they will be able to unite the northern States in one great sectional party; and [since the northern States are] the strongest section, they will thus be enabled to out-vote, conquer, govern, and control the [southern States and their people]." . . .

"Then, my friends I say to you that there is but one path of peace in the [Federation], and that is to administer this [Federal] Government as our fathers made it, divided into [States that exclude bonded African Americans] and [States that include them], allowing each State to decide for itself whether it wants [to include bonded African Americans] or not. If Illinois will settle [for herself the controversy concerning bonded African Americans], and mind her own business and let her neighbors alone, we will be at peace with Kentucky and every other southern State. If every other State in the [Federation] will do the same, there will be peace between the [northern States] and the [southern States], and in the whole [Federation]."

Abe Lincoln then rose to speak in response to Douglas' opening address. Lincoln employed exaggeration, such as:

"But [Douglas] will have it that if we do not confess that there is a sort of inequality between the [European] and [African] races, which justifies us in making them [bonded workers], we must then insist that there is a degree of equality that requires us in making them our wives."

Of course that was nonsense! No one was really debating between two fixed extremes: "make them our bonded workers," or "make them our wives."

Lincoln spent considerable time insisting that African American bonding was wrong, although the only redress he advocated was Exclusionism, and that was no redress at all, for fencing them in the South in no way helped bonded African Americans.

Lincoln again applied his scare-mongering tactic, symbolized by his allegation that "a house divided against itself cannot stand." And, without any reasonable proof, he continued to accuse Douglas of participating in a conspiracy to make African American bonding lawful in the northern States. Surely you agree that it is amazing that such a far-fetched allegation could be taken seriously by a significant fraction of northern States voters. Yet, Lincoln pressed this allegation with consistent determination. At Galesburg he said:

> "[Douglas] is in every possible way preparing the public mind, by his vast influence, for making [African American bonding] perpetual and national." [159]

October 11, 1858 — Jefferson Davis and Family Spend the Summer in the Northeast and He Delivers an Important Speech in Boston

Senator Jefferson Davis of Mississippi was considered the leading Democrat in the Southern States, just as Senator Stephen Douglas was considered the leading Democrat in the Northern States.

Democrat Senator Jefferson Davis of Mississippi, considered the leader of Democrats across the South.

About the end of September, Jeff and Varina Davis, concluded their family summer vacation at Portland, Maine and headed south, stopping in Boston. When a Committee of Boston Democrats asked Senator Davis to speak in famed Faneuil Hall, he was surprised, but he gladly accepted the opportunity to explain the Southern view in Massachusetts. Aiming to arouse feelings of patriotism, Davis planned to avoid criticizing the people of Massachusetts for having threatened to secede when Louisiana was purchased and again when the Nation of Texas merged into the Federation; nor would he talk about the State secession movements that had been prevalent in Massachusetts in 1803-1804 and again in 1815. Biographer Hudson Strode would describe this moving night at Boston's historic Faneuil Hall:

[159] The American Conscience, *The Drama of the Lincoln-Douglas Debates*, edited by Saul Sigelschiffer.

On October 11, 1858, in Faneuil Hall every seat was taken and many stood in the isles. All were eager to hear the message from Senator Davis, the Mississippi farmer and, many thought, the South's most important political leader. Prominent men with distinguished family names occupied the stage as Boston's Caleb Cushing presented Senator Davis glowingly as "a citizen of the southern States, eloquent among the eloquent in debate, wise among the wise in council, and brave among the bravest in the battlefield," referring to Davis' military leadership in the War Against Mexico. Having recently served as President Franklin Pierce's Attorney General, Cushing praised "the surpassing wisdom of Jefferson Davis in the administration of the Federal Government."

As Jefferson Davis took the stand, reported the Boston *Morning Post* of October 12, 1858, "a scene of enthusiasm was presented which defies description. Those who held seats in the galleries rose *en masse*, and joined with those standing on the lower floor in extending a cordial, very cordial, greeting to the honored guest from Mississippi.'"

Jeff Davis then rose to deliver perhaps the most moving speech of his life. He began:

"Countrymen, Brethren, Democrats: Most happy am I to meet you, and to have received here renewed assurance — of that which I have long believed — that the pulsation of the Democratic heart is the same in every parallel of latitude, on every meridian of longitude, throughout these United States."

He spoke of passed days in the Cabinet of President Franklin Peirce:

"It was my fortune lately to serve under a President drawn from the neighboring State of New Hampshire, and I know that he spoke the language of his heart, for I learned it in 4 years of intimate relations with him, when he said he knew 'no North, no South, no East, no West, but sacred maintenance of the common bond and true devotion to the common brotherhood'." [160]

Davis spoke of George Washington and the fight to drive British troops from Boston:

"On the other side [of town] rise the heights of Dorchester where once stood the encampment of the Virginian, the man who came here, and did not ask, 'Is this a town of Virginia?' but 'Is this a town of my brethren?'"

Speaking of the early Massachusetts tradition of State rights, Davis advised Bostonians to go to their historical collections and there find local evidence of "that sacred creed of State rights . . . for "in an early period of our country, you

---

[160] Jefferson Davis had served as Secretary of War under President Franklin Pierce from 1853 to 1857.

find Massachusetts leading the movements, prominent of all the States, in the assertion of that doctrine which has been recently so much belied. . . . You did not surrender your sovereignty" to the British Government. . . . And I have [recently] found that the Democrats [in Maine] asserted the same broad constitutional principle [of States Rights] for which we have been contending, by which we are willing to live, for which we are willing to die!"

Turning his attention to Exclusion and Abolition Agitators, Davis said:

"Why then do you [in Massachusetts] have agitators? With Pharisaical pretension it is sometimes said it is a moral obligation to agitate, and I suppose they are going through a sort of vicarious repentance for other men's sins. With all due allowance for their zeal, we ask, how do they decide that [ownership of bonded African Americans] is a sin? By what standard do they measure it? Not the [Federal] Constitution; [it] recognizes the property in [bonded African Americans] in many forms, and imposes obligations in connection with that recognition. Not the Bible; that justifies it. Not for the good of society; for, if [people prone to agitate] go where [bonded African Americans live], they find that society recognizes it as good. What, then, is [the agitator's] standard? [Is it for] the good of mankind? Is that seen in the diminished resources of the [Federation]? Is that seen in the diminished comfort of the world? Or is not the reverse exhibited? Is there, in the cause of Christianity, a motive for the prohibition of the system which is the only agency through which Christianity has reached that inferior race, the only means by which [people of African descent] have been civilized and elevated? Or is [the agitator's] piety manifested in denunciation of their brethren, who are deterred from answering their denunciation only by the contempt which they feel for a mere brawler, who intends to end his brawling only in empty words? What my friends, must be the consequences? Good or evil? [These agitators] have been evil, and evil they must be only, to the end. Not one particle of good has been done to any man, of any [race or mix of races], by this agitation. It has been insidiously working the purpose of sedition, for the destruction of [the Federation of States] on which our hopes of future greatness depend."

Davis spoke of the sanctity of State sovereignty and the pledge of honor – not the threat of military invasion – that presses a State Government to fulfill its obligations toward the Federal Government:

"I have said that this State sovereignty – this community independence – has never been surrendered, and that there is no power in the Federal Government to [militarily] coerce a State. Will any one ask me, then, how a State is to be held to the fulfillment of its obligations? My answer is, by its honor. . . . The question of a State coercion was raised in the Convention which framed the [Federal]

190

Constitution, and, after discussion, the proposition to give power to the [Federal Government] to enforce, against any State, obedience to the laws was rejected. It is upon the ground that a State cannot be coerced that observance of the compact is a sacred obligation."

Jefferson Davis, Southern Democratic leader and Senator representing Mississippi, then turned his attention to Exclusionism:

"There is another and graver question; it is in relation to the prohibition by [the Federal Government] of [people moving into the National Territories with bonded African Americans]. What power does [the Federal Government] possess in this connection? Has it the right to say what shall be property anywhere? If it has, from what clause of the Constitution does it derive that power? Have other States the power to prescribe the condition upon which a citizen of another State shall enter upon and enjoy [our National Territories] — common property of all? Clearly not! Shall the [settlers] who first go into [a National] Territory deprive any citizen of these United States of those rights, which belong to him as an equal owner of the soil? Certainly not! Sovereign jurisdiction can only pass to the [settlers] when the States, the owners of [every National Territory], shall recognize [those settlers have gained the] right to become an equal member of the [Federation of States]. Until then, the [Federal Constitution] and the laws of the [Federal Government] must be the rule governing within the limits of [each] Territory. The [Federal Constitution] recognizes all property, and gives equal privileges to every citizen of the States; and it would be a violation of its fundamental principles to attempt any discrimination. There is nothing of truth or justice with which to sustain this [Exclusionism] agitation, or [justification] for it, unless it be that it is a good bridge over which [a politician can] pass into [a lucrative government] office; a little stock of trade in politics built up to aid men who are missionaries staying at home; reformers of things which they do not go [off] to learn [about]; preachers without a congregation; [supervisors] without laborers and without wages; war-horses who sniff the battle afar off and cry: 'Aha! Aha! I am afar off'."

Davis took a few moments to explain why most African Americans had lived in the southern States since the birth of our Federation:

"The variety of product, of soil and of climate has been multiplied, both by the expansion of our [Federation] and by the introduction of new tropical products not cultivated in [colonial times]; so that every motive to [join the States together under the Federal Government] — which your fathers had — in a diversity which should give prosperity to [these United States], exists in a higher degree today than when the [Federal Government] was formed, and this diversity is fundamental to the prosperity of the people of the several sections of

191

the country. . . . Originally, [diversity] sprang in no small degree from natural causes. Massachusetts became a manufacturing and commercial State because of her fine harbors — because of her water-power, making its last leap into the sea, so that the ship of commerce brought the staple to the manufacturing power. This made you a commercial and a manufacturing people. In the southern States, great plains interpose between the last leaps of the streams and the sea. Those plains were cultivated in staple crops, and the sea brought their products to your streams to be manufactured. This was the beginning of the differences. Then, your longer and more severe winters [and] your soil [being] not so favorable for agriculture, in a degree kept you a manufacturing and a commercial people. Even after the [initial] cause had passed away — after railroads had been built — after the steam engine had become a motive power for a large part of manufacturing machinery, the natural causes, from which your people obtained a manufacturing ascendancy and ours became chiefly agriculturists, continued to act in a considerable measure to preserve that relation. Your interest is to remain a manufacturing, and ours to remain an agricultural people. Your prosperity, then, is to receive our staple and to manufacture it, and ours to sell it to you and buy the manufactured goods. This is an interweaving of interests, which makes us all the richer and happier."

Davis then pleaded for support for the cause of State rights:

"[If Republicans gain control of the Federal House and Senate and] "attempt to violate the rights of the States; if they should attempt to infringe upon our equality in the [Federation of States] — I believe that even in Massachusetts, though it has not had a [Democrat] in the [Federal House] for many a day, [the Massachusetts Democratic Party], in whose breast beats the spirit of the [past war where we defended our independence], can and will whip the black Republicans. I trust we shall never be [purified], as it were, by fire; but that the peaceful, progressive revolution of the ballot box will answer all the glorious purposes of the [Federal] Constitution and the [Federation of States].

"I have often, elsewhere than in the State of which I am a citizen, spoken in favor of [the Democratic Party], which alone is national, in which alone lies the hope of preserving the [Federal] Constitution and the perpetuation of the [Federal] Government and of the blessings which it was ordained and established to secure."

Then Davis closed, explaining that in Maine and Massachusetts he had found:

"A large mass of as true Democrats as are to be found in any portion of the [Federation]. . . . Their purposes, their construction of the [Federal] Constitution, their hopes for the future, their respect for the past, is the same as that which exists among my beloved brethren in Mississippi.

"[In future days] I shall turn back to my observations here, in this consecrated hall, where men so early devoted themselves to liberty and community independence; and I shall endeavor to impress upon others, who know you only as you are represented in the [Federal House and Senate], how true and how many are the hearts that beat for constitutional liberty, and faithfully respect every clause and guarantee which the [Federal] Constitution contains for any and every portion of [our Federation of States]."

From most accounts, Davis completely captivated his audience at Faneuil Hall. His friends say he was at his absolute best as an orator that night.

Leaving Massachusetts, the Davis family traveled to New York City where, at the Palace Garden, Senator Davis warned New Yorkers of the danger of aggressive sectional politics, the danger of State Secession and a possible war between the states:

"If one section should gain such predominance as would enable it, by modifying the [Federal] Constitution and usurping new power, to legislate for the other, the exercise of that power would throw us back into the condition of the Colonies. And, if in the veins of the sons flows the blood of their sires, they would not fail to redeem themselves from tyranny, even should they be driven to resort to revolution."

Jeff's New York speech concluded his 4-month vacation-and-good-will tour of Maine, Massachusetts and neighboring States. The Davis family would be home in Mississippi on November 16. [161]

October, 13, 1858, Quincy — the Sixth Douglas-Lincoln Debate

The sixth debate between Douglas and Lincoln was held on October 13 at Quincy, located directly west of Springfield, in central Illinois on a bluff overlooking the Mississippi River. Missouri was on the other side. About 12,000 people gathered to hear the debate.

In this debate, Lincoln continued to emphasize that African American bonding was "wrong," while simultaneously assuring everyone that he had no intentions of helping bonded African Americans become independent. His rhetoric was full of awkward and long sentence construction, designed to say little that was meaningful, except: African American bonding is wrong, Exclusionism is right and essential; and we will see Douglas' policies lead to the existence of bonded workers throughout the

---

[161] *Jefferson Davis, American Patriot, 1808-1861*, pages 310-312; *The Rise and Fall of the Confederate Government*, by Jefferson Davis, pages 478-489; *Jefferson Davis, Ex-President of the Confederate States of America, a Memoir by his Wife, Varina Davis*, pages 608-641.

northern States, or we will see African American bonding become extinct (perhaps with deportation) within 100 years.

At one point, Douglas accused Lincoln of leading a crusade that had no helpful purpose:

"Mr. Lincoln thinks that it is his duty to preach a crusade in the [northern] States, against [African American bonding], because it is a crime, as he believes, and ought to be extinguished; and because the people of the [southern] States will never abolish it. How is [Lincoln] going to abolish it?"

October 15, 1858, Alton — the Final Douglas-Lincoln Debate

Finally, the pair of debaters traveled by steamboat down to Alton for the final debate. Alton was in the southern part of central Illinois, on the Mississippi River, about 25 miles north of St. Louis, Missouri. About 5,000 people gathered on October 15 to hear the debaters. Looking tired and losing his voice, Stephen Douglas opened on this final day. Midway during his delivery, he again criticized Lincoln for refusing to speak of Texas:

"The contract we entered into with [the Nation of Texas] when she entered the [Federation of States] obliges us to allow 4 [additional] States to be formed out of the [original] State, and admitted with [bonded African Americans included or excluded], as the respective inhabitants of each may determine. I have asked Mr. Lincoln three times in our joint discussion whether he would vote to redeem that pledge, and he has never yet answered. He is as silent as a grave on the subject." [162]

Toward the end of his remarks, Lincoln spoke of war and peace and the necessity to exclude African Americans from the National Territories:

"Now, irrespective of the moral aspect of this question as to whether there is a right or wrong in [the existence of bonded African Americans within the Federation], I am still in favor of our new [National] Territories being in such a condition that [European American] men may find a home — may find some spot where they can better their condition; where they can settle upon new soil and better their condition in life. I am in favor of this, not merely (I must say it here as I have elsewhere) for our own people who are born amongst us, but as an outlet for [people of the European race] everywhere, the world over — in which Hans, and Baptiste, and Patrick, and all other men [of that race] from all the world, may find new homes and better their conditions in life."

---

[162] Honoring the Federal Government's pledge to divide the newly admitted State of Texas into five States when population growth became sufficient was never honored by Lincoln or any President that followed him in office.

194

During his closing minutes Lincoln spoke of Henry Clay, a key founder of the American Colonization (Deportation) Society, and about "ultimate extinction:"

"Although Henry Clay could say he wished every [bonded African American] in the United States was in [Africa], the country of his ancestors, I am denounced by those pretending to respect Clay for uttering a wish that [African American bonding] might sometime, in some peaceful way, come to an end.

"Whenever the issue can be distinctly made, and all extraneous matter thrown out so that men can fairly see the difference between [Democrats and Republicans], this controversy [concerning African Americans] will soon be settled, and it will be done peaceable too. There will be no war, no violence."

Douglas closed the debate series with a final 30 minutes of oratory. In part he said:

"I assert that this [Federal] Government can exist as [the founders] made it, divided into [States with bonded African Americans and States without, as long as] any one State chooses to retain [them]. [Lincoln] says that he looks forward to a time when [African American bonding] shall be abolished everywhere. I

An 1848 photo of Whig Senator Henry Clay of Kentucky, whose last Senate term expired in 1852. Clay was a friend and neighbor of Mary Todd Lincoln's family in Kentucky. He founded the American Colonization Society, which encouraged the deportation of African Americans to Liberia in West Africa. Also, he was a leader in founding the Whig Party.

look forward to a time when each State shall be allowed to do as it pleases. If [a State] chooses to keep [African Americans bonded for as long as it wishes], it is not my business, but its own; if [a State] chooses to [make them independent], it is its own business – not mine. I care more for the great principle of self-government, the right of people to rule, than I do for all the [Africans] in Christendom. I would not endanger the perpetuity of the [Federation of States], I would not blot out the great inalienable rights of [European American] men, for all the [Africans] that ever existed. Hence, I say, let us maintain this [Federal] Government on the principles that our [founding] fathers made it, recognizing the right of each State to keep [African American bonding] as long as its [voters] determine, or to abolish it when they please." [163]

An Analysis of the Seven Debates

So, even in this last debate, Abe Lincoln continued to refuse to clearly disclose what he wished to happen to bonded African Americans. What did he mean by "ultimate extinction?" Would they be made independent and live only in the South? Would they be made independent and be immediately deported? What was to become of independent African Americans? Would they prosper? Would they be allowed to take up residence in Illinois, a prospect long prohibited by the Illinois Black Code of 1853?

Stephen Douglas did not press for an answer to that all-important question — regarding continuing or rescinding the 1853 Illinois racial prohibition — for he must not have had an answer for it himself.

Fundamentally, the debate was over electing an Illinois senator to serve the next six years. Douglas was encouraging listeners to vote for Democrats in their respective legislative districts so his party would be in the majority in the next Illinois legislature and return him to the United States Senate. Lincoln was encouraging the election of Republicans, presuming that, if his party attained the majority in the next legislature, he would likely be their choice to succeed Douglas in the Senate.

The Douglas-Lincoln debates were extensively and passionately reported in great detail by northern States newspapers, near and far. And the six debates were important political events because Senator Stephen Douglas was recognized as the leader of the Democrat Party all across the Northern States and almost certainly the Democrat that the Republicans would be facing in two years, in 1860, when their candidate, whoever he might be, would be seeking the Presidency of the United States. Yes, in 1860, Douglas would surely be the man to beat. [164]

The 1858 debaters could have argued other serious issues of great importance to a [Federation] that was still emerging from the [Financial] panic of 1857. Important issues before the men of Illinois included: changes to the regulation of banks; should the tax rate on imports be increased; should immigration be restricted moderately; expanding the availability of homesteads for farmers; improving the living conditions for Illinois factory workers, and so forth.

---

[163] The American Conscience, *The Drama of the Lincoln-Douglas Debates*, edited by Saul Sigelschiffer.
[164] *Bloodstains*, Volume 2, by Howard Ray White, pages 342-358, *The American Conscience, The Drama of the Lincoln-Douglas Debates*, by Saul Sigelschiffer, *Lincoln*, by David Donald, pages 215-226, *Jefferson Davis, American Patriot, 1808-1861*, pages 308-312, *Stephen A. Douglas*, by Robert Johannsen, pages 672-676.

Yes, these should have been issues of great interest to Illinois voters concerning their preference for a Federal Senator. Yet their pliable minds were readily diverted away from at-home, practical, governmental problems to the abstract, far-away issue of what to do about those bonded African Americans who lived far away in the Southern States and how to keep them out of the National Territories and all future States.

Since the Illinois Black Code of 1853 prohibited people of color from moving into that State to live, those listening to the debates should have felt assured that African Americans would not become their neighbors. Yet, those listeners seemed drawn to Lincoln's fantastic scare tactic concerning an alleged threat of bonded African Americans coming into the northern States to live and work, and even more far-fetched, that they, themselves might someday be enslaved as well.

Let us reflect on Abe Lincoln's great fear that political opponents might discover that he was born a bastard, fathered by Abraham Enloe of western North Carolina. In the excitement of the debates he had forged ahead with extreme arguments, scooting quickly into and out of Coles County to avoid contact with Sarah Bush Johnston Lincoln and the Hanks. No bastard allegations had surfaced. Now the debates were over. Lincoln had received immense publicity all across the Northern States. His true father had remained a hidden secret. Abe surely breathed a sigh of relief.

Chapter 27: Kansas Territory and the Cooper Union Speech in New York City

In December, 1859 Abraham Lincoln Visited Kansas Territory

In early December, 1859, while Abolitionist terrorist John Brown was scheduled to be hanged for murders in Harpers Ferry, Abe Lincoln was out in the northeastern section of Kansas Territory delivering campaign speeches. His kinsman, Mark Delahay of Leavenworth, was among the organizers of the political visit. Lincoln spoke in Elwood on December 1. On the next day, while Brown was being hanged in Virginia, Lincoln spoke at Troy, Doniphan and Atchison. The third day he spoke in Leavenworth. According to D. W. Wilder, Lincoln's speeches in northeastern Kansas Territory closely matched the speech he would later deliver in New York City at the Great Hall in the Cooper Union for the Advancement of Science and Art. His insistence on excluding bonded African Americans from all National Territory and all future States was undoubtedly cheered by the Exclusionist crowds that gathered to hear the Republican politician from Illinois. Lincoln probably believed a short speaking tour among victorious Kansas Exclusionists would enhance his credentials for the Republican nomination for Federal President, a goal he was considered to have a remote, but possible chance of achieving. Perhaps he imagined his brief trip to Kansas Territory was a trip to the battlefield to review Terrorist gangs and to press the flesh with front-line propagandists. Speaking at Elwood he mentioned, John Brown, the leader of the terrorist gang that the people of Kansas Territory had personally experienced. Republicans felt comfortable in denouncing the aim of inciting an armed revolt against slave owners by African Americans, while at the same time praising the intensity of John Brown's hatred of African American bonding and his courage at inflicting Terrorism. Lincoln also used Brown's execution to illustrate the Republican Party's plan to deal with any Southern State that might dare secede. Of Lincoln's allegation that State Secession resembled Terrorism, a newspaperman for the Leavenworth *Register* wrote, "If [the Republican Party elects] a [Federal] President, and therefore you undertake to [have your State secede], it will be our duty [as Republicans] to deal with you as John Brown has been dealt with [by the Virginia Government]." [165]

February 27, 1860, Abraham Lincoln Delivers a Major Address at the Cooper Institute in New York City

By the winter of 1859-1860, Republican leaders in the Northern States began in earnest their maneuvers toward selection of a candidate for President. Lincoln

---

[165] *Bleeding Kansas*, by Alice Nichols, pages 247-248; *Abraham Lincoln, the Prairie Years and the War Years*, by Carl Sandburg, pages, 159-160; *Lincoln*, by David Herbert Donald, page 239.

was being given significant consideration based on, 1) his widely-reported 1858 debates against the presumed Democrat nominee, 2) his heritage as being honorably born in the South (presumed to have been Kentucky), 3) the absence of a political record at the Federal level that could be challenged, and 4) a tendency to adhere to the same "not a political leader" selection strategy that had led to John Fremont's nomination in 1856. Of course, there were several other candidates, many with important Federal Government experience at Washington City. Perhaps it was advantageous that, like Fremont, Lincoln had no significant experience in the Federal Government, nor as governor of a State. Those two years in Congress and long-ago eight years in the Illinois Legislature were mere peanuts. Fundamentally, he was a lawyer and a politician, just a party leader. So, there was growing support in the northern States for an Abe-Lincoln-for-President movement. This pleased Lincoln. But he had to make every secret effort to hide from Democrat political investigators the true name of his biological father, Abraham Enloe of North Carolina.

To get ahead of the story, Abraham Lincoln was quick to supply his version of his biographical information to the Chester County *Times*, a Pennsylvania newspaper. Based on this account, as supplied by aspiring candidate Lincoln, this Pennsylvania newspaper published a substantial biographical sketch. And, this is important: many newspapers reprinted the biographical sketch, so it was widely read.

But the big break for Lincoln was the invitation he had received in October 1859 to lecture at Henry Ward Beecher's Plymouth Church in Brooklyn, New York, in February, 1860 (the event would be moved to the Great Hall at the Cooper Union for the Advancement of Science and Art). This would be Lincoln's big opportunity to meet face to face with the leading Exclusionists and Abolitionists of the northeastern States on their own turf.

You will recall that his law partner, Billy Herndon, had paved the way in early 1858, during his pilgrimage to New York and Massachusetts two years previously.

Lincoln took the Brooklyn invitation very seriously and began a major effort to study the voting patterns of the men who signed the Federal Constitution and the history of Federal Government legislation concerning the original Northwest Territory, Tennessee, Alabama, Mississippi, the Louisiana Purchase lands and the 36 degrees and 30 minutes 1950 slavery prohibition boundary. He wanted to list legal precedents where the Federal Government had stipulated exclusion of bonded African Americans in past western lands. Although Abe Lincoln had held no elected office since his one-term stint in the Federal Congress 12 years previously, it was purely on the strength of his political activism and his contesting spirit against the Republican's most powerful foe, Stephen Douglas, that he was being seriously mentioned throughout the northern States as a potential Republican candidate for Federal President.

February was naturally filled with earnest maneuvering by other contenders and their supporters for the votes to secure the nomination of the Republican Party:

The person believed most likely to be nominated was **Senator William Seward of New York**, a Whig-turned-Republican who had previously served as New York State Governor. Seward had acquired an earnest Abolitionist reputation through his "higher law" rhetoric, which argued that the citizens and their State Governments could disobey the Federal Constitution if their moral persuasions ran counter to its laws.

Another potential nominee was **Governor Salmon Chase of Ohio**, who had much support from the cadre of the most fervent Abolitionists in the Party.

Senator Simon Cameron had considerable support within his home State of Pennsylvania.

Then there was support among some Republican pragmatists for **Edward Bates, a die-hard Whig in faraway Missouri**. Horace Greeley, publisher of the influential New York *Tribune*, was so eager to stop the nomination of Seward that he was even puffing up enthusiasm for the Missourian.

The New York City Republican organization that sponsored Abe Lincoln's speech was also looking for a political alternative to their State Senator and past Governor, William Seward. Although Seward had become a dedicated Republican, he was not totally to their liking. The organization sponsoring Lincoln included William Cullen Bryant and Horace Greeley. Lincoln would be participating in a lecture series. Two men also opposed to permitting bonded African Americans to settle in the National Territories, Frank Blair of Missouri and Cassius Clay of Kentucky, had already come to New York and delivered their lectures.

Lincoln's lecture would be delivered in the Great Hall at the Cooper Union for the Advancement of Science and Art for best political effect. Peter Cooper of New York had founded the school, locally called "The Cooper Institute," in 1859. The building containing the Great Hall was one of the first buildings in America to be constructed entirely with structural iron beams. Founder Peter Cooper had become very wealthy through his pioneering ironworks facility in Baltimore, Maryland where he had built the first American steam locomotive. The mission of Cooper's school was to unite the teaching of the arts (manual arts, the skills for making useful and attractive objects and machines) and the sciences (the scientific method, the application of rational processes). The curriculum was a blend of trade school and engineering school.

Abe Lincoln had prepared a masterful speech full of historical analysis. Billy Herndon had helped with the research, but he had remained in Illinois. Of the speech, Herndon would write, "It was constructed with a view to accuracy of statement, simplicity of language, and unity of thought. In some respects, like a lawyer's brief, it was logical, temperate in tone, powerful — irresistibly driving conviction home to men's reasons and their souls. No former effort in the line of speech-making had cost Lincoln so much time and thought as this one."

So, on the night of February 27, 1860, William Cullen Bryant warmly introduced Abraham Lincoln to the gathered audience of about 1,500 people in the Great Hall in the Cooper Union.

Lincoln during the time of his Cooper Union address

The first half of Lincoln's speech did truly resemble a lawyer's brief as he built a legal argument to justify his allegation that the Federal Government had, on a few occasions, previously set policy regarding bonded African Americans in lands west of the States. He referred to the Northwest Territory (to become Ohio, Indiana, Illinois and Michigan), which had been given by Virginia to the Confederation Government, and pointed out that the Confederation Congress had voted in 1787 to exclude bonded African Americans in the vast territory given by Virginia, and that this had been later honored by the Federal Government. He referred to Mississippi Territory, established in 1798 and made up of land partly given by Georgia and partly seized from Spain, and pointed out that settlers were prohibited from importing bonded African Americans from Africa or the Caribbean (9 years before the date dictated by the Federal Constitution). He referred to the Louisiana Purchase lands, which had been bought in 1803 during the administration of Thomas Jefferson of Virginia, and pointed out that in 1804 the Federal Government had stipulated that no bonded African Americans could be imported into Louisiana from Africa or the Caribbean (3 years before the date dictated by the Federal Constitution). Lincoln referred to the 1820 Federal policy agreement by which future States north of 36 degrees and 30 minutes would exclude bonded African Americans and argued that that agreement was equivalent to setting policy related to bonded African Americans in the National Territories. Lincoln traced the voting patterns of the 39 men who had signed the Federal Constitution and concluded by that study that 21 had voted at least once in a manner that showed they believed the Federal Government was empowered to include or exclude bonded African Americans in the National Territories. He called the 39 men who signed the Federal Constitution "our fathers." Then he preached:

"As those fathers marked [African American bonding], so let it be again marked, as an evil not to be extended [into any part of the National Territories], but to be tolerated and protected only because of and so far as its actual presence among us [in the southern States] makes the toleration and protection a necessity."

Much of the remainder of Lincoln's address did not resemble a lawyer's brief. It was in the form of role-playing where he paraphrased a complaint by southern States leaders and then provided an answer. In his words:

"I would address a few words to the [southern States] people.

"You say we are sectional. We deny it. . . . The fact that we get no votes in your section is a fact of your making, and not of ours. And if there be fault in that fact, that fault is primarily yours, and remains until you show that we repel you by some wrong principle or practice.

"You say you are conservative – eminently conservative – while we are revolutionary, destructive, or something of the sort. What is conservatism? . . . Some of you are for reviving the [importation of bonded people from Africa]; some for [Federal laws protecting owners of bonded African Americans in the National] Territories; some for [Federal laws mandating that owners may settle in any of the National Territories with bonded African Americans]; some for maintaining [Supreme Court authority for settling in any of the National Territories with bonded African Americans]; some for [what is called Popular Sovereignty]; but never a man among you is in favor of Federal prohibition of [African American bonding] in the Federal Territories, according to the [1787 precedent concerning the Northwest Territory, the gift of Virginia].

"You say we have made the [African American bonding] question more prominent than it formerly was. We deny it. We admit that it is more prominent, but we deny that we made it so.

"You charge that we stir up insurrections among your [bonded African Americans]. We deny it; and what is your proof? Harper's Ferry! John Brown! John Brown was no Republican; and you have failed to implicate a single Republican in his Harper's Ferry enterprise. . . . Republican doctrines and declarations are accompanied with a continual protest against any interference whatever with your [bonded African Americans], or with you about your

202

[bonded African Americans]. . . . Much is said by [southern States] people about the affection of [bonded African Americans] for their [owners and their families]; and a part of it, at least, is true. A plot for an uprising could scarcely be devised and communicated to 20 individuals before some one of them, to save the life of a favorite [owner or family member], would divulge it."

Then, by quoting Thomas Jefferson, Lincoln spoke of the possibility of a massive project to deport African Americans:

"In the language of Mr. Jefferson, uttered many years ago:

"It is still in our power to direct the process of [making bonded African Americans independent] and [deporting them], peaceably, and in such slow degrees, as that the evil will wear off insensibly; and their place be, [at an equal pace], filled up by [independent European American] laborers. If, on the contrary, [bonded African Americans are allowed to remain among us indefinitely], human nature must shudder at the prospect [before us]."

"Mr. Jefferson did not mean to say, nor do I, that the power [to force independence for bonded African Americans] is in the Federal Government. He [had been speaking] of Virginia; and, as to the [State Government's] power [to force independence there]; I speak of the [southern] States only."

A bit later Lincoln spoke bluntly about State secession, again as if he were addressing the southern States people:

"But you will not abide the election of a Republican President! In that supposed event, you say, you will [vote to secede from the Federation of States]; and then, you say, the great crime of having [reduced the extent of the Federation] will be upon us! That is cool. A highwayman holds a pistol to my ear, and mutters through his teeth, 'Stand and deliver, or I shall kill you, and then you will be a murderer!'"

Then, without offering any proof, Lincoln alleged the ridiculous existence of a southern States conspiracy to force the northern States to accept bonded African Americans:

"It is exceedingly desirable that all parts of the great [Federation of States] shall be at peace, and in harmony, one with another. Let us Republicans do our part to have it so. Even though much provoked, let us do nothing through passion and ill temper. Even though the southern [States] people will not so much as listen to us, let us calmly consider their demands, and yield to them, if, in our deliberate view of our duty, we possibly can. . . . Will they be satisfied if the [National] Territories be unconditionally surrendered to them? We know they will not. . . . [They will only be satisfied if we] cease to call [African

203

American bonding] wrong, and join them in calling it right. And this must be done thoroughly – done in acts as well as in words. Silence will not be tolerated – we must place ourselves avowedly with them. Senator Douglas' new sedition law must be enacted and enforced, suppressing all declarations that [African American bonding] is wrong, whether made in politics, in [printed documents] in pulpits, or in private. We must arrest and return [runaway bonded African Americans] with greedy pleasure. We must [amend our State Constitutions to admit bonded African Americans]. The whole atmosphere must be disinfected from all taint of opposition to [African American bonding], before [the people of the southern States] will cease to believe that all their [political] troubles proceed from us. . . . Holding, as they do, that [African American bonding] is morally right, and socially elevating, they cannot cease to demand a full [Federation-wide] recognition of it, as a legal right, and a social blessing."

Another photo of Lincoln during the time of his speech at the Cooper Union in New York City.

You should read the above paragraph again. Study it. Recognize how totally untrue was Lincoln's portrayal of Southern political attitudes and aims.

Then Lincoln closed with an appeal to carry forward the Republican Party political program with religious conviction and without negotiation or compromise:

"Neither let us be slandered from our duty by false accusations against us, nor frightened from it by [threats of State secession] nor of [imprisonment of our people]. Let us have faith that right makes might, and in that faith, let us, to the end, dare to do our duty as we understand it."

I substituted "imprisonment of our people" for Lincoln's precise words, which were, "dungeons for ourselves." I suppose Lincoln was referring to imprisonment of Exclusion Terrorists, Abolition Terrorists and people defying the Return of Runaways Law.

Lincoln's speech was a superb performance. Those present frequently applauded at points within the address. At the close, the crowd stood up and cheered while also waving hats and handkerchiefs.

Noah Brooks of the New York *Tribune* wrote: "He's the greatest man since St. Paul." The next day, four New York newspapers printed Lincoln's address in full. William Cullen Bryant was quoted in the New York *Evening Post* saying that Lincoln's presentation was "most logically and convincingly stated." Horace Greeley reported: "Mr. Lincoln is one of Nature's orators, using his rare powers solely and effectively to elucidate and to convince, though their inevitable effect is to delight and electrify as well."

Abraham Lincoln's February 27, 1860 speech at New York's Cooper Union would be immediately published as Republican campaign pamphlets. In addition, the complete text of the speech would be issued and reissued as a Republican tract by the New York *Tribune*, the Chicago *Press and Tribune*, the Detroit *Tribune*, and the Albany *Evening Journal*. [166]

Abe Lincoln was now fairly confident that he had circumvented the threat that political opponents could find out about his real father, Abraham Enloe of western North Carolina. The nomination of the candidate for President by the Northern States Republican Party was only three months away.

---

[166] *Bloodstains*, Volume 2, by Howard Ray White, pages 406-408, *Lincoln*, by David Donald, pages 239-240, *Abraham Lincoln . . . His Speeches and Writings*, edited by A. P. Basler, pages 517-536.

Chapter 28: The 1860 Northern States Republican Party Nominates Springfield Lawyer Abraham Lincoln for President

May 9-10, 1860: the Illinois Republican State Convention in Decatur — Richard Oglesby, John Hanks and Promoting Lincoln as the "Rail-splitter"

The idea of creating the image of Lincoln as "the rail-splitter" was the inspiration of Illinois politician Richard J. Oglesby, 35. He sought to find "one thing in Mr. Lincoln's unsuccessful career as a laborer that could be made an emblem — [to] make enthusiastic the working people." Oglesby searched for ideas during one or more conversations with Lincoln, probably in the latter's office. Finally, the idea of "Lincoln, the Rail Splitter" was seized upon. To advance that idea, Oglesby met with John Hanks in the Sangamon Bottom to locate and learn about the thousands of fencing rails that he and Abe Lincoln had cut to make split rail fences 30 years ago. John Hanks showed Oglesby the split fencing rails. John Hanks agreed to bring a few rails to Springfield so that Oglesby could use them to promote Abe Lincoln's political image.

Soon afterward, Richard Oglesby took the lead in building a temporary, 2,500-seat "wigwam" against the side of a Decatur building, sheltered by canvas (perhaps obtained temporarily from a circus), and complete with a temporary stage constructed of borrowed lumber. Lincoln's supporters staged a demonstration in the meeting hall at the Decatur Republican convention. And the climax was John Hanks, entering the building with two split fence rails which he claimed he and Lincoln had split long ago. Between the rails was a banner which proclaimed "Abraham Lincoln, the Rail Candidate for President in 1860." The delegates and onlookers wildly cheered the theatrics. [167]

Herndon tells the story in his Lincoln biography:

"The first public movement by the Illinois people in Lincoln's interest was the action of the State Convention, which met at Decatur on the 9th and 10th of May. It was at this convention that Lincoln's friend and cousin, John Hanks, brought in the two historic rails which both had made in the Sangamon bottom in 1830, and which served the double purpose of electrifying the Illinois people and kindling the fire of enthusiasm that was destined to sweep over [the entire

---

[167] *Lincoln's Rail-Splitter: Governor Richard J. Oglesby,* by Mark A. Plummer. See Amazon for the book.

North]. In the words of an ardent Lincoln delegate, "These rails were to represent the issue in the coming contest between democracy and aristocracy."

The delegates to represent Illinois at the Northern States Republican Convention had been selected. Abe Lincoln was not among them. He hoped to be a candidate for President and wanted to remain out of sight in Springfield. By the way, Oglesby would enjoy an illustrious political career: three times Governor of Illinois and United States Senator. [168]

The May 16-18, 1860 Northern States Republican Presidential Nominating Convention in Chicago

One week following the Illinois State Convention in Decatur, Republicans from all across the North gathered in Chicago for their Northern States Convention. Chicago business leaders had financed the construction of a temporary convention hall out of wood, which was capable of accommodating 10,000 people or more. These Chicago men believed attracting fellow business leaders from all across the North to fast-growing Chicago would be good for their interests and that of the city. Only one month was needed by a large force of workmen to construct the building. On May 16, 1860, the Republican Northern States Convention opened in Chicago in the new convention hall.

Abe Lincoln remained in Springfield in the customary manner of hopeful presidential Democrat and Republican nominees. It was up to Lincoln's supporters to win enough votes to put him over the top. All Lincoln could do during the Convention was to wait hopefully in Springfield while frequently checking the news as it came in at the nearby telegraph office. [169]

The arriving Republican Delegates saw a clear path to victory. This was not wishful optimism. All available facts pointed to certain victory for their Republican candidate. All the delegates had to do was to nominate a man whose past political history would not be contentious. Let us look at the facts:

1. The Whig Party was no more.

2. The Democratic Party Convention had convened in Charleston, South Carolina a few weeks previously, only to split over political differences involving State Rights and the rights of citizens to settle in the National Territories with their bonded African Americans.

3. The political success of the Northern States Republican Party had become a major threat to Northern States Democratic politicians, who

---

[168] Herndon's *Life of Lincoln*, by William Herndon and Jesse Weik, pages 372-372.
[169] *Lincoln*, by David Herbert Donald, pages 241-242.

were, in response, moving closer to the Republican agenda in a desperate attempt to save their personal political hides. But saving those personal northern political hides was splitting the National Democratic Party into a Northern States Democratic Party and a Southern States Democratic Party.

4. Republicans hoped the National Democrat Party's destruction would be completed when Democrat delegates reconvened in Baltimore in June.

5. The vacuum across America crying out for a national political party must have been immense.

6. Some patriotic men were organizing a new national political party, which they had named the Constitutional Union Party, but this new party had precious little time to build momentum before the November elections.

So, the Republicans would most likely be running against three newly organized, splintered parties:

The Northern Democrats would likely only be significant in the Northern States.

The Southern Democrats would carry most or all of the lower Southern States.

The Constitutional Union Party would pick up a few of the upper Southern States that bordered on one or more Northern States.

Against such a split field, it was easy to calculate that the Republicans could capture the office of Federal President while only winning less than 40% of the popular vote. All they had to do was win majorities in all of the Northern States. They did not need the votes of any man in the Southern States, and would not seek them.

The Pennsylvania Republican delegation was led by Simon Cameron. As a Federal Senator for the whole State, Cameron had influence throughout Pennsylvania. Thad Stevens, as the Lancaster-area Representative in the Federal House, held influence locally. Stevens arrived in Chicago intent on doing what he could to promote John McLean for President. Stevens thought "the wisest policy" would be to nominate a man who had not been outspoken about either Exclusion or raising import taxes, in hopes that would make it easier to attract votes by Northern Democrats. He wanted to erase fears that the election of a Northern States Republican President would incite voters in the Southern States to vote for their States to secede from the Federal Government.

Overall, the Pennsylvania Delegation arrived with the intention of denying a first ballot victory to William Seward of New York by first voting for their favorite son, Simon Cameron. After that, they expected to get down to the real tug for the prize.

Thad Stevens was happy that the Convention approved the higher import tax Platform Plank that House Representatives within the Pennsylvania Delegation had succeeded in putting through the Platform Committee.

With the Platform approved, the Republican delegates in Chicago then turned their attention to nominating their candidate for President.

The major contenders for the Republican nomination for Federal President were:

Senator and former Governor William Seward of New York.

Lawyer Abraham Lincoln of Illinois.

Governor Salmon Chase of Ohio.

Senator Simon Cameron of Pennsylvania.

Lawyer Edward Bates of Missouri. Although of a Southern State with no significant Republican Party organization, Ed Bates was being considered as a non-controversial candidate.

New York Senator William Seward was a major contender, considered by most the man to beat. His attitude toward Southern States people was unquestionably Republican, but Seward was much less militant than Lincoln and Chase. Horace Greeley, publisher of the influential Republican newspaper, the New York *Tribune*, had earnestly sought a more militant candidate than Seward, so he and his newspaper had been for many months promoting a candidate who could beat Seward of New York in the contest for the nomination.

Salmon Chase of Ohio had a good chance many thought, and he was decidedly uncompromising and militant.

Simon Cameron was a possibility, but he was no idealist.

Edward Bates, the Missouri outlier, was the least likely to get the nod.

Abraham Lincoln was a very strong contender, and most likely to overtake Seward. Lincoln could derail Seward's cautious attitudes. Lincoln could keep the militant fires alive. The former Republican nominee for President, John Fremont, had done very well in the Northern States in 1856, but he had failed to carry Pennsylvania, Indiana and Illinois. So, particular attention was being given to selecting a candidate that would be especially strong in those three States. Lincoln's prospects looked especially favorable in Illinois and Indiana.

Thurlow Weed, who was in charge of the Seward campaign, was established in the Chicago's Richmond House. And David Davis, a Chicago Judge and Lincoln's campaign chief, oversaw the Lincoln campaign from the third floor of the Tremont House, which had been fully reserved for Lincoln promoters. In the thick of the influence trading, David Davis scoffed at cautions about over-committing a future Lincoln Administration and urged his promoters to "pay their price" and "promise them anything. . . . Lincoln ain't here, and don't know what we have to meet, so we will go ahead as if we hadn't heard from him, and he must ratify it."

But Lincoln was such an unlikely candidate on the surface. By applying common sense reasoning, one could only conclude that Lincoln was less prepared to be President of the United States than any other candidate in American history who had previously won that high office (John Fremont did not count; he had lost his election):

1. Lincoln had received only the briefest informal schooling.

2. Although 54 years old (so far he had convinced everyone he was only 50 years old) he had no administrative experience of any sort. The largest organization he had ever managed was a two-man law office.

3. He had never been Governor of his State or even Mayor of Springfield.

4. Although he had impressive knowledge of the United States Constitution, he knew little about the workings of the Federal Government.

5. Since serving in the Illinois Legislature, then as a Representative in the Federal House for one uneventful term ten years previously, he had held no public office.

6. Although he was one of the founders of the Illinois Republican Party and had spoken impressively at the Great Hall at New York's Cooper Union, in states east of Ohio, he had no close friends and only a few acquaintances.

7. Although Lincoln's 1858 debates with Senator Stephen Douglas had brought him national attention, his State's Republican Party had failed to gain the majority in the Illinois legislature, thereby allowing the election of Democrat Douglas, the incumbent, to the U. S. Senate.

May 18, 1860 was the day for balloting for the Republican nominee for Federal President. And what a notorious day it would prove to be. It seems that delegates supporting Lincoln had worked all through the previous night to illegally disrupt the day's proceedings. Yes, the Lincoln Republican Faction was springing an illegal trap upon the other Party Factions. Lincoln's men seemed resolute in their attitude that "the end justifies the means." The story follows:

The previous night Lincoln's friend Ward Lamon had arranged for thousands of counterfeit Convention non-delegate admission tickets to be printed. Lincoln's men had then worked long after midnight signing names of convention officers to make the counterfeit non-delegate admission tickets appear legitimate. Then at sunrise, well before the people who had the valid non-delegate admission tickets figured they ought to arrive, Lincoln's men handed out counterfeit tickets and herded thousands of shouters into the Convention building until they filled every non-delegate seat and occupied much of the standing room. Later, only a small proportion of Seward's cohorts could squirm their way in.

Scheming Ward Hill Lamon helped Lincoln get the nomination at the Northern States Republican Party Convention at Chicago

Under these lawless conditions, the Northern States Republican politicians began to nominate their candidate for Federal President. Every time Lincoln's name was mentioned five thousand people leaped to their seats and shouted with a deafening roar. Yet, among the uproar, delegates proceeded with the business at hand as best they could.

The first ballot tallied: Seward 173-1/2, Lincoln 102, Cameron 50-1/2, Chase 49, and Bates 48. Seward was only 59-1/2 votes shy of the 233 needed to win, but sentiment against Seward ran strong among Delegations supporting Lincoln, Chase, Cameron and Bates.

On the second ballot, some Cameron men who were not in the Pennsylvania Delegation switched to Seward, moving him up a little to 184-1/2 votes. The Pennsylvania Delegation dropped Cameron, too, but sought to keep negotiations open by casting its vote for Thad Stevens's favorite, John McLean.

But the third ballot told the story as Delegations opposed to Seward flocked to Lincoln in a determined move to stop the New Yorker. Lincoln received 231-1/2 votes, including the votes of most of the Pennsylvania Delegation.

At this point Lincoln was a mere 1-1/2 votes short of victory. Then Ohio quickly switched 4 votes from Chase to Lincoln to assure Lincoln's nomination. A subsequent move to make the nomination unanimous was successful.

A man Lincoln had never met, Senator Hannibal Hamlin of Maine, was nominated for Vice President. [170]

Even after his nomination, Abraham Lincoln did not appear before the Chicago Convention, only a few hours away by train. He had already begun his campaign policy of minimum, tightly regulated personal exposure to the public and to newspapermen. He needed to keep secrete the true story about his biological father, should rumors of an Abraham Enloe of North Carolina surface.

The following day, May 19, the official Republican Delegation arrived in Springfield to formally notify Lincoln of his election and seek his acceptance. Playing the role of the reluctant candidate, Lincoln, supposedly deliberating within himself for 4 days, formally accepted the nomination on May 23.

Abraham Lincoln, 54, State Republican Party leader, Springfield, Illinois lawyer, and crusading orator — was on his way to becoming Federal President by the political inflammation of divisive prejudices against Southern States people.

---

[170] Bloodstains, Volume 2, by Howard Ray White, pages 416-418, *Lincoln*, by David Donald, pages 236-251, and *Old Thad Stevens*, by Richard Current, page 133.

Chapter 29: Throughout the Campaign, Abraham Lincoln Sits in a Springfield Office and Submits his Biographical Sketch to Newspapermen who then Publish Lincoln Campaign Biographies

Strangely, Northern States Republican candidate Abraham Lincoln remained in Springfield, Illinois, throughout the duration of the Republican Party campaign across the Northern States. He would just sit in an office loaned to him by Illinois Republican Governor John Wood. He had succeeded thus far in keeping secret the truthful news that the late Thomas Lincoln was not his father, and figured such a policy was wise.

It appears Lincoln figured that staying cooped up in that office was his best strategy to keep that crucial fact secret a few weeks longer. And he had help with mail, outgoing letters

John G. Nicolay, Secretary in Springfield and Washington.

and contact with visitors. Wealthy friends had contributed to a fund to pay John Nicolay to become Lincoln's private Secretary and he and Nicolay corresponded extensively by letter and telegram with campaign workers across the Northern States.

John Hay, Future Lincoln Secretary.

People interested in finding out information about the candidate, or, more likely, in hopes of winning some favor, came to his office in Springfield to see him. Photographers came, fellow politicians came, and newspapermen came. But he stayed put in Springfield.

The Biographies, the Wrong Date of Birth, the Omissions and Herndon's Informants

John Scripps, editor of the Chicago *Press and Tribune,* had prepared an extensive biography based on the autobiographical sketch Lincoln had previously provided to him, and this was receiving wide publication as promotional literature.

William Herndon would later provide the following details about John Scripps in his Lincoln biography:

> "The most complete autobiographical statement which Lincoln ever prepared was written for none other than John Locke Scripps to whom he communicated 'some facts' which he did not wish to be published. Knowing that this statement was to be the basis of a campaign biography, Lincoln wrote it in the third person."

What were those "some facts" that Lincoln wished to keep secret from everyone except John Scripps? It is reasonable to assume that those "some facts" were the revelation that Abe's father was Abraham Enloe and that he had been born prior to his mother's marriage to Thomas Lincoln.

That part which refers to his birth and ancestry follows:

> "Abraham Lincoln was born February 12, 1809, then in Hardin County, now in the more recently formed county of LaRue, Kentucky. [171] His father, Thomas, and grandfather, Abraham, were born in Rockingham County. Virginia, wither they had come from Berks County, Pennsylvania. His lineage has been traced no farther back than this. . . . Abraham, grandfather of the subject of this sketch, came to Kentucky, and was killed there by the Indians, about the year 1784. He left a widow, three sons and two daughters. . . . Thomas, the youngest son, and father of the present subject, by the early death of his father and very narrow circumstances of his mother, even in childhood was a wandering laboring boy and grew up literally without education. He never did more in the way of writing than to bunglingly write his own name. Before he was grown, he passed one year as a hired hand with his Uncle Isaac, on Watauga, a branch of the Holston River in Tennessee. Getting back into Kentucky, and having reached his twenty-eight year, he married Nancy Hanks — mother of the subject — in 1806.

---

[171] Lincoln should have claimed to have been born in Hardin County to match the location of the court house record of the Hanks-Lincoln wedding.

"Nancy Hanks was born in Virginia; and relatives of hers of the name of Hanks, and of other names, now reside in Coles, in Macon, and in Adams Counties, Illinois, and also in Iowa." [172]

In his book, *The Genesis of Lincoln*, published in 1899, James Harrison Cathey reports on a meeting with Captain James W. Terrell, who had been born in 1829 in Rutherford County, North Carolina. Captain Terrell told Cathey of a meeting with Dr. Edgerton, "some years ago." Dr. Edgerton was a relative of Abraham Enloe's wife, Sarah "Sally" Edgerton Enloe. The story in Captain Terrell's words is thus:

"Some time in the early fifties, two young men of Rutherford County moved to Illinois and settled in or near Springfield. One of them, whose name was Davis, became intimately acquainted with Mr. Lincoln. In the fall of 1860, just before the presidential election, Mr. Davis and his friend paid a visit back to Rutherford and spent the night with Dr. Edgerton. Of course, the presidential candidates would be discussed. Mr. Davis told Dr. Edgerton that in a private and confidential talk, which he had with Mr. Lincoln the latter told him that he was of Southern extraction, that his right name was, or ought to have been, Enloe, but that he had always gone by the name of his stepfather." [173]

Again, Candidate Lincoln had advised John Scripps to withhold from publication certain facts concerning his parentage, an event strongly encouraging a belief that his "Thomas Lincoln is my father and I was born after the Hanks-Lincoln marriage" story was a politically motivated lie. [174]

Herndon continued relating the letter's contents using his own words, presenting some birth dates:

"On the 10th day of February, in the following year, 1807, a daughter, Sarah, was born, and two years later, on the 12th of February, 1809, the subject of these memoirs came into this world. After this came the last child, a boy named Thomas after his father — who lived but a few days. No mention of his existence is found in the Bible record.

"Most biographers of Lincoln, in speaking of Mr. Lincoln's sister, call her Nancy. . . . The mistake, I think, arises from the fact that, in the Bible record referred to, all that portion relating to the birth of "Sarah, daughter of Thomas

---

[172] Note that the fact that Nancy Hanks grew up in North Carolina is omitted for obvious reasons. She was just a very little girl when she left Virginia for North Carolina. In Lincoln's adult mind, mention of North Carolina was a "No, No."

[173] *The Genesis of Lincoln*, James H. Cathey, pages 46-53.

[174] Herndon's *Life of Lincoln*, pages 5-6.

and Nancy Lincoln," down to the word Nancy, has been torn away, and the latter name of Nancy has therefore been erroneously taken for that of the daughter." [175]

---

[175] Herndon's *Life of Lincoln*, page 5-6.

Chapter 30: Springfield, Abe's Home Town, was the Location of the Only Campaign Rally to Which he Exposed Himself.

An Example of an 1860 Northern States Republican Party Campaign Poster

The August, 1860 Springfield Republican Rally

The contrast between Lincoln's behavior and that of his political opponent, Democrat Stephen Douglas, was vast, like night and day, extreme to the limits. Northern Democrat Stephen Douglas traveled widely, meeting and speaking — from Illinois, to Kentucky to Pennsylvania, to New York to Chicago. Except for one Springfield Republican political rally, candidate Lincoln would never be seen at a Republican political event prior to the election. Just one rally exposure — his home town:

Yes, Lincoln felt that he had, yes had, to be seen watching the campaign parade at Springfield. The hometown Springfield political rally would be Lincoln's only public appearance between his acceptance of the nomination at his home and his departure to Washington City.

The August 1860 Springfield political rally was indeed immense. Lincoln stood and watched the exhibitions put on by Republican paramilitary groups, such as the Zouave Company, which had been recruited and drilled by his young friend Elmer Ellsworth, who was occasionally supposed to be reading law in the Lincoln and Herndon office. [176]

The Wide Awake Young Republicans' militant-style campaign for Lincoln resembled the later Nazi Party's "Hitler Youths" marchers.

Similar political parades, demonstrations and monster meetings in cities across the Northern States were building enthusiasm for Republican candidates. The Wide-Awake Young Republican clubs, with their frequent meetings, organized drills, and processions, were stimulating immense enthusiasm within the younger voter population and many of that group would be casting their first ballots in the fall.

When asked to speak to the crowd that was also watching the Springfield political rally, Lincoln firmly refused, saying, "It has been my purpose, since I have been placed in my present position, to make no speeches." We ask, why was Presidential candidate Lincoln isolating himself from the campaign? Why did he decline any involvement in any of the gigantic rallies Republicans were holding at most Northern States cities, each featuring processions of young Republican 'Wide-

---

[176] *Lincoln*, by David Donald, page 254 and *Bloodstains*, Volume 2, by Howard Ray White, pages 428-438..

Awakes' clad in black oilcloth capes and caps, carrying split fencing rails decorated with torches? [177]

Perhaps the answer is obvious. Candidate Abraham Lincoln wisely hid himself from campaigning crowds, believing that behavior would better contain his secret — that he was a bastard child of Abraham Enloe of western North Carolina and he desperately needed to keep that truth secret for just a few more weeks.

---

[177] I invite you to compare the Republican Wide Awakes to Adolph Hitler's militant "Youth," who would later be parading in military fashion with straight-arm salutes supporting the Nazi Party.

Chapter 31: Final Campaign Days and the Presidential Electoral College Vote Results

The Amazing Personal Campaign Effort by Northern Democrat Stephen Douglas

Lincoln's political opponent's behavior was strikingly different. Northern States Democrat candidate Senator Stephen Douglas pressed on with his exhausting speaking tour despite his illness. He was dying of throat cancer (too many cigars) but the cause of his illness was not revealed to the public. In early September, he was at Harrisburg Pennsylvania, where he advocated increased taxes on imports. But, all along, he was forced to deliver unusually brief speeches as he nursed his deteriorating voice. On September 10, he was back in New York City where he checked into a hotel for a few days rest and strategy talks with campaign leaders.

On September 16, after the 5 days rest in New York City, Stephen Douglas began a westward campaign swing. He spoke in Syracuse, Rochester, Buffalo, Cleveland, Columbus, and Cincinnati before arriving in Indianapolis on September 28. Crossing into Kentucky he made a brief address in Louisville. His throat suffered terribly from the stress of travel and public speaking. His booming baritone voice in days past, which had carried far into the back row of large crowds, was now only audible in the first few rows.

The next day, in a cold northeast wind, Douglas addressed a huge Chicago crowd – "over 5 acres of densely packed Democrats." Republican William Seward of New York had spoken in town a few days earlier, so Douglas took time to attack Seward and his "irrepressible conflict" doctrine. Then he lambasted Lincoln's "house-divided-against-itself-cannot-stand" doctrine. Lumping both doctrines together, he declared, "Their propositions mean revolution – undisguised revolution," because it would be impossible to implement their policies without driving the people of the Southern States to State secession. Afterward, Chicago Northern States Democrats presented an enormous fireworks display. After a day's rest, Douglas traveled to Iowa, Wisconsin and Michigan to present campaign speeches.

In mid-October Douglas entered Lincoln's hometown of Springfield, Illinois, for a giant rally where he addressed over 5,000 Northern Democratic supporters.

Northern Democrat Candidate Stephen Douglas Campaigns Southward to the Gulf of Mexico

Senator Stephen Douglas departed Springfield for a last-minute tour of the mid-southern States. His wife Adele, her brother James Cutts, and his shorthand secretary, James Sheridan, accompanied him. The party first stopped at St. Louis, Missouri, where Douglas spoke on October 19. Then the Douglas party traveled by train to speak in Memphis, Tennessee, thence to speak in Nashville, Tennessee, thence to speak in Chattanooga, Tennessee, thence to speak in Huntsville, Alabama and thence to speak in Kingston, Georgia. On October 29 Douglas arrived in Atlanta, Georgia. Douglas told the people of Atlanta what he had been telling Southern States crowds for the past 11 days: you should resist Southern States political leaders who advocate State Secession, and it would be a temporary move anyway, because Federal troops would soon force a seceded State to submit to Federal authority. Douglas traveled to speak in Macon and Columbus, Georgia. Then he traveled to Montgomery, Alabama.

Adele Cutts Douglas, age 20, a Washington beauty with famous Southern roots, had married widower Stephen Douglas in 1856.

In the Northern States much was made of how dangerous it was for Douglas to travel through the Southern States, for it was alleged that many men down there were out to kill him. To these alarmists, Montgomery, Alabama, seemed to be the most likely spot for murder. Then, on November 5, the day before the election, Douglas arrived in Mobile, Alabama. At Mobile, far south on the Gulf of Mexico, Douglas made his last speech of the campaign.

Just what was the point of Douglas' campaign swing through Tennessee, Georgia and Alabama during the last two weeks of the campaign for President? There seems to be scant evidence that he was seeking the votes of Southern States men. He went out of his way to admonish them to reject State Secession and to warn them that, should they vote to have their State secede, vast Federal armies from the Northern States would descend upon them and subjugate them. This is the true story:

Douglas had long ago given up on winning the race for President. His campaign goal was to consolidate and defend his control of the Democratic parties in the Northern States. His weak voice would not be a factor in newspaper stories prepared by sympathetic Northern States newspapermen. Physically weakened by his illness, he needed a "David beating Goliath" image. Northern States Democrats read of Douglas (fearless little David) standing up and battling Southern States Secessionists on the enemy's battlefield. So, Douglas was touring Tennessee, Georgia

The Four Candidates for President: John Bell of Tennessee, Abraham Lincoln, John Breckinridge of Kentucky and Stephen Douglas.

and Alabama to cover up his illness and to produce press releases to be telegraphed to Northern States newspapers. His secretary and shorthand expert, James Sheridan, attended every speaking engagement to prepare press releases for Northern States newspapers. This image of little Dug battling Secessionists far to the south capped the Douglas campaign to control the leadership of the Democratic Parties in the Northern States. [178]

Election Day and the Vote Tallies

The next day, November 6, men went to the polls to vote, a rare day of rest for the sick but incessant campaigner, Stephen Douglas.

At about 2 pm the following day, November 7, Abe Lincoln was finally assured in his own mind that he had won the election for President, for it was then that the Springfield telegraph office received the message announcing that New York State had gone for Lincoln. It would take considerable time for the votes to be officially tallied and for the Electoral College vote to be cast and totalled. The final numbers appear below:

---

[178] *Bloodstains*, Volume 2, by Howard Ray White, pages 436-438.

Popular Vote:	Lincoln	1,833,352	40%
	Douglas	1,375,157	29%
	Breckinridge	845,763	18%
	Bell	589,581	13%
Electoral Vote:	Lincoln	180	59%
	Breckinridge	72	24%
	Bell	39	13%
	Douglas	12	4%

States Carried:

Lincoln carried all 16 Northern States and the 2 Pacific States. From east to west they were: Maine, Rhode Island, Massachusetts, New Hampshire, Vermont, Connecticut, New York, New Jersey, Pennsylvania, Ohio, Indiana, Illinois, Michigan, Iowa, Wisconsin, Minnesota, Oregon and California.

Breckinridge carried 11 Southern States. From east to west they were: Delaware, Maryland, North Carolina, South Carolina, Georgia, Florida, Alabama, Mississippi, Louisiana, Arkansas and Texas.

Bell carried 3 Southern States. They were Virginia (including what is now West Virginia), Kentucky, and Tennessee.

Douglas carried 1 Southern State. It was Missouri.

The Republican Party completed its profound sweep of Northern States Governor jobs. With the additions won in the 1860 elections, Republican Governors controlled, or would soon control, the State Militia of the following northern States -— acquiring a large military that was essential to any chance of success in a Northern conquest of the Seceded States:

Maine: Israel Washburn, Jr., Republican Governor from 1861 to 1863, a lawyer. He was preceded by Governor Lot Myrick Morrill, Republican Governor from 1858 to 1860, also a lawyer.

Rhode Island: William Sprague, Republican Governor from 1860 to 1863, an industrialist.

Massachusetts: John Andrew, Republican Governor from 1861 to 1866, a lawyer.

New Hampshire: Nathaniel Berry, Republican Governor from 1861 to 1863. He was preceded by Ichabod Goodwin, Republican Governor from 1859 to 1861.

Vermont: Frederick Holbrook, Republican Governor from 1861 to 1863. He was preceded by Erastus Fairbanks, Republican Governor from 1860 to 1861.

Connecticut: William Buckingham, Republican Governor from 1858 to 1866, an industrialist.

New York: Edwin Morgan; Republican Governor from 1859 to 1863, a wholesale merchant, banker and broker.

New Jersey: Charles Olden, Republican Governor from 1860 to 1863.

Pennsylvania: Andrew Curtin, Republican Governor from 1861 to 1867, a lawyer. He was preceded by William Packer, Democrat Governor from 1858 to 1861.

Ohio: William Dennison, Jr., Republican Governor from 1860 to 1862. He was preceded by Salmon Chase, Free Soil and Republican Governor from 1856 to 1860, a lawyer.

Indiana: Oliver Morton, Republican Governor from 1861 to 1867, a lawyer. He was preceded by Abram Adams Hammond, Republican Governor from 1860 to 1861.

Illinois: Richard Yates, Republican Governor from 1861 to 1865, a lawyer. He was preceded by John Wood, Republican Governor from 1860 to 1861.

Michigan: Austin Blair, Republican Governor from 1861 to 1865, a lawyer. He was preceded by Moses Wisner, Republican Governor from 1859 to 1861.

Iowa: Samuel Kirkwood, Republican Governor from 1860 to 1864, a lawyer.

Wisconsin: Alexander Randall, Republican Governor from 1858 to 1862.

Minnesota: Alexander Ramsey, Republican Governor from 1860 to 1863, a lawyer. He was preceded by Henry Sibley, Democrat Governor from 1858 to 1860, a businessman and politician.

By November 1860 the above Republican-dominated Northern States contained an uninterrupted and unified mass of politically galvanized people.

To the south, four States were placed in immediate harm's way, since a Federal invasion force, which could only be launched from the Republican controlled States, would first have to march through their land. The Republican Party had no significant influence in these four States. Their governors were:

Delaware: William Burton, Democrat Governor from 1859 to 1863, a physician.

Maryland: Thomas Hicks, American Party Governor from 1858 to 1862, a politician and a sheriff.

Kentucky: Beriah Magoffin, Democrat Governor from 1859 to 1862, a lawyer.

Missouri: Claiborne Jackson, Democrat Governor in 1861; forced to flee Missouri by Republican revolutionaries and died a few months later. Preceded by Governor Robert Stewart, Democrat Governor from 1857 to 1861.

Four southern States were positioned immediately south of the above 4 States. Except for a faction in the Appalachian Mountain region, most of the people in these States would surely fight any attempt by the Lincoln Administration to draft their men and force them to join in a Federal invasion of States positioned further south. The governors of these four States were as follows:

Virginia (Including present-day West Virginia): John Letcher, Democrat Governor of Virginia from 1860 to 1863, a lawyer.

The numbered sequence of State secessions

North Carolina: John Ellis, Democrat Governor from 1859 to June 1861, at which time illness would force him to pass authority to Henry Toole Clark, also a Democrat. Clark would hold the office until 1862.

Tennessee: Isham Harris, Democrat Governor from 1857 to 1862, a lawyer.

Arkansas: Henry Rector, Democrat Governor from 1860 to 1862, a lawyer.

Republican Party leaders had not wanted to be significantly listed on ballots in the 15 Southern states, because that would have compromised the purity of their Northern crusade.

Although Abe Lincoln was secure in Springfield, Illinois, he had much reason to worry, and much obligation to reach out to others in the name of peace and good will toward men. But Lincoln would not reach out. He would quietly sit in Springfield while states seceded and the Federation shrunk. [179]

---

[179] *Bloodstains*, Volume 2, by Howard Ray White, pages 439-440.

Seven Southern States Secede, Jefferson Davis is President

After the election of Abraham Lincoln and well before he took power as President of those shrunken United States, seven southern States from South Carolina to Texas were arranging to legally secede from the United States of America and form a new Federation of States whose new Constitution would more thoroughly impede its new federal government from encroaching on individual, local and State Rights. By the time Lincoln would be sworn in as Federal President, seven large States would be gone and out of the reach of new, crusading Republican laws. The Southern Federation of States would be called the Confederate States of America. Before Lincoln arrived in Washington City, the Confederate States of America would have an operating Senate and House of Representatives. Jefferson Davis would have already been sworn in as Provisional Confederate President.

President Jefferson Davis, CSA

Chapter 32: President-Elect Abraham Lincoln Prepares to Leave Springfield; then Boards the "Republican Rally Train" with his Family to become President of the Shrunken United States

Lincoln Prepares to Depart Springfield for Washington

Lincoln would soon be moving to Washington City where he would be sandwiched between two States controlled by the Democratic Party. Lincoln saw the Federation shrinking before his very eyes, yet he would not reach out. The Republican Governors would not reach out. The leaders of the Republican Party would not reach out.

President Lincoln would refuse to meet with President Davis's commissioners in Washington. Furthermore, he would decide to persistently ignore the Supreme Court of his United States with regard to the legality of state secessiom. He knew he commanded the guns and those nearby Justices only wore black robes.

Lincoln would soon send Federal transports and warships to Charleston, South Carolina, inciting Confederates to fire the "first shot," an event he believed to be helpful when, immediately afterward, he intended to ask all Northern States Republican governors to send state militia to reinforce the relatively small Federal army. Vastly reinforced in manpower and weapons, he would then begin his military occupation of four Democrat states — Delaware, Maryland, Kentucky and Missouri — and thereafter launch a military invasion to conquer the seven Southern States that had legally seceded and the four more that would, in response, secede.

The Great American Tragedy would have begun its ugly course. By the time the dying from disease and war would be done, one million Americans, mostly White, but some Black, would, sadly, suffer untimely deaths. With that preamble concluded, we return to Springfield to continue the history.

Mary and Abe Burn their Lincoln Letters and Documents

On February 6, 1861 the Lincolns held a good-bye reception at their Springfield home, saying goodbye to about 700 guests in a long receiving line. They had arranged to lease the house to a retired railroad executive. Some furnishings were sold and the remainder was stored.

During these final days in Springfield, Mary burned stacks of old letters and papers in the back alley. We are left to wonder about the stories those papers told and why the Lincoln's wanted to burn their papers. It appears they wanted to prevent us from knowing the stories contained in those papers. The Lincoln's wanted to arrive in Washington City without the excess political baggage contained in some or many of those burned-up letters.

Abe wrote many letters and received many letters. As President, the history of his Springfield years and rise to the Presidency would be of great national interest to future generations. Did the Lincoln's want to hide the hard reality – the ugliness, greed and racism – of past political maneuvering to permit the future mythical Lincoln to flower? What about his support of Deportation of Black people? What about the confusion, the secrecy, surrounding his age and his true biological father? What about evidence of Abraham Enloe of North Carolina? Burning those papers certainly causes such questions to beg for answers. [180]

As you recall, during November, December and January, 1861 President-elect Abraham Lincoln declined to publicly reveal his intentions for dealing with State Secession even though seven large states had left his county. As President-elect, he remained in Springfield at his home and law office, limiting his communications to biographers, supportive newspapermen and Republican political leaders. He had refused to travel and campaign after being nominated. Likewise, he stayed in Springfield for three months following his election. Historians puzzle over that unusual behavior. Readers of *Rebirthing Lincoln* need not puzzle.

Abraham Enloe of Western North Carolina was Abe's true father and, by staying in Springfield, the President-elect was best able to keep that fact hidden from public view. While a Congressman for two years, he had succeeded in keeping the story hidden. Then, after his step-father, Thomas Lincoln died, he had adroitly penned a Bible record that placed his birth at a day in the calendar long after his mother, Nancy Hanks, and Thomas had married and even after his step-sister, Sarah, had been born.

Mary Goes Shopping in New York City

But, Mary wanted to get away for a while. She wanted to improve her wardrobe. She was looking forward to being First Lady and dreamed of being well dressed. So, for a few days or weeks, Mary Todd Lincoln left Abe in Springfield and took the train to New York City to buy new clothes. Her ancestry was secure. She was of the politically influential Todd family of Lexington, Kentucky. She knew how to dress for her upcoming role. When she returned home, she was well outfitted to host a goodbye reception.

---

[180] *Bloodstains*, Volume 2, by Howard Ray White, pages 455-473

Mary Hosts a Goodbye Reception in their Springfield Home

Shortly before leaving for Washington, Abe and Mary hosted a good-bye reception at their home. Seven states had seceded from the United States Federal Government. Nevertheless, it was a grand affair. Seven hundred attended. Yet, no public word was given regarding the President-elect's future policy toward any seceded state.

Then Abe said "good-bye" to law partner Billy Herndon. Remember, the Lincoln-Herndon law office was the biggest outfit in which Abe had ever worked. Next job: Commander in Chief over the War Between the States.

The Northern States Republican Party Railroad Rally

Plans were now complete to parade the Republican Party's President-elect in a slow-moving special train routed through Republican States — a 12-day trip covering 1,904 miles over tracks of 18 railroad companies, ending in Washington. I call this spectacle the "Republican Railroad Rally," for the intent was to "rally" the people of the Republican states to support Lincoln's future militant stand against Seceded States — to show the new President to thousands and thousands of people across the Northern States in a secure setting. Most who saw Lincoln were just standing alongside the railroad track as the train rolled by, many were watching during frequent brief speeches from the back of the last railroad car, and a few listened to Lincoln during infrequent addresses to state legislatures.

The railroad rally left Springfield on February 11, 1861, routed to Indianapolis; to Cincinnati; to Columbus; to Pittsburgh; to Cleveland; to Buffalo; to Albany, to New York; to Philadelphia; to Harrisburg, to . . . (wait and see). Republican flagmen stood along the track every half-mile, inferring that danger was lurking about. At every significant town it stopped so that Lincoln could be seen and speak to the crowd from the last car. Also, he got off and addressed state legislatures in Indiana, Ohio, New York, New Jersey and Pennsylvania. Never speaking of the Confederate States of America or President Jefferson Davis and never suggesting Confederates just wanted to go their own way in peace, Lincoln deceptively referred to those "misguided citizens" as men who had "mistakenly" supported a "conspiracy by rebellious politicians" who intended "violent injury to the northern States." Those people of whom the new President spoke lived so far away, strangers to residents along that railroad route, that they knew not the truth; they had no way of knowing that those people who lived so far away simply wanted to live separately in peace — that **they intended no harm to the North**. Despite Lincoln's vagueness, it was apparent that he firmly opposed permitting the seceded States to live in peace. There was never a hint of a willingness to negotiate, to even speak to a Confederate emissary, to recognize his existence.

On February 20, the Republican Railroad Rally unofficially concluded in Harrisburg, Pennsylvania. The next day he was to travel part-way through the southern state of Maryland and conclude in Washington City. Since Marylanders would not be cheering this new Northern States Republican Party president, that leg of the official schedule was secretly cancelled. At Harrisburg, after night fell, Allan Pinkerton, of the famous Chicago detective agency, threw a large overcoat across Lincoln's shoulders, concealing his long arms, topped his head with a low felt hat and secretly spirited him aboard a special night train. In disguise the President-elect — the first elected president nominated by the Northern States Republican Party — arrived in Washington in the morning of February 21, 1861. Mary and the others would be following on the Railroad Rally train according to the published schedule.

On February 25, Jeff Davis appointed three men to travel to Washington and attempt to negotiate friendly relations with the Lincoln Administration: Martin Crawford of Georgia, A. B. Roman of Louisiana, and John Forsyth of Alabama. Seeking friendly relations, the Confederate House and Senate also approved a law establishing "free navigation of the Mississippi River without any duty or hindrance except light-money, pilotage, and other like customary charges."

Chapter 33: President Abraham Lincoln Refuses to Negotiate, then Directs the Military Conquest of the Confederate States of America.

The Inauguration

At noon, on March 4, President James Buchanan, Democrat, and Republican Abraham Lincoln rode side-by-side down Pennsylvania Avenue to the Capitol, while sharpshooters looked on from rooftops, soldiers secured intersections and artillery stood at the ready, giving the impression of a military exercise, not a peaceful transition of government leadership. Chief Justice Roger Taney, 84 and frail, administered the oath of office. Then Lincoln stepped forward to deliver his inaugural address. In part he said, "I have no purpose, directly or indirectly, to interfere with [African American bonding] in the States where it exists. I believe I have no lawful right to do so, and I have no inclination to do so." But he warned, "The power confided in me will be used to hold, occupy, and possess the property and places belonging to the [Federal] Government, and to collect the [Federal taxes]; but beyond what may be necessary for these objects, there will be no invasion – no using of force against or among the people anywhere. . . . In your hands, my dis-satisfied countrymen and not in mine,

Senator John J. Crittenden of Kentucky desperately strove to prevent Lincoln's war by his efforts to win votes for his compromise proposal. Sadly, his efforts failed.

is the momentous issue of civil war. The [Federal] Government will not assail you. You can have no conflict, without being yourselves the aggressors." That is what he said, but he meant, "I shall maneuver events to incite you to fire the coveted 'first shot'." [181]

We now tell the story of President Lincoln's "First Shot Strategy."

---

[181] *Bloodstains*, Volume 2, by Howard Ray White, pages 473-488.

Abe Lincoln's First Shot Strategy

Lincoln's Cabinet was soon in place: William Seward of New York, State; Simon Cameron of Pennsylvania, War; Gideon Welles of Connecticut, Navy; Salmon Chase of Ohio, Treasury; Caleb Smith of Indiana, Interior; Edward Bates of Missouri, Attorney General; and Montgomery Blair of Maryland, Postmaster General, the latter two being new-found so-called Republicans from Democrat states. On his eleventh day in office Lincoln consulted his Cabinet about sending the Navy into Charleston harbor, where a small garrison of U. S. troops was occupying Fort Sumter, which was situated on a small island in the middle of the harbor. Charleston was where Lincoln wanted to elicit the coveted "first shot" — the expected Confederate response to his Navy maneuver. If Confederates allowed his Navy to enter and occupy Fort Sumter, then his military would attempt to collect Federal tariff taxes on imports into South Carolina.

Stanton Chase   Lincoln   Welles Seward Smith   Blair   Bates

Lincoln's Postmaster General, Montgomery Blair, the pretend Republican from Maryland, had an idea: his wife's brother-in-law, a former Navy man, already had a proposal for a Navy mission to Charleston harbor. But the rest of the Cabinet opposed Lincoln's proposal to dispatch the Navy to South Carolina. Army Chief Winfield Scott favored peacefully giving up the fort. On the other hand, Lincoln strongly opposed recognition of the existence of the Confederate Government or chatting with the three Confederate commissioners lodging nearby in Washington City.

Republican leaders had no passion for freeing slaves, certainly no passion for freeing slaves and inviting them to come north and be neighbors, but they were passionate about ensuring high taxes on imports, scheduled to soon triple on average. The March 18 issue of the Boston *Transcript* advised, "It is apparent that the people of the principal seceding states are now for commercial independence." The Confederacy would be a free-trade area and Federals worried that the long border between the countries would tempt many Northerners to evade those high U.S. tariffs by sneaking listed goods into the United States from the south. And tariffs on imports were the revenue source that funded the Federal Government, about 80 percent of that revenue being historically collected at seaports in Southern States.

Lacking support from his Cabinet or Army Chief, President Lincoln dispatched three spies to Charleston to snoop around, for he had scant personal knowledge of the Southern States beyond Kentucky. To Charleston he sent the previously mentioned brother-in-law, Gustavus Fox, plus Stephen Hurlbut and the fellow who organized the previously mentioned counterfeit Chicago Convention admission tickets, Ward Lamon. All three men reported back, giving Lincoln greater confidence that his Navy ships would draw the coveted "first shot," that Confederates would not allow his Navy warships and transports into Charleston harbor. Lincoln called another Cabinet meeting on March 29, seeking approval of his navy mission to Charleston. Three approved, but the Army Chief and four opposed. Lincoln was not dissuaded away from his goal because he feared that the longer he delayed the Navy mission, the more likely negotiations with Confederates might gain favor.

So Lincoln proceeded anyway, without Cabinet approval, authorizing Gustavus Fox to direct the outfitting at New York of a fleet of warships and transports to steam south, some to enter Charleston harbor, the remainder to proceed on and re-inforce Fort Pickens at Pensacola, Florida. Those two were the only remaining Federal-occupied forts in the Confederate States — Federals had abandoned all forts within the Confederacy except for Sumter and Pickens. Lincoln cared not about sustaining a Federal post in either Sumter or Pickings. He just wanted that "first shot" to be fired by a Confederate. The fleet heading for Fort Sumter consisted of the warships, *Powhatan, Pawnee, Pocahontas* and *Harriet Lane*; steam-tugs *Uncle Ben, Yankee* and *Freeborn*, and merchant ship *Baltic*. A mission of this size was no secret; Confederate leaders soon knew it was coming to Fort Sumter and other ships to Fort Pickens.

Why, we ask, was this new President in such a hurry to start a war to conquer the Seceded States? Well, the longer he postponed his war, the more time existed for stories about Abraham Enloe to surface from North Carolina and Kentucky, stories that would uncover his lying in his campaign biographies, and thereby weaken his power over Democrats in the Northern States and Northern States militia, crucial to military success. Also, the longer he deferred war, the more time existed for people of the North to realize that the people of the Seceded States just wanted to leave and live in peace, that the Republican warning of a threat to the North from Southern armies was a lie.

Confederate Commissioners in Washington, Roman, Crawford and Forsyth, having never gained an audience, wrote Lincoln their final letter:

Roman   Forsyth   Crawford

> "Your refusal to entertain these overtures for a peaceful solution, the active naval and military preparations . . . can only be received by the world as a declaration of war . . ."

Now, about that small garrison of Federal troops occupying Fort Sumter. Why had they not agreed to come ashore as demanded by Confederates? Because they were loyal to Lincoln's orders to stay put and there was no attempt by Confederates to force them out. But, time was running out. Confederates preferred to fire cannon at the fort than to engage in a firefight with those soon-to-arrive Federal Navy ships. If Lincoln's Navy ships and Federal Tariff agents, representing a foreign country, began collecting tariffs at Charleston, the Confederate States of America would be perceived in Europe as a subjugated nation.

So, as those navy ships gathered offshore, the cannon bombardment of Fort Sumter began. U. S. troops in the fort returned fire. It was quite an artillery show, but no one on either side was hurt. Federal ships remained offshore, their commanders seeing that the coveted "first shot" was achieved.

The garrison then agreed to come ashore and leave for Washington by railroad. Lincoln did not draw blood, but he incited fire. Oh, I almost forgot — the garrison got permission to fire cannon in salute to their flag prior to coming ashore. Fifty firings were planned. But, on the 49th, the barrel exploded killing a soldier. The body went to Washington for display. In a way Lincoln did draw blood. [182]

Citing George Washington's Executive Power to Collect Taxes from Whiskey Distillers, Lincoln Bypasses Congress and Directs Governors of the Remaining States to Send to the Federal Army 75,000 State Militiamen to, 1) Help Occupy Delaware, Maryland, Kentucky and Missouri and to 2) then, Subsequently, Conquer the Seceded States.

The very next day President Lincoln, acting as Commander-in-Chief, issued an Executive Order directing his 16,000 Federal troops and soon to be organized 75,000 state militiamen from the Northern states to subjugate the Democrat States of Delaware, Maryland, Kentucky and Missouri and, subsequently, conquer the States he alleged to be controlled by "combinations too powerful to be suppressed by the ordinary course of judicial proceedings" – an allegation drawn from President George Washington's "1795 Act for Calling forth the Militia," which the country's first President had felt necessary to stop backwoodsmen from selling untaxed whiskey.

If Lincoln had recognized State Secession, he could have sought to conquer a foreign nation. Declaring war on a foreign nation was constitutional. Instead, Lincoln was violating the United States Constitution by making war on a State he pretended to have not seceded. You see, State Secession did not violate the Constitution, but making war on a state within the United States did violate it. However, and this is important, Lincoln had the guns and the Supreme Court just had black robes. He had never allowed and would never allow Justices to judge his decisions.

George had a little spat with back-country whiskey distillers who were skipping out on paying the liquor tax.

Democrat governors lambasted Lincoln and refused to send militia. The Know-Nothing governor of Maryland refused as well. First blood was drawn on the streets

---

[182] Understanding Abe Lincoln's First Shot Strategy (Inciting Confederates to Fire First at Fort Sumter), by Howard Ray White, pages37-40.

of Baltimore as Massachusetts militiamen crossed town while changing trains. Dead were 9 Baltimore protestors and 4 militiamen. Lincoln's response: a Federal blockade of the 3,600-mile Confederate coast. He blockaded his own people, lawyers would argue. All this by April 19, 1861.

Chapter 34: President Jefferson Davis and the Confederate Response

In Response, Virginia, North Carolina, Tennessee and Arkansas Secede

President Lincoln only had access to about 16,000 US troops to stop further secession and to force Seceded States back under the Federal Government — many of those 16,000 destined to resign rather than attack their fellow men. But there was a 1799 law that allowed him to ask governors for state militia on short notice, but it limited the total requested to 75,000. So, on April 15, 1861, President Lincoln had asked the governor of each State that remained under the Federal Government to send militia to reinforce the U. S. Army — submitting the following justification to each governor and to the people of each State:

> "Whereas the laws of the United States have been, for some time past, and now are opposed, and the execution thereof obstructed, in the States of South Carolina, Georgia, Alabama, Florida, Mississippi, Louisiana, and Texas, by combinations too powerful to be suppressed by the ordinary course of judicial proceedings, or by the powers vested in the marshals by law. Now, therefore, I, Abraham Lincoln, President of the United States, in virtue of the power in me vested by the Constitution and the laws, have thought fit to call forth, and hereby do call forth, the militia of the several States of the Union, to the aggregate number of 75,000, in order to suppress said combinations, and to cause the laws to be duly executed. . . . And I hereby command the persons composing the combinations aforesaid to disperse, and retire peaceably to their respective abodes within 20 days from this date. . . ."

At the same time Secretary of War Simon Cameron sent each governor the following telegraphed request for militia:

> "Sir: Under the act of Congress for calling out the militia to execute the laws of the Union to suppress insurrection, repel invasion, &c., approved February 28th, 1795, I have the honor to request your Excellency to cause to be immediately detached from the militia of your state, the **quota** designated in the table below to serve as infantry or riflemen for three months, or sooner, if discharged."

The quota for States with Republican governors totaled 72 regiments (56,160 troops) -- 17 regiments from New York, 16 from Pennsylvania, 13 from Ohio; 6 each from Illinois and Indiana; 4 from New Jersey, 2 from Massachusetts, 1 each from: Maine, New Hampshire, Vermont, Rhode Island, Connecticut, Michigan, Wisconsin, Iowa, and Minnesota, and less than one from the District of Columbia. The quota for states with Democrat governors totaled 21 regiments (16,380 troops) – 4 each from Maryland (Democratic Legislature, but American Party governor), Kentucky, and Missouri; 3 from Virginia, 2 each from North Carolina and Tennessee; 1 each from Delaware and Arkansas. There was to be 37 officers and 743 men in each regiment.

The defiant response from the following Democrat governors helps the student understand why State Secession quickly followed in four more States.

Virginia Governor John Letcher refused to send Lincoln any militia. On the same day, April 17, the Virginia Convention adopted an Ordinance of Secession by a final vote of 103 versus 46. On May 23, Virginians would ratify secession by 78% versus 22%. Most of the no votes were from Virginia's western counties (now in West Virginia), which were economically tied to the Ohio River Valley. Federals were prepared when Virginia quickly seceded. Immediately, the commander of the Federal arsenal at Harper's Ferry directed the destruction by fire of all the buildings, armaments and arms manufacturing and repair machinery. Likewise, the commander of the Federal shipyard at Norfolk directed the torching of all buildings, destroying valuable steam engines and other machinery, the burning of the large warship *Pennsylvania* and the sinking of six more, including the *Merrimac*.

North Carolina Governor John Ellis told Lincoln, "I can be no party to this wicked violation of the laws of the United States, and to this war upon the liberties of a free people. You can get no troops from North Carolina." Anticipating Federal destruction of North Carolina armaments, Ellis shrewdly ordered the State Militia to immediately seize the arsenal at Fayetteville and the 3 Federal forts located within the State. On May 20 the North Carolina Convention would vote, 120 versus 0, to secede.

Tennessee Governor Isham Harris refused to send militia, telegraphing Lincoln he would not send even one man for the purpose of invading the Confederacy, "but 50,000, if necessary, for the defense of our rights, and those of our Southern brothers." The Tennessee State Legislature would approve an Ordinance of Session on May 6, which Tennesseans would vote, 69% versus 31%, to ratify on June 8.

Arkansas Governor Henry Rector refused to send the Federal Government any militia. Rector informed Lincoln, "The people of this Commonwealth are freemen, not slaves, and will defend to the last extremity, their honor, lives and property against Northern mendacity and usurpation." Rector ordered the state militia to immediately seize the Federal military stores at Napoleon, Arkansas. On May 6 the Arkansas Convention would vote, 69 versus 1, to secede.

Virginia, North Carolina, Tennessee and Arkansas joined the Confederate States of America and the Confederate capital would soon be moved from Montgomery,

Alabama to Richmond, Virginia. The addition of these 4 States greatly increased the Confederate economic and military capacity.

You should not be surprised that the people and governments of Virginia, North Carolina, Tennessee and Arkansas — the vast majority being people of the Southern Culture whose ancestors were pioneering colonists — refused to support a military invasion of sister states to their south. The secessions of Virginia, North Carolina, Tennessee and Arkansas expanded the Confederacy to 11 states and doubled the white population. Earlier, all four states had experienced votes against secession.

For the most part, Cherokees, Creeks, Seminoles, Choctaws and Chickasaws supported the Confederacy. To learn why, Google "Cherokee Declaration of Causes, October 28, 1861." Cherokee brigadier general Stand Watie would be the last to surrender to the Yankees. But Northern States politicians would severely punish these five Native American Nations for supporting the Confederacy: the envisioned Native American State would never be permitted; Southern Native Americans would never have a state of their own. There would be a land rush by White people into the land that had, for 55 years, belonged to these five Native American Nations, and they would become a minority people in the State of Oklahoma. [183]

You will now learn how the Democrat states of Delaware, Maryland, Kentucky and Missouri responded to the request for militia to reinforce the Republican military campaign to conquer the Seceded States.

The Response of the People of Maryland

On April 19, 1861, Massachusetts troops, marching through Baltimore between train stations fired on a protesting crowd, killing a number of citizens and increasing Southern sentiment. The Baltimore Mayor, Democrat George Brown, wrote President Lincoln: "Our people viewed the passage of armed troops to another State as an invasion of our soil, and could not be restrained." At the mayor's direction Isaac

American Party Governor of Maryland, Thomas Hicks.

---

[183] *Bloodstains*, Volume 3, page 78.

Trimble, a military veteran, blew up the bridges that Federals had been using to enter Baltimore. Trimble then departed southward to join the Confederate army. Before long, James Ryder Randall would write a song damning the event:

"Maryland, My Maryland! Avenge the patriotic gore that flecked the streets of Baltimore . . ."

Lincoln's militiamen seized Baltimore's mayor, members of the city council, and the police chief. His militiamen also seized many members of the Maryland state legislature. Most legislators were firmly opposed to Lincoln's military actions and a minority sought state secession.

Maryland was forced to remain under the Federal Government. The Federal army and militiamen from Northern States would enforce it. No official efforts were made to legally free any slaves that lived in Maryland. Of coure, runaway slaves found escaping far easier, but making a living elsewhere often more treacherous. Throughout four years of war, the Lincoln administration remained distrustful of Marylanders, suspecting all of supporting the Confederacy and manipulating elections to ensure that the result supported the war cause. John Wilkes Booth, of the famous Booth Shakespearian theatrical family, was of Maryland.

The Response of the People of Delaware and the District of Columbia

Delaware, tiny in size and population, was a Southern state. But she was too small and too far north to consider secession. The Northern States Republican Party had rather ignored the State. It and its people were unable to oppose being subjugated to Federal rule. The Lincoln administration made no effort to outlaw slavery in Delaware.

The people who had long lived in the District of Columbia were treated with suspicion. Going back to President George Washington, the culture there was predominantly Southern. Many slaves lived in the District, mostly servants to residents of the Southern Culture. Directly across the Potomac River with a clear view of the Capitol was the grand home of General Robert E. Lee's wife (a descendant of the wife of President George Washington) and the Lee children. It had been long known as "Arlington House." The house and plantation would soon be seized by the Lincoln administration, forcing Robert E. Lee's wife, Mary, and their children to flee southward.

Representatives and Senators from Maryland and Delaware who had been elected before Lincoln proclaimed war remained in their seats doing what little they could to soften the horrors of the war. After the military occupation withdrew, voters in both Delaware and Maryland elected Democrats to office and opposed the Republican Party's political reconstruction agenda. [184]

The Response of the People of Kentucky

Historically, Kentucky was governed by the Whig Party, supporting the politics of Henry Clay. In fact, the Democratic Party had elected its first Kentucky governor, ten years earlier, in 1851. President Lincoln was determined to prevent, at all costs, the Secession of Kentucky — where Mary was born and raised and where he had experienced his early childhood. The governor of Kentucky, Democrat Beriah Magoffin, in the strongest language, refused Lincoln's demand for Kentucky state militia to join with the Federal army in his fight to conquer the Seceded States. Many Kentuckians had relatives in Southern Ohio, Southern Indiana and Southern Illinois. Its long northern boundary was the Ohio River, the focus of commerce. Therefore, many Kentuckians hoped to **avoid war and promote peace by a policy within their State of "armed neutrality," a policy proclaimed by Governor Beriah Magoffin on May 20, 1861, one month after Lincoln declared war.**

Kentucky Governor, Democrat Beriah Magoffin seeks neutrality.

However, President Lincoln refused Kentucky's "armed neutrality" plea and soon sent Federal troops and Northern States militia into Kentucky as an occupying force. Lincoln appointed one of the largest slave owners in Kentucky, Stephen Burbridge, to rule as military commander at Louisville. Lincoln declared that Kentuckians were a "loyal" people, but, in truth, they felt like an occupied people. During four years of war, Confederate cavalry raided into Kentucky from Tennessee. Each raid was welcomed and resulted in many new recruits and horses for the Confederate military. [185]

The Response of the People of Missouri

The governor of Missouri, Democrat Claiborne Jackson, also denounced Lincoln's call for state militia and refused to send any. He called Lincoln's demand "illegal, unconstitutional, and revolutionary . . . inhuman and diabolical." But Jackson had another problem close to home. A large population of recent German

---

[184] *Bloodstains*, Volume 3, by Howard Ray White, pages 24-30.
[185] *Bloodstains*, Volume 3, by Howard Ray White, pages 31-34.

immigrants in St. Louis, already organized into military-like clubs, wanted to forcefully oppose secession and support the war against Confederates.

On April 26, a Federal officer, Nathaniel Lyon, organized 6,000 St. Louis volunteers, the vast majority recent German immigrants, into a militia-style militant force. Governor Jackson called out the Missouri State militia to put down this unlawful uprising. The bulk of the residents protested against Lyon's upstart militant group and gunfire erupted. This protest resulted in the death of 28 men, women and children. In

Jefferson Davis and Wife Varina are about to face a horrible four-year-long military invasion of the Confederate States, a vast and prosperous region of farmland and formerly the source of 80% of Federal revenue.

response, the legislature authorized a Missouri State Guard under the command of Sterling Price, a former governor. Although, Sterling Price and Federal General William S. Harney agreed to a truce on May 12, a month later, Nathaniel Lyon led a Federal force in an attack on the Missouri State Government at Jefferson City, forcing the whole organization to flee.

Later, Price's Missouri Guard joined with Confederate forces under General Ben McCulloch and defeated Federal forces at Wilson's Creek.

Governor Claiborne Jackson and many State legislators would meet at Neosho, Missouri and enact a Missouri Secession ordinance. During November, 1861, Missouri would be accepted in the Confederate States of America as a government in exile. [186]

The Last Boston Massachusetts Slave Ship

On April 23, 1861, the *Nightingale*, a Massachusetts clipper ship owned and crewed by Bostonians and loaded with 961 African slaves, was captured by the Federal warship *Saratoga* at the mouth of the Congo River in West Africa just before it set out across the Atlantic Ocean. The *Saratoga's* crew unloaded the

---

[186] *Bloodstains*, Volume 3, by Howard Ray White, pages 35-45.

Nightingale's slaves at Liberia to fend for themselves. A Federal warship would never again force a New England slave transport ship to disembark African slaves. [187]

President Davis and Confederates Prepare to Defend a Nation made up of Eleven Large, Legally-Seceded States

Events moved rapidly across the Confederacy in April. Highlights follow. North Carolina militiamen seized the Federal arsenal at Fayetteville; Arkansas militiamen seized Fort Smith forcing the Federals to withdraw; Virginia's military was put "under the chief control and direction of the President of the Confederate States;" Lincoln expanded his blockade to

The Boston-based Nightingale slave transport ship, which was capable of hauling as many as 961 African slaves to the Americas.

include Virginia and North Carolina, but until 1863, the 3,600-mile Confederate coastline would be easily penetrated; the Confederate Congress approved issuance of $50,000,000 in bonds and notes, authorized President Davis to direct all land and sea defensive efforts and approved his defense plans. Also, the Virginia Secession Convention invited the Confederate Government to relocate to Richmond.

Events moved rapidly across the Confederacy during May. I will string together highlights. Thomas Jackson's Virginia militia began salvaging machinery and rifle parts at Harper's Ferry. Since Lincoln ignored the U. S. Supreme Court, Justice John Campbell resigned and returned to Virginia, eventually to become President Davis' Assistant Secretary of War. The Confederate arms industry was emerging rapidly. The Phoenix Iron Works at Gretna, Louisiana cast its first gun for the Confederate Navy. Federals abandoned Fort Arbuckle in the territory long ago given to the Southeastern tribes (Cherokees, Chickasaws, Choctaws, Creeks and Seminoles), most of these Natives eventually supporting the Confederacy. Thousands of volunteers were swarming into Raleigh to join North Carolina militia companies. They were brave men, for the State would suffer more soldier deaths

---

[187] *Bloodstains,* Volume 3, page 51. The trans-ocean slave shipping companies of Massachusetts and Rhode Island were now out business; no more American slavers would operate off the coast of Africa on a route to Brazil and elsewhere in the Caribbean and South America.

than any other. Since a state of war existed, Letters of Marque were authorized for Confederate privateers. Famous London *Times* correspondent William Russell arrived in Montgomery to interview President Davis and his Cabinet, having just completed similar interviews in Washington. He wired back to London "I am convinced that the [Confederates] can only be forced back by such a conquest as that which laid Poland prostrate at the feet of Russia." But the British would only recognize the Confederate States as "belligerents," not as an independent nation. James Bulloch left for England to purchase or have constructed 6 steam-powered warships for up to $1,000,000 total. Congress also authorized $2,000,000 to purchase two new ironclad battleships in England or France. President Davis put Robert Lee in command of all Confederate troops in Virginia. At Pensacola, Davis directed General Bragg to retain only enough men along the shore opposite Fort Pickens to discourage Federals from landing and to send the remainder to Virginia to reinforce General Lee's troops.

The Confederate Congress approved moving the capital to Richmond and planned to meet there on July 20. Militarily important were the naval shipyards at Norfolk and the Tredegar Iron Works at Richmond. Citizens were prohibited from paying debts owed to U. S. merchants. On May 29, Jeff Davis arrived in Richmond to an enthusiastic reception complete with a 15-gun salute. There, he told Confederate troops, "I look upon you as the last best hope of liberty. . . . Upon you rest the hopes of our people."

Senator Stephen Douglas Dies of Throat Cancer

This chapter concludes in early June. On June 1 the nation's mail service required Confederate postage. Illinois Senator Stephen Douglas died on June 3 at his hotel suite in Chicago. Once Lincoln had declared war, Douglas passionately supported it. Only one week earlier he had delivered a war-mongering speech before the Illinois Legislature in Springfield. He died of throat cancer. An amazing Democratic leader, he was only 48.
188

Senator Stephen Douglas memorial in Chicago, Illinois.

---

188 *Bloodstains*, Volume 3, pages 48-91.

Chapter 35: Republican President Abraham Lincoln Directs a Horrendous Four-Year War to Conquer the Confederate States of America and it's Democratic People

The First Year of President Lincoln's Four-Year War to Conquer the Seceded States

What about the African Americans?

At the start of his military invasion, Lincoln made sure no efforts were launched to free slaves in any Southern State. Instead, he advocated "Colonization." Kentuckian Henry Clay, an important leader in founding the Whig Party and the American Colonization Society, was a hero to Abe and his wife's family. In the famous debate series with Senator Stephen Douglas, Lincoln predicted slavery would not come to an end in less than 100 years (1958). Since 1853, Illinois, had forbade free people of color from moving there to live as neighbors. People of noticeable African ancestry were not welcome in the Northern States. That's why the "Underground Railroad" hurried Southern runaway slaves beyond the Northern States into Canada.

July 1861: Manassas Junction, northern Virginia. By mid-July the Federal invasion force amassed just south of Washington, D. C. was then the largest army ever gathered at one spot in American history, consisting of 40,000 well-armed men and the best field artillery the world had ever seen. Commander Irvin McDowell of Ohio intended to fight all the way to Richmond and crush the Confederate Government. Excited Republican political leaders had gathered a safe distance behind their army to enjoy a picnic and witness the invasion's historic launch. At Manassas Junction, an important Virginia railroad hub, Confederates under Pierre Beauregard of Louisiana, prepared to meet the attack.

General Stonewall Jackson of Virginia.

On the 17th, Beauregard telegraphed Richmond, "The enemy has assailed my outposts in heavy force," prompting President Davis to order Thomas Jackson's troops to hurry eastward, cross over the

Blue Ridge Mountains and reinforce Manassas. Intense fighting erupted on the 20th; a Confederate defeat seemed likely. But, Thomas Jackson's tough troops arrived by noon. Joe Johnston's troops arrived by train from Winchester at mid-afternoon. Now re-enforced, with Jackson's men firing in support, many other Confederates charged forward like furies and drove the Federals from the field in disorganized panic. Abandoning cannon, firearms and most everything, the Federals scampered back to Washington in disarray, struggling with Republican picnickers to get across congested bridges. After a few miles of pursuit, Confederates pressed no farther. President Davis arrived by railroad at the climax of the victory. He and his generals agreed their orders were to defend Virginia, not invade Washington. And many wounded needed attention. Here Thomas Jackson was nicknamed "Stonewall." His troop's fire was an important part of the victory.

October 1861: Western Virginia. The Virginia counties located in the Appalachian Mountains proved impossible to defend with available resources. Steep ridges greatly impeded travel to and from the east; travel to and from the north was a simple ride down the valleys, and access to and from the Ohio River was straightforward. Many western Virginians were more tied economically to the north and west than to the east. The Kanawha Valley was an industrial region (annual capacity of 1,500,000 bushels of salt; almost 2,000,000 gallons of coal oil; valuable niter deposits for making gunpowder, and more). By early September, Federals controlled western Virginia, unopposed. By October Confederates under Robert E. Lee had retreated to make a defensive stand at Sewell Mountain. Since Rosecrans' Federals chose not to attack and cold weather arrived, Lee then ordered a retreat out of western Virginia. Soon afterward Federals organized a rigged an unconstitutional voting process to allegedly justify the secession of 39 western Virginia counties from the State of Virginia.

February 1862: Forts Donelson and Henry, Tennessee. Riverboats manufactured by James Eads of St. Louis are credited for the defeat of Forts Donelson and Henry in February. Having received a contract for 7 iron-clad river gunboats, Eads' accomplishment was one of the war's greatest feats. An engineer and river wrecks salvager, Eads designed the crafts, hired crews and supplied riverboats in time to lead the capture of Fort Henry on the Tennessee River and Fort Donelson on the Cumberland River, both just south of the Kentucky state border. The fall of the Confederate forts was a disaster, resulting in the capture and imprisonment at Chicago of 4,459 Confederates. Indefensible, Nashville, where I grew up and graduated from Vanderbilt University, surrendered without a fight. Tennessee lay exposed.

Early April 1862: Pittsburg Landing and Island #10, Tennessee. Corinth was the junction of the Mobile and Ohio and the Memphis and Charleston railroads and its defense was vital. But not far away was the Tennessee River, which steamboats could access from the Ohio River. By late March, Confederates under Albert Sidney Johnston were concentrated into a huge army of 40,000 troops. But, by this time Federals under Ulysses Grant had landed 40,000 troops at the Tennessee River port town of Pittsburg Landing and would soon be reinforced by 40,000 more. On the morning of April 6 Johnston decided to attack before those reinforcements arrived. The surprise attack drove many Federals back toward the river bank in panic, and many prisoners and weapons were captured. But, when reinforcements arrived, Confederates had to retreat. Federals suffered 13,047 casualties and Confederates suffered 10,694. It was the bloodiest battle ever fought on either American continent. Sadly, General Albert Sidney Johnston was killed leading a charge. That same day, Federals to the west on the Mississippi River captured over 6,000 Confederates who had been defending against downriver traffic at Island Number 10. James Eads' gunboats, with larger, longer range artillery, had been decisive by blocking Confederate retreat, and would give the Federals a great advantage on the western rivers. Being a retired licensed professional engineer myself, I must admire what Eads accomplished in such short time. [189]

The Second Year of President Lincoln's War to Conquer the Seceded States

Late April 1862: New Orleans, Louisiana. The Federal navy also held a major advantage over Confederates. On April 24 a Federal invasion fleet gathered into formation and ran past the two Confederate forts that were defending the mouth of the Mississippi River, most surviving to reach the city of New Orleans. Confederate forces under Mansfield Lovell burned the warehoused cotton and

President Lincoln during the war. Notice his unusually long legs, one crossed over the other, for him a comfortable way to sit in a chair – a physical characteristic inherited from Abraham Enloe's parents.

withdrew with their arms. Benjamin Butler of Massachusetts accepted the surrender of Mayor John Monroe.

---

[189] *Bloodstains*, Volume 3, *The Bleeding*, pages 101 to 109; 127 to 146; 168 to 176, and 192 to 195.

June 1862: Seven Days' before Richmond, Virginia. By June 23, a 105,000-man, well-equipped Federal army under George McClellan was in position to lay siege on Richmond. Robert E. Lee, realizing a siege could not be withstood, gathered his top commanders and planned a fierce attack to drive the Federals away. The attack would include Stonewall Jackson's Confederates, who had been in the Valley, keeping Federals there occupied and defeated. On June 26, Confederates forced the Federals at Mechanicsville to retreat to Gaines' Mill. On the 27th, they drove them back further. On the 28th, Federals began withdrawing from around Richmond toward Savage's Station. On the 29th, Confederates drove them back to Frayser's Farm. On the 30th, they drove them back to Malvern Hill. But, at that point Federals were protected by artillery on Malvern Hill and on warships in the James River. Should Confederates charge again considering the artillery they now faced? Hard decision! The victory was won and Richmond was saved, but General Lee ordered a massive charge up Malvern Hill, hoping to help Northern Peace Democrats in the upcoming election. His brave troops charged forth. The death toll was awful. But Lincoln learned that Confederates were determined and fearless. Richmond would be successfully defended for 34 more months. Confederates captured 52 artillery pieces and 35,000 muskets, but suffered 20,141 casualties versus 15,849 for the Federals.

July 1862: Republicans Authorize $500,000 to Deport African Americans: On July 16, the Republican-dominated Federal House and Senate authorized $500,000 to fund the deportation of African Americans to Liberia, Haiti or elsewhere. Now, President Lincoln had the money to begin the deportation program he had long advocated. Was he now planning deportation to Haiti as the start of his long-held vision for making slavery "extinct?" On August 14, he invited a delegation of prominent Washington, D. C. African American leaders to the White House to try to win their support of his major deportation program. He told them, "You and we are different races," and, since nowhere are your people treated as equals, "It is better for us both, therefore, to be separated." Every one of his guests, considering themselves Americans, refused to support Lincoln's deportation scheme. Blacks were Americans! Plan B? But, Lincoln would carry on!

September 1862: Sharpsburg, Maryland. Confederates under Robert E. Lee defeated Federals under John Pope in the second battle of Manassas Junction, again forcing Federals to abandon supplies and retreat to Washington, the 75,000-man army suffering 16,054 casualties. This time, with mid-term elections less than two months off, Lee advocated a counter-offensive into Federal territory in hopes of encouraging votes for Peace Democrats. Davis agreed. The invasion began with troops singing "My Maryland." Lee's effort climaxed, near Sharpsburg, along Antietam Creek. At most 40,000 Confederates faced 87,000 Federals. Federals suffered 12,469 casualties, Confederates, 13,724, the latter retreating in order to

Virginia. Attacking was a bad idea: Democrats elected the New York Governor and gained a few Congressional seats, but too few to matter.

Murfreesboro, Tennessee, End of 1862 and Start of 1863. Let me first explain what the war meant to me as a 10-year-old boy in 1948 when my family lived for a year at my grandfather's farm near Murfreesboro while my father built our new house in Nashville. I slept in an upstairs room where bloodstains covered the floor. The Battle of Murfreesboro had been fought on this farm and others nearby as 1862 ended and 1863 began. In that upstairs room, 85 years earlier, a Federal surgeon had amputated arms and legs off of scores of wounded soldiers, the blood soaking into the wooden floor. A huge graveyard just down the road displayed more than 6,100 Federal tombstones as far as the eye could see. That political nightmare became quite personal and I swore to, someday, better understand what had caused it. I am now 82 years old,

A small sampling of the more than 6,100 graves of Lincoln's soldiers at the Military graveyard at Murfreesboro, Tennessee.

and have written four volumes of *Bloodstains* and eight other books relevant to Southern history. I hope you find my accumulated knowledge, now being applied to a true biography of Abraham Lincoln, helpful toward your improved knowledge of that horrible era in our American history.

January 1, 1863: Lincoln's "War Measure," the Emancipation Proclamation.

By late 1862, it was obvious to President Lincoln and the Republican governors that the conquest of the Confederate States was two or more years away. No slaves had been freed to date in Delaware, Maryland, Kentucky, Missouri, or Confederate regions thus far under Federal military rule such as Middle Tennessee. **Lincoln's promise to refrain from freeing slaves had been kept**. Now desperate, he figured he must break that promise and **proclaim free those slaves living beyond his military control**. He could do that **without disturbing the social order in regions within his control**. Abe hoped news about freedom would surge across Confederate-held regions and slaves would revolt, kill their masters and the resulting horror would cause Confederate soldiers to abandon their posts and flee for home to protect their families. Lincoln figured demands for deportation of all Blacks across America would follow. So on January 1, 1863, Lincoln issued his "Emancipation Proclamation." It freed no slaves. He called it his "War Measure."

However, slaves under Confederate rule would remain faithful; they would not rise up and kill their masters. The aim of those slaves was simply to survive during the horrific war surrounding them. Lincoln's war to conquer the Seceded States would continue, becoming more bloody by the month. [190]

The Third Year of President Lincoln's War to Conquer the Seceded States

March 1863: Lincoln Escalates the Military Campaign to Include a War Against Civilians.

During January and February it became obvious that Lincoln's Emancipation Proclamation scheme was a failed "War Measure." By and large, slaves who remained with their owners were loyal to them and realized that, by supporting each other, all could best survive the war raging about them. These feelings of interdependence would grow as simply getting enough to eat would become more desperate. Lincoln and people across the Northern States would be more and more amazed and puzzled over the total failure of Lincoln's Emancipation Proclamation "War Measure" to incite a race war across the South — the anticipated race war that many hoped would justify a major deportation program to remove people of noticeable African ancestry from North America.

"The Butcher," Lincoln's most destructive general, U. S. Grant.

So, in March of 1863, General Ulysses Grant wrote: "Rebellion has assumed the shape now that it can only terminate by the complete subjugation of the South. It is our duty to weaken the enemy, by destroying their means of subsistence, withdrawing their means of cultivating their fields, and in every other way possible." Grant was advocating making war against Confederate armies **and also against the Southern people**, both White and Black, their food, cattle, plows and shelter.

April, 1863: Lincoln Deports 430 to Haiti. During April, Lincoln ordered Federals at Fortress Monroe, Virginia to select 430 African American men, women and children from among those gathered around the fortress seeking food, tell them

---

[190] *Bloodstains*, Volume 3, *The Bleeding*, pages 196 to 197; 214 to 217; 233; 246 to 250; 280 to 294 and 294 to 296.

they were free when deported and load them aboard the *Ocean Ranger*. Two wealthy New York men, Paul Forbes and Charles Tuckerman, had contracted, at $50 each, to oversee the former slaves' resettlement at Ile A'Vache, a 100 square mile island off the Haitian coast. The plan was to deport 5,000 people of color to this island. Many of the first 430 would get sick, 39 would die and starvation would become a problem. No more would be deported. Eleven months later survivors would disembark near Washington, D. C. That would be March 4, 1864. By then the slave deportation idea would be dead because Republicans would be developing plans to free Confederate slaves and organize them into Republican voting blocks to enable the party to control the government of each politically reconstructed Southern State.

May 1863: Fredericksburg and Chancellorsville, Virginia. Federals under Joe Hooker, a force of 133,868 men, advanced southward toward Richmond. First stop Fredericksburg. Hooker spit his army, leaving 64,000 behind and leading 70,000 westward to the vicinity of Mr. Chancellor's house, where he set up headquarters. Robert E. Lee, making an audacious decision, split his 47,000-man Confederate army, sending 26,000 under Stonewall Jackson to attack Hooker's 70,000. Jackson's men caught Hookers' men by surprise and overwhelmed the far larger army, which retreated back toward Fredericksburg. There was more fighting at Fredericksburg before Federals withdrew toward Washington. A huge Federal offensive toward Richmond had again failed. Federal casualties were 17,287; Confederate were 12,764. But Stonewall Jackson would die of wounds, a loss greatly felt.

The general most credited for denying the conquest of the Confederate capital, Richmond, Virginia, for four long years, General Robert E. Lee of Virginia.

July 1863: Gettysburg, Pennsylvania. On June 25, with Confederate cavalry already occupying Gettysburg and York, Pennsylvania, and in hopes of winning votes for Peace Democrats, Lee led his troops into Maryland. From its post in northern Virginia the huge Federal army headed north to defend Pennsylvania and Washington. On July 1 Oliver Howard's Federals failed to reclaim Gettysburg and retreated up Cemetery Ridge. George Meade's main army arrived during the night. The Confederate advantage was lost. There was bloody fighting on July 2 and both armies held their ground. Determined to strike a decisive blow, Lee order a frontal attack against the re-enforced, dug-in Federals. By July 3, following a big Confederate artillery attack, troops under George Pickett, James Pettigrew and Isaac Trimble ran the one-mile gauntlet up the hillside. It was deadly. That night Lee's Confederates began their retreat into Virginia, taking wounded as they could. Meade's Federals were slow to pursue. Lee's men returned to Virginia to fight another 22 months. Of 85,000 Federals engaged, casualties totaled 23,049; of 65,000 Confederates it was 20,451. Peace Democrats acquired no political advantage.

July 1863: Vicksburg and Port Hudson, Mississippi. It had been a long siege of these two last impediments to total Federal control of the Mississippi River. Inside the heavily fortified river town of Vicksburg were 31,000 Confederates under John Pemberton. Grant commanded far more Federals along the siege line who were raining artillery on the defenders. On May 23, Grant had ordered a frontal attack by 45,000 Federals. It had failed and his men suffered 3,199 casualties. Further down the river, the Siege of fortified Port Hudson had begun two days earlier where 33,000 Federals under Nathaniel Banks surrounded 7,000 Confederates under Franklin Gardner. Banks had ordered frontal attacks on May 27 and June 10, together resulting in 3,787 Federal casualties. But, as July approached, citizens and troops in Vicksburg were suffering starvation. Pemberton negotiated the surrender of Vicksburg and, four days later, Gardner surrendered Port Hudson. Troops were allowed to go home by promising to not rejoin the fight until exchanged. Some officers were imprisoned.

November 1863: The Graveyard Ceremony at Gettysburg

On November 19, 1863, President Lincoln followed Edward Everett, the primary speaker, in adding a few remarks while the assembled crowd listened. Lincoln's few remarks, delivered in two minutes, are known as his "Gettysburg Address." This event was an important propaganda tool for the Northern States Republican Party, delivered at the site of the only major military battle fought within a state that was under the political control of Lincoln's Northern States Republican Party. Gettysburg lay only 32 miles north of the border with Maryland, a Southern State. You remember how, during the 1860 campaign, Lincoln and other Northern States Republican politicians warned the people of their respective States about the likelihood of a military invasion advancing from the South with intentions of conquering the North. Of course, that fearmongering accusation was pure nonsense. Finally, there, in Gettysburg was so-called proof of that long-ago threat of a military invasion from the South. Lincoln used the ceremony to justify his past refusal to negotiate a peaceful settlement with President Jefferson Davis and, instead, initiate a bloody war against those Democrat States that had seceded before he was sworn into office.

On the day of Lincoln's brief speech, people viewed the new graves of 1,188 Federal soldiers that had so far been unearthed from temporary graves and reburied in organize rows in the new designated graveyard each grave marked by a wooden board rising above the ground. Today, the count is 3,512. Names of 979 remain unknown. Many decades later, organizations in the former Confederate States would unearth hundreds of Confederate dead around the Gettysburg battlefield area and reinter them in Southern graveyards in Richmond and elsewhere.

In President Lincoln's brief address at the Gettysburg grave dedication ceremony, he referred to the declaration by the thirteen British Colonies of their independence from the government of Great Britain. He referred to the phrase "all men are created equal," which denounced the European tradition of naming and elevating Kings and Lords, and Dukes, and Princes, etc. The thirteen colonies would forever prohibit the practice of naming Kings, Princes, Lords, Dukes, etc. as a superior class. "All men are created equal" in no way referred to elevating one race of people above another race. Furthermore, Confederates were not trying to change the Constitution of Mr. Lincoln's country. His focus was not on freeing slaves or making Black men the equal of White men. His focus was

President Abraham Lincoln at the Gettysburg graveyard dedication. Eventually his war would result in one million unnecessary deaths.

on the North's fight to militarily conquer and politically dominate the lawfully seceded States. Somehow, he supposed that, with eleven States seceded, his dreadful war was needed to ensure, "that this nation, under God, shall have a new birth of freedom — and that government of the people, by the people, for the people, shall not perish from the earth." If "new birth of freedom" was his way of saying "my army will free the Southern slaves," we must remember that, so far, he had done little toward advancing that goal except, as a "war measure," having proclaimed free slaves living on land controlled by Confederates. Lincoln presumed there was a threat that the reduced nation of which he had become President might "perish from the earth," if his army failed to conquer the Confederate States. But the Confederate States army was merely defending its right to be a new nation, to defend its independency from an abusive tyrannical government. In no way was it fighting to upset the structure of the government of the United States and Lincoln's presidency. Nevertheless, Lincoln's brief address at the Gettysburg graveyard, 32 miles above Maryland, a Southern State, would be widely quoted as justifying the war he was waging against eleven Seceded States, a war that was destined to result in one million unnecessary American deaths, including his own.

The Fourth Year of the President Lincoln's War to Conquer the Seceded States

June 1864: Cold Harbor, Virginia. Of the battles presented here, none reeked more of politics than Cold Harbor. Seeking to retain political control, Republicans had rebranded themselves as the "Union Party," selected Democratic Baltimore for their nominating Convention and aimed to select former Tennessee Democrat Andrew Johnson as Vice President. But Republicans wanted another campaign boost four days before the June 6 Convention opening. They wanted a major victory at Cold Harbor, only 9 miles from Richmond. Lee's Confederates, 25,000 strong, were ready and protected behind earthworks. Ulysses Grant, with a force of 50,000, ordered the charge. It was a

General U. S. Grant, Cold Harbor's "Butcher"

slaughter. Don't count the dead! Don't wire news to Baltimore! For four days Grant allowed his wounded to suffer on the battlefield, crying out for "water," many dying of non-fatal wounds. On June 7, Grant finally asked Lee for permission to gather his dead and wounded. That day Republicans nominated the Lincoln-Johnson ticket. Federal dead and wounded at Cold Harbor was about 13,000. Since May 5, the beginning of Grant's advance toward Richmond, his troops had suffered 54,929 killed, wounded and missing, a number almost equaling Robert E. Lee's total fighting army. Grant was called "The Butcher." Richmond remained free.

August 1864: Atlanta, Georgia. By late August, John Hood decided his Confederates were unable to defend Atlanta against encirclement by William Sherman's huge force. To save his army, Hood evacuated to the south on September 1. Sherman's Federals moved into the city and ordered all African Americans to remain and all Whites to evacuate with little more than the clothes on their backs. The conquest of Atlanta gave Republicans a Lincoln re-election boost. Sherman would be preparing a "March to the Sea" after the November elections.

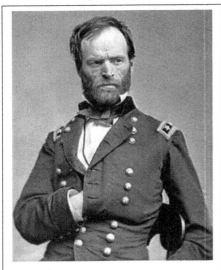

General William Sherman was as destructive as General Grant.

April 1865: The fall of Petersburg and Richmond. We now come to the climatic end: the conquest of Petersburg and nearby Richmond. The effort to conquer Petersburg had begun 11 months earlier, on May 5, 1864, when 30,000 Federals under Benjamin Butler landed at City Point on the south bank of the James River, aiming to get to Richmond by way of Petersburg. Reinforced two weeks later by Grant's surviving Cold Harbor troops, Federals repeatedly attacked, suffering 8,150 killed and wounded. On June 18, 1864 Grant decided to lay siege and attempt to cut railroad connections. It would be a long campaign. Federal miners dug a 586-foot tunnel under the Confederate earthworks and detonated a huge explosion; then Federal troops rushed into the resulting crater, bogged down and suffered under intense Confederate fire, resulting in 4,000 killed and wounded, many being African American troops. The siege continued into 1865. On March 25, 1865 a surprise attack from the Fort Stedman section of the defensive works failed. But, on March 31, Lee advised President Davis to flee Richmond with the government.

U. S. President Abraham Lincoln, with son, Tad, walking through the capital of the Confederate States of America after the conquest of the city.

On March 31, 1865, the day before U. S. Colored Troops swarmed into Richmond to begin occupation, President Davis, his family and the Confederate civil government left the city on a guarded train bound for mid-state North Carolina. The government was fleeing toward Mexico, hoping to set itself up in exile. The next day, at the Battle of Five Forks, Federals cut railroad access from the south and Lee and his army retreated west, giving up Petersburg and Richmond. On April 4, with 12-year-old son Tad at his side (it was his birthday), President Lincoln proudly entered conquered Richmond, rode to the former Davis residence, the Confederate White House, stepped into President Davis' office and set in his desk chair. Then, perhaps, Abe Lincoln reflected on what an illegitimate boy born in North Carolina to an illegitimate mother had just accomplished, grinned and gloated.

April 14, 1865: President Lincoln is Killed, One of a Million Deaths Caused by His War. On April 14, 1865, famous Maryland stage actor, John Wilkes Booth, entered the back of Ford's Theater, climbed the back stairs to the presidential booth, opened the door, stepped inside and shot Abraham Lincoln in the back of the head. That was four years and two days after Abe got his coveted first shot at Fort Sumter in Charleston harbor. Springfield Lawyer Abraham Lincoln had prosecuted the war of conquest that caused one million to unnecessarily die. He now joined them in the grave. Many would praise him as "America's Greatest President," the man of humble beginnings who "Saved the Union" and "Emancipated the Slaves." Others would curse him for inciting Southern States to secede and pursuing a four-year war of conquest that resulted in one million unnecessary American deaths. [191]

Public viewing of President Abraham Lincoln's body at the Illinois State House in Springfield, prior to burial in a temporary grave nearby. The body had arrived in Springfield on May 3, 1865, 19 days after he was killed by John Wilkes Booth.

[191] *Bloodstains*, Volume 3, *The Bleeding*. Pages 409 to 415; 440 to 441; 512 to 534, and 539-545.

Chapter 36: We Close with a Talley of the Death Toll — One Million Unnecessary American Deaths

Making Sense of It All.

We hope your heart and mind were moved by the history that you have devoted many hours to reading. In closing, let's look at some numbers — of the 3,653,770 people of African descent living in the Confederate States, 3.6% were free, the remainder were slaves (1860 census). Together, people of African descent (slave and free) were 33% of the total population of the South. In the 1858 debate with Senator Stephen Douglas, Abraham Lincoln predicted more than 100 years would pass before all Southern slaves would be free (sometime beyond 1958). Of course, it only took 8 years and 1,000,000 unnecessary deaths to accomplish that goal. As an 82-year-old Southerner, Southern historian and Christian, I believe that, if the Confederacy had been allowed to go its own way, avoiding that horrific war, all Confederate slaves would have been free by 1890 (Brazil freed its last in 1888). The idea that over a million young men of the North, many just-arrived immigrants, took up arms, invaded the South, many giving their lives, on a crusade to free mostly well-cared-for slave families is preposterous.

Counting the One Million Unnecessary Deaths

President Lincoln's War to Conquer the Seceded States of the Confederacy was the most horrific conflict ever fought by Americans. Lincoln's Federal military dead totaled, 400,000 men. If you laid Lincoln's 400,000 Federal military dead with arms over their heads, with a bouquet of flowers in each right hand, then another, and another, toe to flower, beginning at Washington, heading southward down the road toward Charleston, the last of those flower decorations would dip into the seawater in Charleston harbor, within sight of Fort Sumter. That is the image of the war that I hope you always remember, for those Federal dead had been duped into going to war to enable political domination of the South by a Northern States Republican Party — a sad cause for which to die.

For a more complete presentation on this subject, read Chapter 29 by the late William Cawthon in the book titled, *Understanding the War Between the States*, produced by The Society of Independent Southern Historians, which I co-founded in 2013. I honor Mr. Cawthon by drawing heavily on his work while writing a condensed version here.

The long-standing "official" death toll is 360,000 Union dead and 260,000 Confederate dead, totaling 620,000 deaths, approximations computed by two Union veterans in the late 1800's. There were errors: only 54% of Northern deaths were named individuals and many Confederate records were lost during the final year of war.

The December, 2011 issue of *Civil War History*, a scholarly journal published quarterly by The Kent State University Press, presented a highly praised, 41-page census quantitative study by J. David Hacker, titled "A Census-Based Count of the Civil War Dead." Hacker, presently at the University of Minnesota, reports that his study indicates that our ancestors suffered 750,000 soldier deaths instead of the 620,000 traditional number, an increase of 130,000. He believes the Confederate deaths from disease and accidents have been seriously undercounted. Due to the North's scorched earth policy, food, clothing and shoes were often scarce, increasing the death rate from exposure and disease, so we assign 70% of those 130,000 deaths to Confederates, elevating their death total from 260,000 to 350,000. The death toll for Lincoln's invaders rises to 400,000. Hacker's figures include war injuries that resulted in death up to 4 years after surrender.

A death toll of 350,000 Southern men represents 30 percent of the White male population, age 18 to 48, that were living in the Seceded States when Lincoln launched his invasion. And a death toll of 400,000 Northern men, many, many just-arriving immigrants, represents 9 percent of that population, age 18 to 48. Applying 30 percent to today's American population (2010 census), calculates to 21 million deaths — a war-death toll that today's Americans cannot comprehend. Only the region between the Rhine and the Volga in World War II suffered greater mortality. My wife's ancestor and three brothers fought for South Carolina troops. Three brothers were killed defending the Confederacy. My wife and our children live today because the fourth brother lived.

White civilian deaths during Lincoln's invasion and the first four years of the Political Reconstruction that followed are a very sad historical story. William Cawthon estimated that 35,000 White civilians died. Historian James McPherson calculates that the North's war against civilians destroyed two-thirds of the assessed value of wealth in the Confederate States, two-fifths of their livestock and over half of their farm machinery, resulting in a destitute people, struggling to find enough to eat, unable to control their future.

Jim Downs' 2012 book, *Sick from Freedom,* proves with abundant contemporary sources the truly heart wrenching experiences of the freedpeople, the newly independent former slaves. Many Black people who rushed to the Northern armies as they penetrated deeper into the Confederate States in hopes of sustenance, suffered inadequate food, clothing, shelter, and medical care. Lincoln's Army and the Freedman's Bureau together put many Black men to work on their projects, leaving the Black women and children behind to fend for themselves. Concentrating Blacks together at "contraband camps" promoted sickness and death by disease. A smallpox epidemic was first noted in 1862 among Blacks congregated around Washington, D. C. It subsequently spread south reaching epidemic levels among Blacks and arriving in Texas in 1868. A few Whites contracted smallpox, but the disease mostly took the lives of Blacks. Two dreadful examples: "800 freed Blacks a week died on the Sea Islands in November and December 1865" and "caskets of the Black dead were lined up on the streets of Macon, Georgia during Political Reconstruction." William Cawthon estimated 200,000 Blacks died as a result of the war and Political Reconstruction and "The mortality rate of contraband camps may have reached 25 percent."

Adding together deaths in the Confederacy for soldiers, White citizens and Blacks (350,000 + 35,000 + 200,000) comes to 585,000. Adding in 400,000 Northern soldier deaths comes to 985,000. White and Black civilians also died unnecessarily in the subjugated Democrat States: Delaware, Maryland, Kentucky and Missouri. **Adding in those deaths increases total war deaths beyond one million.**

Closing a Tragic American Biography

Many Abolitionists and Exclusionists had wrongly believed that, when all Blacks were made independent, their population would steadily decline. They believed free Blacks would follow the fate of the Indians. Observing that, in each of the three decades prior to 1860, the free black population of the United States had, percentage-wise, increased less than had the slave population, some analysts had incorrectly projected that the black population of America "is doomed to comparatively rapid absorption or extinction."

William Cawthon lamented, "The old Southern civilization which produced George Washington, Thomas Jefferson, John C. Calhoun, and a host of other eminent Americans and a rich, vibrant intellectual culture amidst an organic society rooted in family, the land, religion, tradition, honest agrarian self-sufficiency and a fierce legacy of self-government was swept away."

Selected References to Other Books and Records about Abraham Enloe, about Nancy Hanks and about Abraham Lincoln's Birth, his Law Practice, his Family, his Political Career, and his Rise to become President of those Remaining United States

The best Lincoln biography

Lincoln, by David Herbert Donald (winner of the Pulitzer Prize), Simon & Schuster, 1995. This is by far the best Lincoln biography. Donald recognizes the possibility of Abraham Enloe fathering Lincoln, and then set's it aside.

The best Herndon biography

Lincoln's Herndon, a Biography, by David Herbert Donald, first published in 1948. I used the Da Capo Press paperback published in 1988. This is by far the best Herndon biography. Donald researched and wrote this definitive Herndon biography long before writing *Lincoln.*

The best Douglas Biography

Stephen A. Douglas, by Robert W. Jahannsen, Oxford University Press, 1973. This is the best Douglas biography.

William Herndon's Research and Subsequent Books

Abraham Lincoln's long time law partner and political supporter, Billy Herndon, started gathering information to support a biography immediately after the President's death. All of those records, unaltered, were published in one large book in 1998:

> *Herndon's Informants, Letters, Interviews, and Statements about Abraham Lincoln*, edited by Douglas L. Wilson and Rodney O. Davis, published in 1998 by University of Illinois Press. This fine hardbound book contains all of Herndon's original Lincoln source material, 827 pages, in a convenient form.

For two to three years following Lincoln's death, Herndon was very busy gathering the bulk of the information published above for our convenience. But he seemed to have had difficulty in assembling this large body of information into a Lincoln biography. Eventually, Ward Hill Lamon paid Herndon between $2,000 and $4,000 for a bound copy of all of Herndon's biographical records. Lamon then teamed with an excellent writer, Chauncey F. Black, and wrote and published the following book:

The Life of Abraham Lincoln, From His Birth to His Inauguration as President, by Ward H. Lamon, published in 1872. This was reprinted in 1999 by University of Nebraska Press with an introduction by Rodney O. Davis.

Herndon's original biographical records sat in boxes in the back of his law office, until, many years later. As he approached old age, he partnered with a young writer, Jesse W. Weik, who proceeded to write Herndon's version of the biography of Lincoln. With Lamon's book as a guide, with Herndon's boxes of letters, interviews and statements before him and Herndon to proof-read, Weik proceeded to write Herndon's biography of Lincoln up to the time the subject left Springfield for Washington:

Herndon's Life of Lincoln, the History and Personal Recollections of Abraham Lincoln, by William H. Herndon and Jesse W. Weik, published in 1889. Reprinted in 1983 by Da Capo Press, Inc. with an introduction by Henry Steele Commanger.

Lincoln's North Carolina Parentage

The Genesis of Lincoln, by James Harrison Cathey, published in 1899. A 1999 reprint by the Confederate Reprint Company is recommended. James Cathey was the original investigator to gather memories and records pointing to baby Abraham's parentage. Since the birth event was only 85 years ago when Cathey was investigating, his work was decidedly advantaged.

The Eugenics of Lincoln. By James Caswell Coggins, published in 1940. A 2001 reprint by The Confederate Reprint Company is recommended. Coggins' study took place 41 years after Cathy's. It broadly validates Cathy's work and adds important new findings.

The Tarheel Lincoln, North Carolina's Origins of "Honest" Abe, by Jerry A. Goodnight and Richard Eller both of North Carolina, printed by Westmoreland Printers, published in 2003. This is a fairly recent retelling of the story by two North Carolina writers. It adds important new information.

Abraham Enloe of Western North Carolina, the Natural Father of Abraham Lincoln, by Don Norris of North Carolina, published in 2008. This is another recent retelling of the story and it also adds new information.

The Bostic Lincoln Center, Inc., dedicated to collecting, documenting, researching and preserving the generational lore in support of evidence that President Abraham Lincoln was born near Bostic, North Carolina, in a cabin on "Lincoln Hill," to Nancy Hanks about two years before she would meet and marry Kentuckian Thomas Lincoln. You are encouraged to visit the Bostic Lincoln Center. Check online for the days and hours when the Center is open for visitors.

The Abraham Lincoln Genesis Cover-up, The Censored Origins of an Illustrious Ancestor, by R. Vincent Enlow, published in 2001, by Genealogy Today Publications, New Providence, New Jersey.

The Paternity of Abraham Lincoln, Was He the Son of Abraham Lincoln?, by William Eleazar Barton, published by George H. Doran Company, New York, 1920. Here, Barton struggles as he attempts to allege that the Abraham Enloe parentage is false. Generally, historians allege that Barton proved that all illegitimate stories about Lincoln were false, **but he did not, in reality, prove his case**.

Books about the War Between the States

Bloodstains, An Epic History of the Politics that Produced and Sustained the American Civil War and the Political Reconstruction that Followed, Volume 1, *The Nation Builders,* by Howard Ray White, published in 2002. See Amazon. This volume presents American history from the founding of Jamestown, Virginia Colony in 1607 through to March, 1848, when the Republic of Texas transitioned to the State of Texas — a 241-year era in America. It includes glimpses of Abraham Lincoln's early life.

Bloodstains, An Epic History of the Politics that Produced and Sustained the American Civil War and the Political Reconstruction that Followed, Volume 2, *The Demagogues,* by Howard Ray White, published in 2003. See Amazon. This volume continues the history presented in Volume 1, *The Nation Builders.* This volume includes the history of Lincoln's marriage and his political rise to become President. It concludes with Lincoln's success at drawing the "first shot" at Charleston.

Bloodstains, An Epic History of the Politics that Produced and Sustained the American Civil War and the Political Reconstruction that Followed, Volume 3, *The Bleeding,* by Howard Ray White, published in 2007. See Amazon. This volume continues the history presented in Volume 2, *The Demagogues.* Here you learn about the four-year-long War Between the States with particular emphasis on the North's accompanying political transformation.

Other Books by Howard Ray White that should interest you

A Quick-Read You Must Engage

Why and How the North Conquered the South, by Howard Ray White, a new concise, yet complete book telling relevant truthful American history in 31 facing-page chapters, which takes only three hours to read. You must read this and encourage others to also read it. Go to Amazon.

How to Study History when Seeking Truthfulness and Understanding: Lessons Learned from Outside of Academia, by Howard Ray White, 2019, paperback and e-book, Amazon, another quick read.

Bloodstains, Volume 4:

Bloodstains, An Epic History of the Politics that Produced and Sustained the American Civil War, Volume 4, *Political Reconstruction and the Struggle for Healing*, by Howard Ray White, 2012, paperback and e-book, Amazon.

Other Histories:

How American Families Made America, Colonization, Revolution, and Expansion from Virginia Colony to The Republic of Texas, 1607 to 1836, by Howard Ray White, 2020, paperback and e-book, Shotwell Publishers and Amazon.

Understanding Abe Lincoln's First Shot Strategy (Inciting Confederates to Fire First at Fort Sumter, 2011, paperback and e-book, Amazon.

Understanding "Uncle Tom's Cabin" and "The Battle Hymn of the Republic"— How Novelist Harriet Beecher Stowe and Poet Julia Ward Howe Influenced the Northern Mind, by Howard Ray White, 2012, paperback and e-book, Amazon.

A History of Mankind:

Understanding Creation and Evolution, by Howard Ray White, 2018, Shotwell Publishing, paperback, e-book and audiobook (read by author), Amazon and Audible. I encourage Christians to read this study, which supports both God's creation **and** the evolution we observe today.

Alternate History/Historical Novel:

The CSA Trilogy, An Alternate History/Historical Novel about Our Vast and Beautiful Confederate States of America – A Happy Story in Three Parts of What Might Have Been – 1861 to 2011, by Howard Ray White, 2018, paperback and e-book, Amazon. This is a pleasant read that helps one dream of what the South might have been like, going forward to today, if the Confederate States had successfully defended their independence.

Historical Novel set in Wartime Virginia

R. E. Lee, Edmund Ruffin and Slavery: During Four Years of Civil War across Virginia, a Slave Family Struggles to Keep Safe and Stay Together as They Ask, "Who are Our True Friends, White People of the North or White People of the South," by Howard Ray White, 2019, see Amazon. This novel allows the reader to experience a capable and literate slave family struggling to keep safe, stay together and survive the war in Virginia that raged about them over the course of four years. Major real-life characters are Mrs. R E. Lee and Edmund Ruffin.

Enjoy the Above Books Authored by Howard Ray White and These Below as Well

Histories jointly written by sixteen members of the Society of Independent Southern Historians, Howard Ray White and Dr. Clyde N. Wilson, co-founders and co-editors:

Understanding the War Between the States, by sixteen Society members, 2015, paperback, e-book and audio-book, Amazon and Audible.

American History for Home Schools, 1607 to 1885, with a Focus on Our Civil War, by sixteen Society members, 2018, paperback, e-book and audio-book, Amazon and Audible.

Thanks for your interest in Truthful American History

Howard Ray White, Southern Historian

Index for Rebirthing Lincoln, a Biography

Made in the USA
Middletown, DE
22 October 2021

50379794R00150